2025

ZERO POINT
WEIGHT LOSS

COOKBOOK for Beginners

Delicious, Lose Weight & Stress-Free No Point Recipes without Counting Calories for a Healthier Lifestyle | Includes 30-Day Plan

Emuyoilija Deitubeljak

TABLE OF CONTENTS

INTRODUCTION

In today's fast-paced world, the quest for effective weight loss solutions often leads to a cycle of frustration, restrictive diets, and feelings of deprivation. However, the Zero Point Weight Loss Cookbook presents a refreshing alternative—a sustainable approach that emphasizes enjoyment, satisfaction, and the pleasure of eating delicious meals while achieving your weight loss goals. This cookbook invites you to embark on a culinary journey that will not only help you shed pounds but also transform your relationship with food.

The Concept of Zero Points

The idea of "zero points" is rooted in the revolutionary Weight Watchers program, which encourages individuals to focus on consuming foods that are low in calories but high in nutritional value. Zero point foods, such as fruits, vegetables, lean proteins, and whole grains, allow you to enjoy abundant servings without the guilt that often accompanies traditional dieting. This approach redefines the way we think about weight loss, shifting the emphasis from restriction to abundance. It empowers you to fill your plate with nutrient-dense foods that nourish your body, promote satiety, and support overall well-being.

Imagine indulging in a bowl of vibrant vegetable soup, rich with the flavors of fresh herbs and seasonal produce, or delighting in a luscious fruit salad bursting with natural sweetness. With zero point foods, these satisfying and wholesome meals become staples in your diet, making it easier to stay on track with your weight loss journey. This philosophy opens up a world of culinary possibilities, allowing you to explore a diverse range of flavors and textures that keep meals exciting and enjoyable.

A Balanced Approach to Nutrition

The Zero Point Weight Loss Cookbook emphasizes the importance of a balanced diet filled with whole, unprocessed foods. It promotes a lifestyle that encourages healthy eating habits while ensuring that you never feel deprived. Within these pages, you will discover a plethora of recipes tailored to accommodate various dietary preferences, from hearty meat dishes to flavorful vegetarian options. Each recipe is crafted with the understanding that food should be a source of joy, not just sustenance.

The focus on meal planning and preparation is crucial in today's busy lifestyles, where convenience often leads to unhealthy choices. This cookbook not only provides delicious recipes but also offers practical tips for effective meal planning. By dedicating a little time each week to prepare your meals, you can set yourself up for success. With zero point options readily available, you will be less tempted to resort to less nutritious alternatives when hunger strikes.

Recipes for Every Occasion

One of the greatest strengths of the Zero Point Weight Loss Cookbook is its versatility. Whether you are hosting a dinner party, enjoying a cozy family meal, or needing a quick lunch to take to work, this cookbook has something for every occasion. You will find a variety of recipes ranging from scrumptious appetizers and satisfying main courses to delightful desserts and snacks—all designed to fit into the zero point framework.

For example, you can prepare a creamy and comforting cauliflower soup that feels indulgent while being low in calories. A refreshing quinoa salad featuring seasonal vegetables and a zesty dressing is perfect for lunch or dinner. For those sweet moments, our fruit-based desserts will satisfy your cravings without jeopardizing your progress. Each recipe includes clear instructions, tips for ingredient substitutions, and pairing suggestions, making it easy for you to create meals that align with your lifestyle and preferences.

Building a Healthy Mindset

Weight loss is as much about the mental aspect as it is about physical changes. The Zero Point Weight Loss Cookbook encourages you to cultivate a positive mindset around food and body image. This journey is about celebrating progress, no matter how small, and understanding that lasting change takes time. Mindfulness in eating is a key principle emphasized in this cookbook; taking the time to savor each bite and listen to your body's hunger cues can enhance your overall eating experience.

Additionally, we recognize that challenges often arise on the path to weight loss. This cookbook provides strategies to navigate common obstacles, from social situations to managing cravings. You will find practical advice to help you stay motivated and committed to your goals, reinforcing the idea that this is not merely a diet but a lifelong commitment to health and wellness.

The Importance of Community and Support

As you embark on this journey, remember that you are not alone. Community and support are vital components of successful weight loss. Engaging with friends, family, or support groups can provide encouragement and accountability. Sharing meals, experiences, and tips can enhance your journey and make it more enjoyable. The **Zero Point Weight Loss Cookbook** also aims to foster this sense of community by encouraging you to share your culinary creations and inspire others in their weight loss journeys.

Conclusion

The Zero Point Weight Loss Cookbook is more than just a collection of recipes; it is a comprehensive guide to transforming your relationship with food and embracing a healthier lifestyle. By focusing on zero point eating, you can nourish your body with satisfying meals while achieving your weight loss goals. Each recipe serves as an invitation to explore new flavors, celebrate fresh ingredients, and discover the joy of cooking.

As you begin this culinary adventure, remember that every meal is an opportunity to nurture your body and spirit. Embrace the freedom that comes with zero point eating, and let this cookbook inspire you to create meals that not only support your weight loss aspirations but also bring happiness and fulfillment to your dining experiences. Welcome to a healthier, happier you, where delicious food and weight loss go hand in hand!

Embracing the Zero Point Lifestyle

Chapter 1: Embracing the Zero Point Lifestyle

Understanding the Zero Point Philosophy

The journey to a healthier lifestyle begins with a fundamental shift in how we perceive food. The Zero Point philosophy is built on the understanding that we don't have to sacrifice taste or satisfaction to achieve our weight loss goals. Instead, we can indulge in an array of nutrient-rich, delicious foods that support our bodies and satisfy our cravings. This chapter explores the principles of the Zero Point lifestyle and how to integrate them into your daily routine.

At the heart of this philosophy is the concept of zero point foods. These are items that carry little to no point value in the Weight Watchers system, allowing you to enjoy them without counting calories or feeling guilty. By incorporating these foods into your meals, you can fill your plate generously, ensuring that you remain full and satisfied throughout the day.

Identifying Zero Point Foods

Zero point foods include a variety of fruits, vegetables, lean proteins, and whole grains. Understanding which foods fall into this category is essential for making informed choices.

♦ Fruits and Vegetables: Most fresh fruits and vegetables are zero points, making them the perfect choice for snacking or adding to meals. Think of colorful berries, crunchy carrots, crisp cucumbers, and hearty leafy greens. These foods are not only low in calories but

also packed with vitamins, minerals, and fiber that are essential for overall health.

♦ Lean Proteins: Foods like chicken breast, turkey, fish, and eggs are excellent sources of protein that are generally considered zero points. Protein plays a crucial role in keeping you feeling full and maintaining muscle mass, especially during weight loss.

♦ Whole Grains: While some grains may carry points, certain options like brown rice and quinoa can be included as zero point foods when portioned correctly. They provide energy and are a great source of fiber, aiding in digestion and keeping you satisfied longer.

Meal Planning for Success

A successful weight loss journey requires planning and preparation. By taking the time to plan your meals, you set yourself up for success and minimize the temptation to reach for unhealthy options when hunger strikes.

1. Create a Weekly Menu: Dedicate time each week to outline your meals. Include a variety of zero point foods to keep things interesting and enjoyable. Consider planning for breakfasts, lunches, dinners, and snacks. This not only helps you stay organized but also allows you to try new recipes and flavors.

2. Make a Grocery List: Once you have your menu, create a grocery list based on the ingredients you need. This helps prevent impulse purchases and ensures that you have everything on hand

to prepare your meals. Stick to the perimeter of the grocery store, where fresh produce, meats, and dairy products are typically found, and limit your time in the processed food aisles.

3. Prep Ahead of Time: Preparing meals in advance can save you time and effort during busy weekdays. Spend a few hours on the weekend washing and chopping vegetables, cooking proteins, and portioning out snacks. Having ready-to-eat meals and snacks on hand will make it easier to stay on track and avoid the temptation of quick, unhealthy options.

Building Balanced Plates

As you begin to incorporate zero point foods into your meals, focus on building balanced plates that include a variety of food groups. A well-rounded meal should consist of:

♦ A Lean Protein: This could be grilled chicken, baked fish, or a veggie-based protein like beans or lentils.

♦ Colorful Vegetables: Fill half your plate with a mix of colorful vegetables, whether they are raw, steamed, roasted, or sautéed. The more variety, the better!

♦ Whole Grains: Include a small serving of whole grains, like brown rice or quinoa, to provide energy and keep you full.

♦ Healthy Fats (in moderation): While most fats carry points, small amounts of healthy fats from sources like avocado or olive oil can enhance flavor and help with satiety.

Mindful Eating Practices

Beyond what you eat, how you eat can significantly impact your weight loss success. Mindful eating is the practice of being present during your meals, allowing you to fully enjoy and appreciate the flavors and textures of your food. Here are some tips for cultivating mindful eating habits:

♦ Slow Down: Take your time to chew your food thoroughly and savor each bite. This not only enhances the eating experience but also helps your body recognize when it's full.

♦ Listen to Your Body: Pay attention to your hunger and fullness cues. Eat when you are hungry, and stop when you feel satisfied, rather than finishing everything on your plate out of habit.

♦ Limit Distractions: Try to avoid eating in front of the TV or while scrolling through your phone. Focus on your meal, and enjoy the company of those you're dining with if applicable.

The Importance of Community and Support

Embarking on a weight loss journey can be challenging, but having a supportive community can make a world of difference. Whether it's friends, family, or online support groups, sharing your experiences and goals with others can provide motivation and encouragement. Surround yourself with people who understand your journey and can help you celebrate your successes, no matter how small.

Conclusion

Chapter 1 of the Zero Point Weight Loss Cookbook sets the foundation for your journey toward healthier living. By embracing the principles of the zero point lifestyle, identifying zero point foods, and planning your meals effectively, you are taking significant steps toward achieving your weight loss goals. Remember that this journey is about progress, not perfection, and every small change you make adds up to a healthier, happier you. Let's move forward together into the delicious recipes that await you in the chapters to come!

30-Day Meal Plan

DAYS	BREAKFAST	LUNCH	DINNER	SNACK/DESSERT
1	Keto Breakfast Delight Sandwiches 11	Mediterranean Tuna & Pepper Salad 26	Hearty Sausage-Stuffed Bell Peppers with Provolone Melt 33	Almond Flour Blueberry Crumble 66
2	Crispy Bacon-Infused Radish Medley 12	Creamy Bacon Clam Chowder 21	Zesty Shrimp Cauliflower Fried Rice 22	Coconut Strawberry Bliss Ice 71
3	Spicy Bacon-Jalapeño Egg Bites 14	Zesty Ahi Tuna Hand Rolls 26	Jerk Pulled Pork with Avocado 35	Cinnamon Hazelnut Bliss Cookies 85
4	Avocado Egg Boats 13	Golden Turmeric Salmon & Cauliflower 20	Herb-Infused Cilantro Pork Shoulder 31	Decadent Keto Birthday Cheesecake 85
5	Garden Fresh Tofu Scramble 13	Crispy Shrimp Lettuce Tacos 20	Layered Alfredo Chicken Bake 42	Coconut-Chocolate Almond Bliss Bites 87
6	Hearty Cowboy Cauliflower Breakfast 18	Glazed Salmon with Savory Noodles 22	Apple Cider Herb-Infused Pork Tenderloin 33	Low-Carb Cream Cheese Delight 86
7	Creamy Pumpkin Spice Shake 12	Flounder with Lemon Brown Butter Drizzle 20	Creamy Cheddar-Dill Chicken 37	Rich and Creamy Erythritol Crème Brûlée 93
8	Berry Bliss Smoothie 15	Crispy Parmesan-Crusted Pork Chops 29	Air-Fried Herb-Crusted Lamb Chops 30	Fluffy Toasted Coconut Marshmallows 86
9	Frothy Butter Coffee Bliss 16	Mediterranean Grilled Pork Skewers 34	Zesty Lemon Butter Chicken Piccata 40	Zesty Lime Delight Muffins 89
10	Silky Smooth Scrambled Eggs 16	Creamy Power Greens Soup 75	Smoky Paprika-Grilled Pork Chops 33	Coconut Flour Vanilla Bliss Scones 92
11	Keto Air Fryer Everything Bagels 18	Thai Coconut Curry Mussels 21	Creamy Salsa Verde Chicken Soup 78	Decadent Dark Chocolate Brownies 93
12	Cheesy Broccoli Egg Bites 15	Creamy Cheddar Cauliflower Soup 76	Spicy Cajun Chicken and Sausage Gumbo 41	Easy Almond Butter Bliss Cookies
13	Crispy Parmesan Pork Rind Zucchini Sticks 47	Crispy Sesame-Crusted Tuna Steaks 25	Creamy Chicken and Garden Vegetable Delight 79	Frozen Strawberry Cream Cheesecake
14	Cheesy Keto Waffle Bites 12	Classic Ahi Poke with Sesame 27	Creamy Garlic Mashed Cauliflower 48	Pecan Bourbon Delight Bites
15	Creamy Almond-Infused Beef Stew 31	Garlic Butter Sautéed Spinach 51	Spicy Chorizo-Beef Burgers 30	Refreshing Electrolyte Gelatin Bites 87
16	Zesty Lemon-Blueberry Air Muffins 14	Sautéed Herbed Radishes with Chives 49	Layered Caprese Eggplant Stacks 55	Decadent Almond Cocoa Fat Bombs 88

DAYS	BREAKFAST	LUNCH	DINNER	SNACK/DESSERT
17	Fluffy Oven-Baked Pancake Puff 17	Garlic & Herb Flank Steak Delight 32	Crispy Parmesan Artichokes 57	Savory Roasted Garlic Bulbs 70
18	Hearty Veggie-Beef Skillet with Baked Eggs 16	Crispy Balsamic Brussels Sprouts 50	Spiced Roasted Salmon with Fresh Avocado Salsa 21	Creamy Coconut Almond Popsicles 90
19	Cheesy Cream-Filled Muffins 11	Zesty Lemon-Pepper Chicken Drumsticks 68	Instant Pot Chicken Carnitas 43	Nutty Sesame Delight Cookies 91
20	Crispy Zucchini and Spinach Croquettes 57	Cheesy Cauliflower Rice Medley 69	Creamy Garlic Butter Broccoli 50	Creamy Cardamom Bliss Rolls 89
21	Creamy Ranch Chicken Bake 43	Garlic Basil Portobello Pizzas 45	Cheesy Mackerel & Broccoli Bake 24	Coconut Pistachio Dream Fudge 91
22	Keto Cinnamon Swirl Rolls 13	Garlic-Parmesan Pan-Roasted Green Beans 46	Thai Coconut Shrimp Soup with Mushrooms 76	Decadent Vanilla Crème Brûlée 92
23	Bacon-Wrapped Avocado & Egg Bomb 12	Steamed Salmon with Fresh Dill Butter 22	Savory Sun-Dried Tomato Turkey Meatballs 40	Cheesy Quiche-Stuffed Bell Peppers 57
24	Spicy Pulled Pork Breakfast Hash 17	Spaghetti Squash Ramen Delight 74	Lemon Herb Whole Roasted Cauliflower 61	Creamy Cheese-Stuffed Bell Peppers 56
25	Cheesy Italian Chicken Bake 41	Cheesy Cauliflower Hash Brown Bake 45	Air-Fried Short Ribs with Fresh Chimichurri 34	Spicy Loaded Cauliflower Steaks 60
26	Crispy Eggplant Parmesan with Marinara 58	Crispy Parmesan Pork Rind Green Beans 47	Creamy Garlic Zucchini Rolls 54	Refreshing Lemon Tea Gummies 90
27	Crispy Almond-Cauliflower Gnocchi 62	Creamy Cheddar Baked Zucchini 61	Coconut Cauliflower Shrimp Curry Soup 74	Almond Flour Strawberry Delight 91
28	Creamy Cauliflower Tikka Masala 60	Garlic Herb Roasted Broccoli with Dipping Sauce 59	Spicy Jalapeño Cod 24	Creamy Cheesecake Poppers 88
29	Cheesy Broccoli-Stuffed Chicken 38	Mediterranean Cheese Pan Pizza 61	Coconut Curry Broccoli Bliss Soup 83	Coconut Flour Butter Biscuits 51
30	Garlic Herb Roasted Spaghetti Squash 58	Zesty Air-Fried Lemon Salmon 21	Spicy Buffalo Chicken Soup 73	Chocolate Walnut Delight 89

Chapter 2

Breakfasts

Chapter 2 Breakfasts

Keto Breakfast Delight Sandwiches

Prep time: 5 minutes | Cook time: 10 minutes | Makes 2 sandwiches

- 1 tablespoon butter
- 4 eggs
- 2 cooked breakfast sausage patties
- 2 slices Cheddar cheese
- Salt and freshly ground black pepper, to taste

1. Begin by heating a large nonstick skillet over medium heat. Add the butter and allow it to melt completely. 2. Crack each egg into a round metal biscuit cutter, a silicone mold, or the ring of a mason jar lid. Give the eggs a quick stir as they cook, gently breaking the yolks. Cook for about 3 to 4 minutes or until the eggs are set. Carefully remove the eggs from the mold and set aside. Repeat this process until all eggs are cooked. 3. In the same skillet, add the sausage and heat for 1 to 2 minutes to warm through. Top each sausage piece with a slice of cheese. Cover the skillet with a lid to help the cheese melt more quickly. 4. Assemble your sandwiches by placing a cheesy sausage on top of one egg, then topping it with a second egg. Continue this process with the remaining ingredients to make all the sandwiches. Serve immediately and enjoy!

Per Serving:
1 sandwich: calories: 397 | fat: 34g | protein: 23g | carbs: 1g | net carbs: 1g | fiber: 0g

Cheesy Cream-Filled Muffins

Prep time: 10 minutes | Cook time: 10 minutes | Makes 6 muffins

- 4 tablespoons melted butter, plus more for the muffin tin
- 1 cup almond flour
- ¾ tablespoon baking powder
- 2 large eggs, lightly beaten
- 2 ounces cream cheese mixed with 2 tablespoons heavy (whipping) cream
- Handful shredded Mexican blend cheese

1. Preheat your oven to 400°F (200°C) and grease six cups of a muffin tin with butter. 2. In a small bowl, combine the almond flour and baking powder, mixing them together well. 3. In a separate medium bowl, whisk together the eggs, cream cheese and heavy cream mixture, shredded cheese, and 4 tablespoons of melted butter until fully combined. 4. Gradually add the flour mixture to the egg mixture, then use a hand mixer to blend until the batter is smooth and well incorporated. 5. Carefully pour the batter into the prepared muffin cups, filling each about three-quarters full. 6. Bake for approximately 12 minutes or until the tops are golden brown. Remove from the oven and serve warm.

Per Serving:
calories: 247 | fat: 23g | protein: 8g | carbs: 4g | net carbs: 4g | fiber: 2g

Creamy Bacon & Spinach Cashew Dip

Prep time: 10 minutes | Cook time: 8 minutes | Makes 2 cups

- 6 strips bacon (about 6 ounces/170 g)
- 1 cup (160 g) raw cashews, soaked for 4 hours, then drained and rinsed ⅔ cup (160 ml) full-fat coconut milk
- ¼ cup (17 g) nutritional yeast
- 3 tablespoons apple cider
- vinegar
- 1 teaspoon finely ground gray sea salt
- 1 teaspoon onion powder
- ½ teaspoon garlic powder
- ½ teaspoon ground mustard
- ¼ teaspoon ground black pepper
- 1 cup (70 g) spinach, chopped

1. In a large skillet over medium heat, cook the bacon until it's nice and crispy. Once cooked, remove the bacon from the pan, letting it cool slightly before crumbling it into pieces. Reserve the bacon grease in the skillet; don't wash the pan, as you'll need it again soon. 2. In a food processor or blender, combine the reserved bacon grease with the soaked cashews, coconut milk, nutritional yeast, vinegar, salt, and spices. Blend everything together until the mixture is completely smooth and creamy. 3. While the mixture is blending, sauté the spinach in the same skillet over medium-low heat until just wilted, which should take about 30 seconds. 4. Add the crumbled bacon and wilted spinach to the blender or food processor, pulsing the mixture just until everything is combined but still a bit chunky. 5. Transfer the mixture to a serving bowl and enjoy!

Per Serving:
calories: 132 | fat: 11g | protein: 4g | carbs: 5g | net carbs: 4g | fiber: 1g

Cheesy Keto Waffle Bites

Prep time: 5 minutes | Cook time: 10 to 15 minutes | Serves 1

◆ Nonstick cooking spray, butter, or oil for greasing the waffle maker	◆ 1 large egg
	◆ ⅓ cup grated Cheddar cheese, divided

1. Lightly grease and preheat your waffle maker. 2. In a small bowl, whisk together the egg and one-third of the cheese until well combined. 3. Sprinkle a layer of grated cheese directly onto the waffle maker surface, then pour in half of the egg-cheese mixture. Add another sprinkle of cheese on top before closing the lid. 4. Cook the waffle for 4 to 5 minutes, checking for desired crispness. If needed, flip and cook an additional 1 to 2 minutes for extra crispiness. Repeat the process with the remaining egg mixture and cheese.

Per Serving:

calories: 222 | fat: 17g | protein: 16g | carbs: 1g | net carbs: 1g | fiber: 0g

Bacon-Wrapped Avocado & Egg Bomb

Prep time: 5 minutes | Cook time: 17 minutes | Serves 1

◆ 1 large egg	◆ Fresh parsley, for serving (optional)
◆ 1 avocado, halved, peeled, and pitted	◆ Sea salt flakes, for garnish (optional)
◆ 2 slices bacon	

1. Lightly spray the air fryer basket with avocado oil and preheat the air fryer to 320°F (160°C). Prepare a small bowl with cool water. 2. To soft-boil the egg, place it in the air fryer basket and cook for 6 minutes for a runny yolk or 7 minutes for a firmer yolk. Transfer the egg to the bowl of cool water and let it sit for 2 minutes before peeling. Set aside. 3. Carefully scoop out extra flesh from the center of each avocado half to create enough space for the soft-boiled egg. Place the egg in the hollow of one avocado half, then top with the other half, reassembling the avocado to look whole. 4. Wrap the avocado completely with bacon, starting at one end and securing with toothpicks as needed to keep the bacon in place. 5. Place the bacon-wrapped avocado in the air fryer basket and cook for 5 minutes. Flip it over and cook for an additional 5 minutes, or until the bacon reaches your desired crispness. Serve on a bed of fresh parsley, if desired, and sprinkle with salt flakes for added flavor. 6. Enjoy fresh. Store leftovers in an airtight container in the refrigerator for up to 4 days. To reheat, place in a preheated 320°F (160°C) air fryer for 4 minutes, or until warmed through.

Per Serving:

calories: 380 | fat: 32g | protein: 13g | carbs: 14g | net carbs: 2g | fiber: 12g

Creamy Pumpkin Spice Shake

Prep time: 5 minutes | Cook time: 0 minutes | Serves 2

◆ 1 cup full-fat coconut, nut, or dairy milk	◆ 1 teaspoon pure vanilla extract
◆ ¾ cup canned pumpkin	◆ Small handful of ice (optional)
◆ ½ cup frozen riced cauliflower	◆ 2 scoops collagen peptides
◆ 1 cup water	◆ ⅛ teaspoon green stevia, or 2 or 3 drops stevia extract (optional)
◆ 1 teaspoon ground cinnamon, plus extra for garnish if desired	◆ 1 tablespoon coconut chips, for garnish (optional)
◆ 1 teaspoon pumpkin pie spice	

1. Add all ingredients, except for the coconut chips, into a blender and blend until the mixture is completely smooth. For a thinner consistency, adjust with extra water or milk as desired. 2. Pour into a glass, and sprinkle ground cinnamon and coconut chips on top as a garnish, if preferred. Serve immediately.

Per Serving:

calories: 302 | fat: 24g | protein: 13g | carbs: 12g | net carbs: 9g | fiber: 3g

Crispy Bacon-Infused Radish Medley

Prep time: 10 minutes | Cook time: 25 minutes | serves 4

◆ 1 (16 ounces) bag radishes	pepper
◆ 6 slices bacon	◆ Chopped fresh flat-leaf parsley, for garnish (optional)
◆ Salt and ground black	

1. Begin by trimming the tops off the radishes and cutting them into small pieces. 2. In a large skillet set over medium heat, cook the bacon until it becomes crispy, which should take about 5 minutes. Remove the bacon from the skillet but keep the drippings in the pan. Crumble the bacon and set it aside for later. 3. Add the chopped radishes to the skillet and cook over medium-high heat for 10 minutes. Then, reduce the heat to medium and stir in the crumbled bacon. Continue cooking for an additional 10 minutes, stirring occasionally, until the radishes are slightly crispy and caramelized around the edges. 4. Season the dish with salt and pepper to taste, and serve immediately. If desired, garnish with fresh parsley before serving.

Per Serving:

calories: 100 | fat: 7g | protein: 6g | carbs: 4g | net carbs: 2g | fiber: 2g

Cheesy Bacon Breakfast Calzones

Prep time: 15 minutes | Cook time: 12 minutes | Serves 4

♦ 2 large eggs	♦ 2 ounces (57 g) cream cheese, softened and broken into small pieces
♦ 1 cup blanched finely ground almond flour	
♦ 2 cups shredded Mozzarella cheese	♦ 4 slices cooked sugar-free bacon, crumbled

1. Beat eggs in a small bowl. Pour into a medium nonstick skillet over medium heat and scramble. Set aside. 2. In a large microwave-safe bowl, mix flour and Mozzarella. Add cream cheese to the bowl. 3. Place bowl in microwave and cook 45 seconds on high to melt cheese, then stir with a fork until a soft dough ball forms. 4. Cut a piece of parchment to fit air fryer basket. Separate dough into two sections and press each out into an 8-inch round. 5. On half of each dough round, place half of the scrambled eggs and crumbled bacon. Fold the other side of the dough over and press to seal the edges. 6. Place calzones on ungreased parchment and into air fryer basket. Adjust the temperature to 350°F (177°C) and set the timer for 12 minutes, turning calzones halfway through cooking. Crust will be golden and firm when done. 7. Let calzones cool on a cooking rack 5 minutes before serving.

Per Serving:
calories: 398 | fat: 32g | protein: 24g | carbs: 5g | net carbs: 3g | fiber: 2g

Keto Cinnamon Swirl Rolls

Prep time: 10 minutes | Cook time: 20 minutes | Makes 12 rolls

♦ 2½ cups shredded Mozzarella cheese	♦ ½ teaspoon vanilla extract
♦ 2 ounces (57 g) cream cheese, softened	♦ ½ cup confectioners' erythritol
♦ 1 cup blanched finely ground almond flour	♦ 1 tablespoon ground cinnamon

1. In a large microwave-safe bowl, mix together the Mozzarella cheese, cream cheese, and almond flour. Microwave on high for 90 seconds, stirring halfway, until the cheese has fully melted. 2. Stir in vanilla extract and erythritol, blending continuously for about 2 minutes until a smooth dough forms. 3. Let the dough cool slightly until manageable, about 2 minutes, then spread it into a 12 × 4-inch rectangle on parchment paper without greasing. Sprinkle cinnamon evenly over the dough surface. 4. Carefully roll the dough from one long side to create a log shape. Cut the log into twelve equal slices. 5. Arrange the rolls in two ungreased round nonstick baking dishes. Place one dish in the air fryer basket, set the temperature to 375°F (191°C), and cook for 10 minutes. 6. Rolls are ready when golden-brown on the edges and mostly firm. Repeat with the second batch.

Let the rolls cool in the dish for 10 minutes before serving warm.

Per Serving:
calories: 123 | fat: 9g | protein: 7g | carbs: 3g | net carbs: 2g | fiber: 1g

Garden Fresh Tofu Scramble

Prep time: 10 minutes | Cook time: 10 minutes | serves 4

♦ 1 (14-ounce) block firm sprouted organic tofu, pressed and drained	coconut oil
	♦ ⅓ cup diced yellow onion
♦ 2 tablespoons tahini	♦ ⅓ cup diced green bell pepper
♦ 2 tablespoons nutritional yeast	♦ ¼ teaspoon garlic powder
♦ 1 tablespoon chia seeds	♦ ¼ cup olives
♦ ¼ teaspoon turmeric powder	♦ 2 cups coarsely chopped fresh spinach
♦ ⅛ teaspoon kala namak salt	♦ 1 teaspoon hot sauce (optional)
♦ 2 tablespoons cold-pressed	

1. Use a paper towel to press out excess moisture from the tofu, then crumble it into a large mixing bowl by hand. 2. Add tahini, nutritional yeast, chia seeds, turmeric, and kala namak salt to the bowl, gently mixing everything until well combined. Set aside. 3. Warm coconut oil in a large skillet over medium heat. 4. Add diced onion, chopped bell pepper, and a sprinkle of garlic powder to the skillet. 5. When the vegetables are softened and lightly caramelized, add in the olives along with the tofu mixture. 6. Let the tofu cook undisturbed for around 4 minutes to achieve a lightly crispy texture, then stir once to evenly toast. 7. When the tofu is golden, remove the skillet from heat, adding spinach and stirring until it wilts slightly. 8. Serve immediately with a dash of hot sauce, if desired.

Per Serving:
calories: 253 | fat: 18g | protein: 15g | carbs: 11g | net carbs: 7g | fiber: 4g

Avocado Egg Boats

Prep time: 10 minutes | Cook time: 10 minutes | Serves 4

♦ 2 large avocados, halved and pitted	♦ Salt and black pepper to season
♦ 4 small eggs	♦ Chopped parsley to garnish

1. Set the oven to preheat at 400°F. 2. Carefully crack an egg into each avocado half, arranging them on a greased baking sheet. Place the sheet in the oven and bake for 8-10 minutes, or until the eggs reach your desired doneness. 3. Sprinkle with salt and pepper, then garnish with fresh parsley before serving.

Per Serving:
calories: 221 | fat: 18g | protein: 7g | carbs: 9g | net carbs: 3g | fiber: 6g

Crab & Egg Scramble with Fresh Herb Salsa

Prep time: 10 minutes | Cook time: 10 minutes | Serves 3

◆ 1 tablespoon olive oil	flaked
◆ 6 eggs, whisked	◆ Salt and black pepper to taste
◆ 1 (6 ounces) can crabmeat, For the Salsa:	
◆ ¾ cup crème fraiche	◆ Salt and black pepper to taste
◆ ½ cup scallions, chopped	
◆ ½ teaspoon garlic powder	◆ ½ teaspoon fresh dill, chopped

1. Heat olive oil in a sauté pan over medium heat. Crack the eggs directly into the pan, scrambling them as they cook. Add the crabmeat, seasoning with salt and black pepper, and cook until everything is heated through and fully cooked. 2. In a separate bowl, mix together all the salsa ingredients until well combined. Divide the egg and crab mixture evenly onto serving plates, and serve with the salsa and sliced scallions on the side.

Per Serving:
calories: 364 | fat: 26g | protein: 25g | carbs: 5g | net carbs: 5g | fiber: 0g

Spicy Bacon-Jalapeño Egg Bites

Prep time: 5 minutes | Cook time: 25 minutes | Makes 6 egg cups

For The Bacon:	
◆ 6 bacon slices	◆ 1 tablespoon butter
For The Eggs:	
◆ 2 jalapeño peppers	◆ Pink Himalayan salt
◆ 4 large eggs	◆ Freshly ground black pepper
◆ 2 ounces cream cheese, at room temperature	◆ ¼ cup shredded Mexican blend cheese

To Prepare the Bacon: 1. Set the oven to 375°F to preheat. 2. As the oven heats, place a large skillet on medium-high and add the bacon strips, cooking them until they're partially done, about 4 minutes. Remove the bacon and lay it on a plate lined with paper towels. 3. Grease six sections of a standard muffin tin with butter. Fit one piece of partially cooked bacon around the sides of each prepared cup.
To Prepare the Eggs: 1. Slice one jalapeño lengthwise, remove seeds, and mince finely. Slice the other jalapeño into rings, discarding the seeds, and set aside. 2. In a mixing bowl, use a hand mixer to beat the eggs until fully combined. Add cream cheese and minced jalapeño, season with pink Himalayan salt and black pepper, and blend until smooth. 3. Carefully pour the egg mixture into the muffin tin, filling each cup about two-thirds to allow room for rising. 4. Sprinkle shredded cheese over each egg cup, add a

jalapeño ring on top, and bake for 20 minutes. 5. Let cool for 10 minutes before serving warm.

Per Serving:
calories: 159 | fat: 13g | protein: 9g | carbs: 1g | net carbs: 1g | fiber: 0g

Zesty Lemon-Blueberry Air Muffins

Prep time: 5 minutes | Cook time: 20 to 25 minutes | Makes 6 muffins

◆ 1¼ cups almond flour	◆ 3 tablespoons melted butter
◆ 3 tablespoons Swerve	◆ 1 tablespoon almond milk
◆ 1 teaspoon baking powder	◆ 1 tablespoon fresh lemon juice
◆ 2 large eggs	◆ ½ cup fresh blueberries

1. Preheat the air fryer to 350°F (177°C) and lightly grease 6 silicone muffin cups with vegetable oil. Set aside. 2. In a large bowl, mix together almond flour, Swerve, and baking soda until well combined. Set aside. 3. In a small bowl, whisk the eggs, melted butter, milk, and lemon juice until smooth. Pour this wet mixture into the dry ingredients and stir until just incorporated. Gently fold in the blueberries, allowing the batter to rest for 5 minutes. 4. Fill each muffin cup with batter, filling them about two-thirds of the way. Place the cups in the air fryer and cook for 20 to 25 minutes, or until a toothpick inserted in the center comes out clean. 5. Carefully remove the air fryer basket and let the muffins sit for 5 minutes before transferring them to a wire rack to cool completely.

Per Serving:
calories: 188 | fat: 15g | protein: 6g | carbs: 7g | net carbs: 5g | fiber: 2g

Golden Turmeric Scramble

Prep time: 5 minutes | Cook time: 5 minutes | Serves 2

◆ 3 large eggs	◆ Salt, to taste
◆ 2 tablespoons heavy cream (optional)	◆ Freshly ground black pepper, to taste
◆ 1 teaspoon ground turmeric	◆ 1 tablespoon butter

1. In a small bowl, whisk together the eggs and cream until combined, then add the turmeric, salt, and pepper. 2. Heat butter in a skillet over medium heat until it begins to foam slightly. Pour in the egg mixture carefully, stirring frequently as the eggs start to set, cooking for 2 to 3 minutes. 3. Remove from heat, taste, and adjust salt and pepper as desired. Serve immediately.

Per Serving:
calories: 213 | fat: 18g | protein: 10g | carbs: 2g | net carbs: 2g | fiber: 0g

Instant Pot Gruyère & Asparagus Frittata

Prep time: 10 minutes | Cook time: 22 minutes | Serves 6

◆ 6 eggs	◆ 1 clove garlic, minced
◆ 6 tablespoons heavy cream	◆ 1¼ cup shredded Gruyère cheese, divided
◆ ½ teaspoon salt	
◆ ½ teaspoon black pepper	◆ Cooking spray
◆ 1 tablespoon butter	◆ 3 ounces (85 g) halved cherry tomatoes
◆ 2½ ounces (71 g) asparagus, chopped	
	◆ ½ cup water

1. In a large mixing bowl, combine the eggs, cream, salt, and pepper, whisking until smooth. 2. Set the Instant Pot to Sauté mode and melt the butter. Add the asparagus and garlic, sautéing for about 2 minutes until the garlic is fragrant and the asparagus remains crisp. 3. Transfer the asparagus and garlic into the bowl with the egg mixture, stirring in 1 cup of cheese. Wipe out the Instant Pot to prepare for the next step. 4. Lightly coat a baking pan with cooking spray, then spread the tomatoes in a single layer at the bottom of the pan. Pour the egg mixture over the tomatoes and sprinkle the remaining ¼ cup of cheese on top. Cover the pan tightly with aluminum foil. 5. Pour water into the Instant Pot, place the trivet inside, and set the baking pan on the trivet. 6. Secure the lid and select Manual mode, setting it to cook on High Pressure for 20 minutes. Once done, perform a quick pressure release and carefully open the lid. 7. Remove the baking pan from the Instant Pot, uncover, and gently blot away any excess moisture. Allow the frittata to cool for 5 to 10 minutes before transferring it to a plate for serving.

Per Serving:
calories: 204 | fat: 17g | protein: 11g | carbs: 2g | net carbs: 2g | fiber: 1g

Keto Mini Chocolate Chip Muffins

Prep time: 5 minutes | Cook time: 20 minutes | Serves 7

◆ 1 cup blanched almond flour	◆ ½ cup Swerve, or more to taste
◆ 2 eggs	
◆ ¾ cup sugar-free chocolate chips	◆ 2 tablespoons salted grass-fed butter, softened
◆ 1 tablespoon vanilla extract	◆ ½ teaspoon salt
	◆ ¼ teaspoon baking soda

1. Pour 1 cup of filtered water into the Instant Pot's inner pot and place the trivet inside. Using an electric mixer, blend together the flour, eggs, chocolate chips, vanilla, Swerve, butter, salt, and baking soda until well mixed. Spoon the batter into a well-greased muffin or egg bites mold suitable for the Instant Pot. 2. Carefully place the filled mold onto the trivet, using a sling if desired for easy removal, and loosely cover with aluminum foil. Secure the lid, set the

pressure release to Sealing, and select Manual mode. Set to cook on High Pressure for 20 minutes. 3. After cooking, allow the pressure to release naturally for 10 minutes, then carefully turn the pressure release to Venting to release any remaining pressure. 4. Open the lid, remove the pan, and let the muffins cool before serving. Enjoy!

Per Serving:
calories: 204 | fat: 17g | protein: 3g | carbs: 10g | net carbs: 9g | fiber: 1g

Berry Bliss Smoothie

Prep time: 5 minutes | Cook time: 0 minutes | Serves 5

◆ 2 cups unsweetened vanilla almond milk	sweetener blend (1:1 sugar replacement)
◆ 2 cups (9 ounces / 255 g) raspberries, fresh or frozen	◆ ½ cup almond butter, no sugar added
◆ 1 cup (3½ ounces / 99 g) blueberries, fresh or frozen	◆ ½ cup lemon juice
	◆ ¼ cup chia seeds
◆ ½ cup monk fruit/erythritol	

1. Place all ingredients in a blender and blend until the mixture is completely smooth. For an extra refreshing smoothie, chill in the refrigerator for 30 minutes if you used fresh berries.
Per Serving:
calories: 256 | fat: 18g | protein: 8g | carbs: 39g | net carbs: 11g | fiber: 28g

Cheesy Broccoli Egg Bites

Prep time: 10 minutes | Cook time: 10 minutes | Serves 7

◆ 5 eggs, beaten	◆ 1 ounce (28 g) finely chopped broccoli
◆ 3 tablespoons heavy cream	
◆ ⅛ teaspoon salt	◆ 1 ounce (28 g) shredded Cheddar cheese
◆ ⅛ teaspoon black pepper	
	◆ ½ cup water

1. In a blender, combine the eggs, heavy cream, salt, and pepper, pulsing until smooth and well-mixed. 2. Evenly distribute the chopped broccoli across the egg cups, then pour the egg mixture over the broccoli, filling each cup about three-fourths full. Top each with a sprinkle of Cheddar cheese. 3. Cover the egg cups securely with aluminum foil. 4. Pour water into the Instant Pot and place the trivet inside. Arrange the egg cups on the trivet. 5. Secure the lid, select Manual mode, and set to cook on High Pressure for 10 minutes. When the timer goes off, allow a natural pressure release for 5 minutes, then carefully release any remaining pressure and open the lid. 6. Serve the egg cups immediately for best results.

Per Serving:
calories: 89 | fat: 7g | protein: 6g | carbs: 1g | net carbs: 1g | fiber: 0g

Spinach & Bacon Breakfast Wraps

Prep time: 5 minutes | Cook time: 11 minutes | Makes 3 roll-ups

- 4 large eggs
- ¼ cup heavy whipping cream
- ½ teaspoon pink Himalayan salt
- 6 ounces fresh spinach
- 6 slices bacon, cooked
- 2 ounces fresh (soft) goat cheese

1. Warm a 12-inch skillet over low heat and coat it lightly with coconut oil spray. 2. In a medium bowl, whisk together the eggs, cream, and a pinch of salt until smooth. 3. Pour a ⅓-cup portion of the egg mixture into the center of the hot skillet, tilting to evenly coat the surface. Cover with a lid and cook for 2 to 3 minutes, or until the wrap is fully set. Repeat this process with the remaining egg mixture to make a total of 3 wraps. 4. Increase the heat to medium-high, re-spray the skillet with coconut oil, and add the spinach. Cover and cook for 1 to 2 minutes, until the spinach wilts. Remove from the skillet. 5. Evenly distribute the cooked spinach across the 3 egg wraps, laying it along one edge. Place 2 slices of bacon on each wrap over the spinach, and sprinkle the goat cheese evenly. 6. Roll each wrap from the edge with the fillings, folding in the ends like a burrito, or simply rolling it like a crepe. Serve warm for the best flavor.

Per Serving:
calories: 299 | fat: 24g | protein: 20g | carbs: 4g | net carbs: 2g | fiber: 2g

Hearty Veggie-Beef Skillet with Baked Eggs

Prep time: 5 minutes | Cook time: 35 minutes | Serves 4

- 2 tablespoons good-quality olive oil
- ½ pound grass-fed ground beef
- ½ red bell pepper, diced
- ½ zucchini, diced
- ¼ onion, diced
- 2 teaspoons minced garlic
- 1½ cups low-carb tomato sauce
- 1 tablespoon dried basil
- 1 teaspoon dried oregano
- ⅛ teaspoon sea salt
- ⅛ teaspoon freshly ground black pepper
- 4 eggs

1. Prepare the beef. In a large, deep skillet over medium-high heat, heat the olive oil. Add the beef, stirring occasionally, and cook until fully browned, around 10 minutes. 2. Create the sauce. Add bell pepper, zucchini, onion, and garlic to the skillet, sautéing for 3 minutes. Mix in the tomato sauce, basil, oregano, salt, and pepper, bringing it to a boil, then let it cook for 10 minutes. 3. Cook the eggs. Using the back of a spoon, make four wells in the beef mixture. Crack an egg into each well, cover the skillet, reduce the heat to medium-low, and let the eggs cook until set, about 10 minutes. 4. Serve. Spoon the beef and vegetable mixture into four bowls, ensuring each portion has an egg.

Per Serving:
calories: 275 | fat: 19g | protein: 18g | carbs: 8g | net carbs: 6g | fiber: 2g

Frothy Butter Coffee Bliss

Prep time: 5 minutes | Cook time: 0 minutes | Serves 1

- 1 cup (8 ounces / 227 g) brewed coffee
- ½ tablespoon unsalted butter
- ½ tablespoon MCT oil
- 3 tablespoons unsweetened vanilla almond milk

1. In a blender, add the coffee, butter, MCT oil, and almond milk. Blend the mixture until it becomes frothy and well combined. (Avoid simply stirring the ingredients, as this will result in an oily coffee rather than a frothy texture.) 2. Pour the frothy coffee into a mug and enjoy!

Per Serving:
calories: 119 | fat: 13g | protein: 0g | carbs: 0g | net carbs: 0g | fiber: 0g

Silky Smooth Scrambled Eggs

Prep time: 5 minutes | Cook time: 5 minutes | Serves 2

- 4 eggs
- 1 to 2 tablespoons water
- 1 tablespoon butter
- Salt and freshly ground
- black pepper, to taste
- Sliced scallion, green parts only, or chopped fresh chives, for topping (optional)

1. Preheat a large nonstick skillet over medium-high heat. 2. In a medium bowl, crack the eggs, add the water, and whisk thoroughly until the whites and yolks are fully blended, aiming for a smooth, lump-free consistency that flows continuously when lifted. 3. Add butter to the skillet, using a spatula to coat the entire surface as it melts. Pour in the eggs, stirring briefly, then lower the heat to medium. Gently stir the eggs while tilting the skillet so the uncooked portions spread and make contact with the hot surface. 4. As the eggs set, about 3 to 4 minutes, reduce the heat to low and fold the eggs over gently with the spatula until cooked to your preference. 5. Season with salt and pepper, and serve hot. Garnish with sliced scallions if desired.

Per Serving:
calories: 177 | fat: 15g | protein: 11g | carbs: 1g | net carbs: 1g | fiber: 0g

Spicy Pulled Pork Breakfast Hash

Prep time: 10 minutes | Cook time: 15 minutes | Serves 4

- 4 eggs
- 10 ounces (283 g) pulled pork, shredded
- 1 teaspoon coconut oil
- 1 teaspoon red pepper
- 1 teaspoon chopped fresh cilantro
- 1 tomato, chopped
- ¼ cup water

1. Begin by melting the coconut oil in the Instant Pot using the Sauté mode. 2. Next, add the pulled pork, diced red pepper, chopped cilantro, water, and chopped tomato to the pot. 3. Allow the mixture to cook for 5 minutes, stirring occasionally. 4. After 5 minutes, give it a good stir with a spatula, then crack the eggs directly over the mixture. 5. Secure the lid on the Instant Pot. 6. Switch to Manual mode (High Pressure) and set the cooking time for 7 minutes. Once the timer goes off, perform a quick pressure release to release the steam.

Per Serving:
calories: 275 | fat: 18g | protein: 22g | carbs: 6g | net carbs: 5g | fiber: 1g

Zesty Shakshuka with a Mediterranean Kick

Prep time: 5 minutes | Cook time: 30 minutes | Serves 3

- 1 tablespoon avocado oil
- ½ cup (2 ounces / 57 g) diced onion
- 2 cloves garlic, minced
- 1 (10-ounce / 283-g) can no-salt-added diced tomatoes with green chilies
- ½ cup tomato sauce
- 1 teaspoon paprika
- 1 teaspoon ground cumin
- ½ teaspoon sea salt, plus more for taste
- 6 large eggs
- 2 tablespoons chopped fresh parsley

1. In a 12-inch sauté pan, warm the oil over medium-low heat. Add the diced onion and cook for about 10 minutes until it becomes golden brown. Stir in the minced garlic and sauté for another minute until aromatic. 2. Add the diced tomatoes (with their juices), tomato sauce, paprika, and cumin to the pan. Season with sea salt, then cover and let it simmer for 12 to 15 minutes, or until the tomato mixture has thickened and most of the liquid has reduced. If needed, uncover and cook for a few more minutes to achieve the desired consistency. 3. Crack the eggs directly into the pan, spacing them out in the sauce. If you prefer, make small wells in the sauce for each egg. Lightly sprinkle the eggs with a bit more sea salt. 4. Cover the pan and cook for 4 to 6 minutes, until the whites are set but the yolks remain runny. If you prefer firmer eggs, cook them a bit longer to your liking. 5. Garnish with fresh parsley and serve hot.

Per Serving:
calories: 248 | fat: 15g | protein: 16g | carbs: 10g | net carbs: 8g | fiber: 2g

Fluffy Oven-Baked Pancake Puff

Prep time: 5 minutes | Cook time: 20 minutes | serves 4

- 2 tablespoons salted butter
- 4 large eggs
- ¼ cup water
- ¼ cup heavy whipping cream
- 2 tablespoons coconut flour
- 2 tablespoons granular erythritol
- ½ teaspoon vanilla extract
- ¼ teaspoon salt

For Garnish (optional):
- Fresh blueberries
- Confectioners'-style erythritol

1. Preheat the oven to 425°F. 2. Place the butter in a 10-inch cast-iron or other oven-safe skillet, then put it in the oven to melt. Once the butter is melted, carefully remove the skillet from the oven. 3. In a medium bowl, whisk the eggs thoroughly, then add the water, cream, coconut flour, erythritol, vanilla extract, and salt, stirring until the batter is smooth and well combined. 4. Pour the prepared batter into the hot skillet and bake for 18 to 20 minutes, or until the pancake is puffed and golden brown. Cut into quarters and serve with fresh blueberries and a dusting of confectioners' erythritol, if desired.

Per Serving:
calories: 164 | fat: 14g | protein: 7g | carbs: 2g | net carbs: 1g | fiber: 1g

Quick & Fluffy Mug Biscuits

Prep time: 2 minutes | Cook time: 1 minutes | Serves 4

- 1 large egg
- 3 tablespoons blanched almond flour
- 1 tablespoon coconut flour
- 1 tablespoon unsalted butter,
- softened
- 1 teaspoon avocado oil
- ¼ teaspoon baking powder
- Pinch of salt

1. Combine all ingredients in a microwave-safe mug, stirring thoroughly with a fork until the mixture is smooth. Use the back of a spoon to level off the top. 2. Microwave for 1 minute, adjusting the time as needed depending on your microwave's power. 3. Carefully remove the hot mug from the microwave, cover with a plate, and flip it over to release the biscuit onto the plate. Lay the biscuit on its side and slice it evenly into 4 pieces.

Per Serving:
calories: 182 | fat: 17g | protein: 6g | carbs: 5g | net carbs: 2g | fiber: 3g

Savory Beef Jerky Bites

Prep time: 10 minutes | Cook time: 6 hours | Serves 18

◆ 1 pound (455 g) ground beef (10% fat)	◆ 1 teaspoon ground black pepper
◆ 2 tablespoons coconut aminos	◆ ½ teaspoon garlic powder
◆ 1 teaspoon smoked sea salt	◆ ½ teaspoon red pepper flakes

1. Position two oven racks as close to the center as possible and preheat the oven to 170°F (77°C). Line two baking sheets with parchment paper or silicone baking mats. 2. In a medium bowl, use your hands to mix all ingredients thoroughly until well blended. 3. Scoop a heaping tablespoon of the mixture, roll it into a ball, then flatten it into a 2-inch (5-cm) round. Place on the prepared baking sheet and repeat with the remaining mixture. 4. Bake for 6 hours, flipping each cookie halfway through. Occasionally switch the baking sheets between racks to promote even cooking. The cookies are ready when they have a jerky-like chewiness. 5. Move the cookies to a cooling rack and let them cool for 30 minutes before serving.

Per Serving:
calories: 47 | fat: 2g | protein: 8g | carbs: 1g | net carbs: 1g | fiber: 0g

Hearty Cowboy Cauliflower Breakfast Skillet

Prep time: 20 minutes | Cook time: 42 minutes | serves 8

Crust:

◆ 1 (12-ounce) bag frozen riced cauliflower	◆ ½ cup grated Parmesan cheese
◆ 1 large egg	◆ ¼ teaspoon salt

Filling:

◆ 8 ounces bulk breakfast sausage	green onions
◆ 6 slices bacon, chopped	◆ 6 large eggs
◆ ½ cup diced bell peppers (any color)	◆ ¼ teaspoon salt
◆ 2 tablespoons chopped	◆ ½ teaspoon ground black pepper

To prepare the crust: 1. Set the oven to 425°F and lightly oil a 12-inch cast-iron or other oven-safe skillet. 2. Cook the cauliflower as directed on the package, then allow it to cool briefly. Use cheesecloth or paper towels to press out any excess moisture. 3. In a mixing bowl, combine the cauliflower, egg, Parmesan cheese, and salt until well mixed. Press this mixture evenly into the bottom of the prepared skillet. Par-bake the crust for about 12 minutes, until the edges begin to brown, then remove from the oven and let cool. Keep the oven on for the filling.

To make the filling: 1. In a skillet over medium heat, cook the sausage, bacon, bell peppers, and green onions, breaking up the sausage as it cooks. Continue until the meats are browned and the vegetables are softened, about 10 minutes, then remove from heat. 2. In a separate bowl, whisk together the eggs, salt, and pepper. Add the cooked meat and vegetables to the eggs, stirring to combine. 3. Pour the filling evenly over the par-baked crust. 4. Place the skillet back in the oven and bake for 20 minutes, or until the eggs are set and slightly firm to the touch. Run a knife along the edges of the skillet before slicing. Serve warm. Store any leftovers in the refrigerator for up to 5 days, reheating gently to avoid rubbery eggs.

Per Serving:
calories: 338 | fat: 26g | protein: 20g | carbs: 6g | net carbs: 3g | fiber: 3g

Keto Air Fryer Everything Bagels

Prep time: 15 minutes | Cook time: 14 minutes | Makes 6 bagels

◆ 1¾ cups shredded Mozzarella cheese or goat cheese Mozzarella	vinegar
	◆ 1 cup blanched almond flour
◆ 2 tablespoons unsalted butter or coconut oil	◆ 1 tablespoon baking powder
	◆ ⅛ teaspoon fine sea salt
◆ 1 large egg, beaten	◆ 1½ teaspoons everything bagel seasoning
◆ 1 tablespoon apple cider	

1. Prepare the dough: Place the Mozzarella cheese and butter in a large microwave-safe bowl and heat for 1 to 2 minutes until fully melted. Stir thoroughly, then add the egg and vinegar. Mix on medium with a hand mixer until well incorporated. Add almond flour, baking powder, and salt, and continue mixing until the dough is well-combined. 2. Place a sheet of parchment paper on the counter and turn the dough onto it. Knead for about 3 minutes until it becomes smooth and slightly sticky. If too sticky, refrigerate for an hour or overnight to firm up. 3. Preheat the air fryer to 350ºF (177ºC) and lightly coat a baking sheet or pie pan that fits your air fryer with avocado oil spray. 4. Divide the dough into 6 equal pieces. Roll each piece into a 6-inch log about ½ inch thick, forming each into a circle and sealing the edges to shape a bagel. Repeat with the remaining dough to make 6 bagels. 5. Arrange the bagels on the greased baking sheet. Spray the tops with avocado oil and sprinkle generously with everything bagel seasoning, pressing gently to help it adhere. 6. Air fry the bagels for 14 minutes, flipping them after 6 minutes, until they are golden brown and cooked through. 7. Let the bagels cool slightly after removing from the air fryer, then slice and serve. Store leftovers in an airtight container in the refrigerator for up to 4 days or freeze for up to a month.

Per Serving:
calories: 290 | fat: 25g | protein: 13g | carbs: 7g | net carbs: 4g | fiber: 3g

Chapter
3

Fish and Seafood

Chapter 3 Fish and Seafood

Golden Turmeric Salmon & Cauliflower

Prep time: 10 minutes | Cook time: 25 minutes | Serves 4

♦ 1 pound (454 g) salmon fillet, diced	♦ 1 tablespoon coconut oil, melted
♦ 1 cup cauliflower, shredded	♦ 1 teaspoon ground turmeric
♦ 1 tablespoon dried cilantro	♦ ¼ cup coconut cream

1. In a mixing bowl, combine the salmon, cauliflower, dried cilantro, ground turmeric, coconut cream, and coconut oil, stirring until well mixed. 2. Place the salmon mixture into the air fryer basket and cook at 350ºF (177ºC) for 25 minutes, stirring every 5 minutes to ensure even cooking and prevent burning.

Per Serving:
calories: 295 | fat: 20g | protein: 21g | carbs: 7g | net carbs: 5g | fiber: 2g

Crispy Shrimp Lettuce Tacos

Prep time: 10 minutes | Cook time: 9 minutes | Makes 8 tacos

♦ 2 large eggs	and tails removed
♦ 1 teaspoon prepared yellow mustard	♦ ½ cup finely shredded Gouda or Parmesan cheese
♦ 1 pound (454 g) small shrimp, peeled, deveined,	♦ ½ cup pork dust
For Serving:	
♦ 8 large Boston lettuce leaves	cabbage
♦ ¼ cup pico de gallo	♦ 1 lemon, sliced
♦ ¼ cup shredded purple	♦ Guacamole (optional)

1. Preheat the air fryer to 400ºF (204ºC). 2. In a large bowl, crack the eggs, add mustard, and whisk until smooth. Add the shrimp, stirring to coat them evenly. 3. In a separate bowl, mix the cheese and pork dust until well blended. 4. Take each shrimp from the egg mixture and roll it in the pork dust mixture, pressing firmly to coat. Lightly spray the coated shrimp with avocado oil and arrange them in the air fryer basket, leaving some space between each. 5. Cook the shrimp in the air fryer for 9 minutes, flipping halfway through, until they're opaque and cooked through. 6. To serve, place a lettuce leaf on a plate, arrange several shrimp on top, and add 1½ teaspoons of pico de gallo and purple cabbage. Squeeze lemon juice over the top and serve with guacamole if desired. 7. Store any leftover shrimp in an airtight container in the fridge for up to 3 days. Reheat in a 400ºF (204ºC) air fryer for about 5 minutes until warmed through.

Per Serving:
calories: 260 | fat: 14g | protein: 22g | carbs: 10g | net carbs: 6g | fiber: 4g

Flounder with Lemon Brown Butter Drizzle

Prep time: 10 minutes | Cook time: 10 minutes | Serves 4

For The Sauce

♦ ½ cup unsalted grass-fed butter, cut into pieces	♦ Sea salt, for seasoning
♦ Juice of 1 lemon	♦ Freshly ground black pepper, for seasoning

For The Fish

♦ 4 (4-ounce) boneless flounder fillets	♦ ¼ cup almond flour
♦ Sea salt, for seasoning	♦ 2 tablespoons good-quality olive oil
♦ Freshly ground black pepper, for seasoning	♦ 1 tablespoon chopped fresh parsley

To Make the Sauce: 1. Begin by browning the butter. In a medium saucepan over medium heat, melt the butter, stirring occasionally until it turns a rich golden brown, about 4 minutes. 2. Remove the pan from heat and stir in the lemon juice. Season with salt and pepper to taste, then set the sauce aside.

To Prepare the Fish: 1. Start by seasoning the fish fillets. Pat them dry with a paper towel, then lightly season with salt and pepper. Place the almond flour on a plate and coat each fillet by rolling them through the flour until covered. 2. In a large skillet over medium-high heat, warm the olive oil. Add the fish fillets and cook for 2 to 3 minutes on each side, until they are golden and crispy. 3. Arrange the fish on a serving plate, drizzle the browned butter sauce over the top, and garnish with fresh parsley. Serve immediately while hot.

Per Serving:
calories: 389 | fat: 33g | protein: 22g | carbs: 1g | net carbs: 1g | fiber: 0g

Spiced Roasted Salmon with Fresh Avocado Salsa

Prep time: 10 minutes | Cook time: 12 minutes | Serves 4

For The Salsa

- 1 avocado, peeled, pitted, and diced
- 1 scallion, white and green parts, chopped
- ½ cup halved cherry tomatoes
- Juice of 1 lemon
- Zest of 1 lemon

For The Fish

- 1 teaspoon ground cumin
- ½ teaspoon ground coriander
- ½ teaspoon onion powder
- ¼ teaspoon sea salt
- Pinch freshly ground black pepper
- Pinch cayenne pepper
- 4 (4-ounce) boneless, skinless salmon fillets
- 2 tablespoons olive oil

To Make the Salsa: 1. In a small bowl, combine the avocado, scallion, tomatoes, lemon juice, and lemon zest, stirring until well blended. 2. Set aside to let the flavors meld.

To Make the Fish: 1. Preheat the oven to 400°F and line a baking sheet with aluminum foil. 2. In a separate small bowl, mix together the cumin, coriander, onion powder, salt, black pepper, and cayenne. 3. Rub the spice mixture evenly over the salmon fillets, then place them on the prepared baking sheet. 4. Drizzle the fillets with olive oil and roast for about 15 minutes, or until the salmon is just cooked through. 5. Serve the salmon with a generous topping of the avocado salsa.

Per Serving:
calories: 320 | fat: 26g | protein: 22g | carbs: 4g | net carbs: 1g | fiber: 3g

Creamy Bacon Clam Chowder

Prep time: 10 minutes | Cook time: 4 minutes | Serves 2

- 5 ounces (142 g) clams
- 1 ounce (28 g) bacon, chopped
- 3 ounces (85 g) celery,
- chopped
- ½ cup water
- ½ cup heavy cream

1. Set the Instant Pot to Sauté mode and cook the bacon for 1 minute until it begins to release its flavor. 2. Add the clams, celery, water, and heavy cream to the pot, stirring briefly to combine. 3. Secure the lid and ensure it is sealed. 4. Switch to Steam mode (High Pressure) and cook for 3 minutes. Once done, perform a quick pressure release. 5. Ladle the clams and creamy broth into bowls and serve warm.

Per Serving:
calories: 221 | fat: 17g | protein: 7g | carbs: 10g | net carbs: 9g | fiber: 1g

Thai Coconut Curry Mussels

Prep time: 15 minutes | Cook time: 12 minutes | Serves 6

- 3 pounds mussels, cleaned, de-bearded
- 1 cup minced shallots
- 3 tablespoons minced garlic
- 1½ cups coconut milk
- 2 cups dry white wine
- 2 teaspoons red curry powder
- ⅓ cup coconut oil
- ⅓ cup chopped green onions
- ⅓ cup chopped parsley

1. In a large saucepan, pour in the wine and add the shallots and garlic. Cook over low heat until softened, then stir in the coconut milk and red curry powder, cooking for 3 minutes to blend the flavors. 2. Add the mussels to the pan and steam for about 7 minutes or until their shells open. Use a slotted spoon to transfer the open mussels to a bowl, leaving the sauce in the pan. Discard any mussels that remain closed. 3. Stir the coconut oil into the sauce, then turn off the heat and mix in the parsley and green onions. Serve the warm sauce alongside a butternut squash mash for a complete meal.

Per Serving:
calories: 275 | fat: 19g | protein: 23g | carbs: 3g | net carbs: 2g | fiber: 1g

Zesty Air-Fried Lemon Salmon

Prep time: 30 minutes | Cook time: 10 minutes | Serves 4

- 1½ pounds (680 g) salmon steak
- ½ teaspoon grated lemon zest
- Freshly cracked mixed peppercorns, to taste
- ⅓ cup lemon juice
- Fresh chopped chives, for garnish
- ½ cup dry white wine
- ½ teaspoon fresh cilantro, chopped
- Fine sea salt, to taste

1. To make the marinade, add all ingredients, except the salmon steak and chives, to a deep pan. Bring to a boil over medium-high heat, then simmer until the mixture has reduced by half. Remove from heat and let it cool. 2. Place the salmon steak in the cooled marinade and refrigerate for about 40 minutes. Discard the marinade afterward, and transfer the marinated salmon steak to a preheated air fryer. 3. Air fry at 400°F (204°C) for 9 to 10 minutes. Once done, brush the hot salmon steak with fresh marinade, garnish with chopped chives, and serve immediately.

Per Serving:
calories: 319 | fat: 17g | protein: 37g | carbs: 3g | net carbs: 2g | fiber: 1g

Steamed Salmon with Fresh Dill Butter

Prep time: 7 minutes | Cook time: 8 minutes | Serves 2

♦ 1 teaspoon salt	fillet
♦ 2 tablespoons chopped fresh dill	♦ ¼ cup butter
♦ 10 ounces (283 g) salmon	♦ ½ cup water

1. Place butter and salt in a baking pan. 2. Lay the salmon fillet on top and sprinkle with fresh dill. Cover the pan tightly with foil. 3. Add water to the Instant Pot, then carefully place the baking pan with the salmon inside. 4. Set to Steam mode and cook for 8 minutes. 5. Carefully remove the foil, plate the salmon, and serve warm!

Per Serving:
calories: 399 | fat: 32g | protein: 28g | carbs: 2g | net carbs: 2g | fiber: 0g

Glazed Salmon with Savory Noodles

Prep time: 5 minutes | Cook time: 20 minutes | Serves 4

♦ ¼ cup plus 2 tablespoons (75 ml) avocado oil, divided	sea salt
♦ ¼ cup (60 ml) coconut aminos	♦ 1 pound (455 g) salmon fillets, cut into 4 equal portions
♦ 2 tablespoons plus 2 teaspoons tomato paste	♦ 2 (7-ounce/198-g) packages konjac noodles or equivalent amount of other low-carb noodles of choice
♦ 2 tablespoons apple cider vinegar	
♦ 1 (2-in/5-cm) piece fresh ginger root, grated	♦ 2 green onions, sliced
♦ 4 cloves garlic, minced	♦ Handful of fresh cilantro leaves, roughly chopped
♦ ½ teaspoon finely ground	♦ 1 teaspoon sesame seeds

1. In a large frying pan over medium heat, warm 2 tablespoons of oil. 2. While the oil heats, prepare the sauce: In a small bowl, whisk together the remaining ¼ cup of oil, coconut aminos, tomato paste, vinegar, ginger, garlic, and salt until smooth. 3. Place the salmon fillets in the heated pan, reduce the heat to low, and generously brush with the sauce. Pour any leftover sauce directly into the pan. Cover and cook on low for 15 minutes, until the salmon is seared and cooked through. 4. Once the salmon is ready, move it to one side of the pan, creating space for the noodles. Add the noodles and green onions to the pan, tossing them in the sauce until well coated. Lay the cooked salmon on top of the noodles and cook for an additional 3 to 5 minutes to warm the noodles. 5. Garnish the salmon with fresh cilantro and sesame seeds. Divide the noodles and salmon across 4 plates, drizzling each with any extra pan sauce, and serve. Enjoy your meal!

Per Serving:
calories: 333 | fat: 22g | protein: 25g | carbs: 8g | net carbs: 5g | fiber: 4g

Zesty Shrimp Cauliflower Fried Rice

Prep time: 15 minutes | Cook time: 15 minutes | Serves 4

♦ ¼ teaspoon cayenne pepper	♦ ½ medium-sized white onion, finely chopped
♦ ¼ teaspoon chili powder	♦ 2 teaspoons minced fresh ginger
♦ ¼ teaspoon paprika	
♦ ¼ teaspoon pink Himalayan salt	♦ 1 cup fresh broccoli florets, chopped
♦ ¼ teaspoon ground black pepper	♦ 3 tablespoons soy sauce
♦ 1 pound medium-sized shrimp, peeled and deveined	♦ 1 tablespoon Sriracha sauce
	♦ 1½ teaspoons unseasoned rice wine vinegar
♦ 2 tablespoons ghee, divided	♦ 2 large eggs
♦ 4 cups riced cauliflower (see Tip)	♦ 2 teaspoons toasted sesame oil

For Garnish (Optional):

♦ Sliced scallions	♦ Black and white sesame seeds

1. In a medium bowl, combine the cayenne, chili powder, paprika, salt, and pepper. Add the shrimp and toss to coat them evenly in the seasoning mix. 2. Heat 1 tablespoon of ghee in a large skillet over medium-high heat. Place the seasoned shrimp in the skillet and cook until pink, about 2 minutes per side. Transfer the cooked shrimp to a small bowl and set aside. 3. Add the remaining tablespoon of ghee to the skillet, then spread the riced cauliflower in an even layer. Cook for 3 to 5 minutes until it begins to crisp. 4. Stir the cauliflower rice, then add the onion and ginger, cooking for 2 minutes until the onion softens slightly. Add the broccoli and cook for 1 to 2 minutes until it turns bright green. Pour in the soy sauce, Sriracha, and vinegar, mixing well. 5. Create a well in the center of the skillet and crack the eggs into it. Scramble the eggs with a spatula, then stir them into the rest of the skillet contents. 6. Return the shrimp to the skillet and toss everything together. Drizzle with sesame oil and garnish with sliced scallions and sesame seeds, if desired. Serve hot. 7. Store any leftovers in an airtight container in the refrigerator for up to 4 days, and reheat in the microwave for 60 to 90 seconds.

Per Serving:
calories: 283 | fat: 13g | protein: 32g | carbs: 13g | net carbs: 9g | fiber: 4g

Spicy Coconut-Braised Squid

Prep time: 10 minutes | Cook time: 20 minutes | Serves 3

- 1 pound (454 g) squid, sliced
- 1 teaspoon sugar-free tomato paste
- 1 cup coconut milk
- 1 teaspoon cayenne pepper
- ½ teaspoon salt

1. Place all the ingredients listed above into the Instant Pot. 2. Secure the lid, ensuring it is sealed, and set to Manual mode on High Pressure. Cook the squid for 20 minutes. 3. Once cooking is complete, perform a quick pressure release to release the steam. 4. Serve the squid warm with the coconut milk gravy from the pot. Enjoy!

Per Serving:
calories: 326 | fat: 21g | protein: 25g | carbs: 10g | net carbs: 8g | fiber: 2g

Air-Fried Blackened Salmon

Prep time: 10 minutes | Cook time: 8 minutes | Serves 2

- 10 ounces (283 g) salmon fillet
- ½ teaspoon ground coriander
- 1 teaspoon ground cumin
- 1 teaspoon dried basil
- 1 tablespoon avocado oil

1. In a shallow bowl, combine ground coriander, ground cumin, and dried basil, mixing until evenly blended. 2. Coat the salmon fillet thoroughly in the spice mixture, then drizzle with avocado oil. 3. Place the salmon in the air fryer basket and cook at 395°F (202°C) for 4 minutes on each side, until cooked through. Serve hot.

Per Serving:
calories: 270 | fat: 17g | protein: 25g | carbs: 2g | net carbs: 0g | fiber: 2g

Steamed Cod with Olive Topping

Prep time: 15 minutes | Cook time: 10 minutes | Serves 2

- 8 ounces (227 g) cod fillet
- ¼ cup sliced olives
- 1 teaspoon olive oil
- ¼ teaspoon salt
- 1 cup water, for cooking

1. Pour water into the Instant Pot and place the steamer rack inside. 2. Cut the cod fillet into two portions and season each with salt and a drizzle of olive oil. 3. Place each portion on a piece of foil, top with sliced olives, and wrap securely. Transfer the wrapped fish onto the steamer rack. 4. Close and seal the lid, then set to Manual mode on High Pressure and cook for 10 minutes. 5. Allow a natural pressure release for 5 minutes before carefully opening the lid. Serve immediately.

Per Serving:
calories: 130 | fat: 5g | protein: 20g | carbs: 1g | net carbs: 1g | fiber: 0g

Air-Fried Classic Crab Cakes

Prep time: 10 minutes | Cook time: 10 minutes | Serves 4

- 2 (6 ounces / 170 g) cans lump crab meat
- ¼ cup blanched finely ground almond flour
- 1 large egg
- 2 tablespoons full-fat mayonnaise
- ½ teaspoon Dijon mustard
- ½ tablespoon lemon juice
- ½ medium green bell pepper, seeded and chopped
- ¼ cup chopped green onion
- ½ teaspoon Old Bay seasoning

1. In a large bowl, mix all the ingredients until well combined. Shape the mixture into four equal balls, then flatten each into a patty. Place the patties in a single layer in the air fryer basket. 2. Set the air fryer to 350°F (177°C) and cook for 10 minutes. 3. Flip the patties halfway through to ensure even cooking. Serve warm and enjoy.

Per Serving:
calories: 181 | fat: 9g | protein: 20g | carbs: 4g | net carbs: 2g | fiber: 2g

Air-Fried Lemon Dill Mahi-Mahi

Prep time: 5 minutes | Cook time: 14 minutes | Serves 2

- Oil, for spraying
- 2 (6-ounce / 170-g) mahi-mahi fillets
- 1 tablespoon lemon juice
- 1 tablespoon olive oil
- ¼ teaspoon salt
- ¼ teaspoon freshly ground black pepper
- 1 tablespoon chopped fresh dill
- 2 lemon slices

1. Line the air fryer basket with parchment paper and lightly spray with oil. 2. Place the mahi-mahi fillets in the prepared basket. 3. In a small bowl, mix the lemon juice and olive oil, then brush it evenly over the fish. 4. Season the mahi-mahi with salt and black pepper, and sprinkle with fresh dill. 5. Air fry at 400°F (204°C) for 12 to 14 minutes, depending on the thickness of the fillets, until the fish flakes easily with a fork. 6. Transfer to plates, garnish each fillet with a lemon slice, and serve warm.

Per Serving:
calories: 233 | fat: 9g | protein: 35g | carbs: 2g | net carbs: 2g | fiber: 0g

Baked Seafood Zoodle Fideo

Prep time: 15 minutes | Cook time: 20 minutes | Serves 6 to 8

♦ 2 tablespoons extra-virgin olive oil, plus ½ cup, divided	♦ ½ cup crumbled goat cheese
	♦ ½ cup crumbled feta cheese
♦ 6 cups zucchini noodles, roughly chopped (2 to 3 medium zucchini)	♦ 1 (28-ounce / 794-g) can chopped tomatoes, with their juices
♦ 1 pound (454 g) shrimp, peeled, deveined and roughly chopped	♦ 1 teaspoon salt
	♦ 1 teaspoon garlic powder
	♦ ½ teaspoon smoked paprika
♦ 6 to 8 ounces (170 to 227 g) canned chopped clams, drained	♦ ½ cup shredded Parmesan cheese
♦ 4 ounces (113 g) crabmeat	♦ ¼ cup chopped fresh flat-leaf Italian parsley, for garnish

1. Preheat the oven to 375°F (190°C). 2. Drizzle 2 tablespoons of olive oil into the bottom of a 9-by-13-inch baking dish, swirling to coat evenly. 3. In a large mixing bowl, combine the zucchini noodles, shrimp, clams, and crabmeat. 4. In a separate bowl, mix the goat cheese, feta, and ¼ cup of olive oil until well blended. Stir in the canned tomatoes with their juices, salt, garlic powder, and paprika, and mix thoroughly. Add this cheese and tomato mixture to the zucchini and seafood, stirring until evenly combined. 5. Transfer the mixture to the prepared baking dish, spreading it out in an even layer. Sprinkle shredded Parmesan over the top, then drizzle with the remaining ¼ cup of olive oil. Bake for 20 to 25 minutes, or until the dish is bubbly and golden. Serve warm, garnished with chopped parsley.

Per Serving:

calories: 390 | fat: 22g | protein: 36g | carbs: 16g | net carbs: 12g | fiber: 4g

Grilled Spicy Shrimp with Cilantro Mojo Verde

Prep time: 20 minutes | Cook time: 8 minutes | Serves 4

♦ ½ cup lime or lemon juice	deveined and butterflied
♦ 3 teaspoons minced garlic	♦ 2 teaspoons cayenne pepper
♦ ¼ red onion, thinly sliced	♦ 1 teaspoon ground cumin
♦ 12 jumbo shrimp (peels on),	♦ 1 teaspoon fine sea salt
Dipping Sauce:	
♦ 3 loosely packed cups fresh cilantro leaves	♦ 2 tablespoons minced garlic
	♦ 2 teaspoons coconut vinegar
♦ ½ cup MCT oil or extra-virgin olive oil	♦ 1 teaspoon fine sea salt
	♦ ½ teaspoon ground cumin

1. Preheat a grill to medium-high heat. Meanwhile, soak 4 wooden skewers in water. 2. Pour lime juice into a shallow baking dish and add garlic, onion, and shrimp. Let the shrimp marinate for 15 minutes while preparing the spice blend and dipping sauce. 3. In a small dish, mix cayenne pepper, cumin, and salt until well combined, then set aside. 4. For the dipping sauce, place all sauce ingredients in a food processor or blender and blend until smooth. Adjust salt to taste if needed. 5. Remove shrimp from the marinade, sprinkle generously with the spice mixture, and thread 3 shrimp onto each skewer. Grill for 3 to 4 minutes on each side, until the shrimp are pink and fully cooked. Serve each skewer with ¼ cup of the dipping sauce. 6. Enjoy fresh, though leftovers can be stored in an airtight container in the refrigerator for up to 3 days. Serve cold or reheat by sautéing in a skillet over medium heat until warmed through.

Per Serving:

calories: 365 | fat: 29g | protein: 21g | carbs: 5g | net carbs: 4g | fiber: 1g

Cheesy Mackerel & Broccoli Bake

Prep time: 15 minutes | Cook time: 15 minutes | Serves 5

♦ 1 cup shredded broccoli	cheese
♦ 10 ounces (283 g) mackerel, chopped	♦ 1 cup coconut milk
	♦ 1 teaspoon ground cumin
♦ ½ cup shredded Cheddar	♦ 1 teaspoon salt

1. Season the chopped mackerel with ground cumin and salt, then place it in the Instant Pot. 2. Layer the shredded broccoli and Cheddar cheese over the fish. 3. Pour the coconut milk over the top. Secure the lid, ensuring it is sealed. 4. Set the Instant Pot to Manual mode on High Pressure and cook for 15 minutes. 5. Once done, let the pressure release naturally for 10 minutes before carefully opening the lid.

Per Serving:

calories: 312 | fat: 25g | protein: 18g | carbs: 4g | net carbs: 2g | fiber: 2g

Spicy Jalapeño Cod

Prep time: 5 minutes | Cook time: 14 minutes | Serves 4

♦ 4 cod fillets, boneless	♦ 1 tablespoon avocado oil
♦ 1 jalapeño, minced	♦ ½ teaspoon minced garlic

1. In a shallow bowl, combine the minced jalapeño, avocado oil, and minced garlic, stirring well. 2. Place the cod fillets in a single layer in the air fryer basket and spoon the jalapeño mixture over each fillet, spreading it evenly. 3. Air fry the cod at 365°F (185°C) for 7 minutes on each side, until cooked through and flaky.

Per Serving:

calories: 130 | fat: 3g | protein: 23g | carbs: 0g | net carbs: 0g | fiber: 0g

Crispy Sesame-Crusted Tuna Steaks

Prep time: 5 minutes | Cook time: 8 minutes | Serves 2

- 2 (6 ounces / 170 g) tuna steaks
- 1 tablespoon coconut oil, melted
- ½ teaspoon garlic powder
- 2 teaspoons white sesame seeds
- 2 teaspoons black sesame seeds

1. Brush each tuna steak with coconut oil and sprinkle with garlic powder. 2. In a large bowl, add the sesame seeds, then press each tuna steak into the seeds, coating them thoroughly on all sides. Place the sesame-coated tuna steaks in the air fryer basket. 3. Set the air fryer to 400ºF (204ºC) and cook for 8 minutes. 4. Flip the tuna steaks halfway through cooking to ensure even doneness. For well-done steaks, the internal temperature should reach 145ºF (63ºC). Serve warm and enjoy.

Per Serving:
calories: 308 | fat: 16g | protein: 37g | carbs: 2g | net carbs: 1g | fiber: 1g

Garlic Butter Foil-Baked Halibut

Prep time: 10 minutes | Cook time: 20 minutes | Serves 4

- Coconut oil, for greasing
- 4 (4-ounce / 113-g) halibut fillets, about 1-inch thick
- ½ cup (1 stick) butter, cut into squares
- 2 tablespoons finely
- chopped scallion
- 1 tablespoon minced garlic
- ½ lemon
- Sea salt and freshly ground black pepper, to taste

1. Preheat the oven to 400ºF (205ºC). 2. Cut four 12-inch squares of aluminum foil and lightly grease each with coconut oil. Place one halibut fillet in the center of each foil square. Add two pats of butter on top of each fillet. Evenly sprinkle scallion and garlic over the fillets, then squeeze lemon juice over each, finishing with a generous sprinkle of salt and pepper. 3. Fold up the sides of each foil square to create a sealed pouch around the halibut, leaving a little room inside for steam to circulate. Place the foil pouches on a large baking sheet. 4. Bake for approximately 20 minutes, until the halibut is opaque and flakes easily with a fork. 5. Carefully remove the fish from the foil before serving, reserving any cooking juices to drizzle over vegetables or as desired. Enjoy!

Per Serving:
1 fillet: calories: 313 | fat: 25g | protein: 21g | carbs: 1g | net carbs: 1g | fiber: 0g

Baked Asiago Garlic Salmon

Prep time: 10 minutes | Cook time: 12 minutes | Serves 4

- ½ cup Asiago cheese
- 2 tablespoons freshly squeezed lemon juice
- 2 tablespoons butter, at room temperature
- 2 teaspoons minced garlic
- 1 teaspoon chopped fresh basil
- 1 teaspoon chopped fresh oregano
- 4 (5-ounce) salmon fillets
- 1 tablespoon olive oil

1. Preheat the oven to 350°F and line a baking sheet with parchment paper. Set aside. 2. In a small bowl, combine the Asiago cheese, lemon juice, butter, garlic, basil, and oregano, mixing until well blended. 3. Pat the salmon fillets dry with paper towels and place them skin-side down on the prepared baking sheet. Evenly distribute the cheese mixture over each fillet, using a knife or spoon to spread it across the surface. 4. Drizzle olive oil over the fillets, then bake for about 12 minutes, or until the topping is golden and the fish is cooked through. 5. Serve immediately.

Per Serving:
calories: 357 | fat: 28g | protein: 24g | carbs: 2g | net carbs: 2g | fiber: 0g

Red Curry Perch with Lemon & Rosemary

Prep time: 5 minutes | Cook time: 6 minutes | Serves 4

- 1 cup water
- 2 sprigs rosemary
- 1 large-sized lemon, sliced
- 1 pound (454 g) perch fillets
- 1 teaspoon cayenne pepper
- Sea salt and ground black pepper, to taste
- 1 tablespoon red curry paste
- 1 tablespoons butter

1. Pour the water into the Instant Pot, then add rosemary and lemon slices. Place a trivet inside the pot. 2. Season the perch fillets with cayenne pepper, salt, and black pepper. Spread the red curry paste and butter evenly over each fillet. 3. Place the seasoned fillets on the trivet in a single layer. 4. Secure the lid, select Manual mode, and set to cook for 6 minutes at Low Pressure. 5. Once cooking is complete, perform a quick pressure release. Carefully remove the lid and serve the fillets with your favorite keto sides.

Per Serving:
calories: 142 | fat: 4g | protein: 23g | carbs: 3g | net carbs: 2g | fiber: 2g

Mediterranean Tuna & Pepper Salad

Prep time: 10 minutes | Cook time: 4 minutes | Serves 4

◆ 1½ cups water	◆ 2 tablespoons Kalamata olives, pitted and halved
◆ 1 pound (454 g) tuna steaks	
◆ 1 green bell pepper, sliced	◆ 2 tablespoons extra-virgin olive oil
◆ 1 red bell pepper, sliced	
◆ 2 Roma tomatoes, sliced	◆ 2 tablespoons balsamic vinegar
◆ 1 head lettuce	◆ ½ teaspoon chili flakes
◆ 1 red onion, chopped	◆ Sea salt, to taste

1. Pour the water into the Instant Pot and place a steamer basket inside. 2. Arrange the tuna steaks in the basket, then layer the bell pepper and tomato slices on top of the tuna. 3. Secure the lid, select Manual mode, and set to cook for 4 minutes on High Pressure. 4. Once the timer beeps, perform a quick pressure release and carefully remove the lid. 5. Use a fork to flake the tuna. 6. Prepare 4 serving plates by layering lettuce leaves to create a bed for the salad. Add onion slices and olives on top. Drizzle with olive oil and balsamic vinegar. 7. Sprinkle with chili flakes and salt, then arrange the flaked tuna, tomatoes, and bell peppers over the salad. 8. Serve immediately for the freshest taste.

Per Serving:

calories: 170 | fat: 5g | protein: 24g | carbs: 8g | net carbs: 6g | fiber: 2g

Zesty Ahi Tuna Hand Rolls

Prep time: 10 minutes | Cook time: 0 minutes | Serves 6

Tuna:

◆ 12 ounces sushi-grade ahi tuna, finely chopped	◆ 1 tablespoon mayonnaise, homemade or store-bought
◆ 2 tablespoons Sriracha sauce	◆ 1 teaspoon toasted sesame oil

Hand Rolls:

◆ 3 sheets nori	◆ Black and white sesame seeds, for garnish (optional)
◆ 1 medium-sized avocado, thinly sliced	◆ Soy sauce, for serving
◆ ½ cucumber, julienned	

1. In a small bowl, combine the tuna, Sriracha, mayonnaise, and sesame oil, mixing thoroughly with a spoon until smooth. 2. Slice each nori sheet in half lengthwise, creating 6 rectangular wrappers. 3. Place a nori wrapper on the palm of your hand. Add 2 ounces of the tuna mixture along with 3 to 4 slices each of avocado and cucumber on the left end, angling them diagonally to make rolling easier. Starting from the bottom-left corner, tightly roll the nori

into a cone shape, dampening the edge slightly to seal. Garnish with sesame seeds, if desired. Repeat with the remaining nori and fillings. 4. Serve immediately with soy sauce on the side. These rolls are best enjoyed fresh, as they don't store well.

Per Serving:

calories: 133 | fat: 6g | protein: 15g | carbs: 4g | net carbs: 2g | fiber: 2g

Herb-Infused Italian Salmon

Prep time: 10 minutes | Cook time: 4 minutes | Serves 2

◆ 10 ounces (283 g) salmon fillet	◆ 1 teaspoon Italian seasoning
	◆ 1 cup water

1. Add water to the Instant Pot and insert the trivet. 2. Rub the salmon fillet with Italian seasoning, then wrap it securely in foil. 3. Place the wrapped salmon on the trivet and close the lid. 4. Set to Manual mode on High Pressure and cook for 4 minutes. 5. Once finished, perform a quick pressure release and carefully remove the salmon from the foil. 6. Slice the salmon into individual servings and enjoy.

Per Serving:

calories: 195 | fat: 10g | protein: 27g | carbs: 0g | net carbs: 0g | fiber: 0g

Lemon-Dill Foil-Packet Salmon

Prep time: 2 minutes | Cook time: 7 minutes | Serves 2

◆ 2 (3-ounce / 85-g) salmon fillets	◆ ¼ teaspoon pepper
	◆ ¼ teaspoon dried dill
◆ ¼ teaspoon garlic powder	◆ ½ lemon
◆ 1 teaspoon salt	◆ 1 cup water

1. Place each salmon fillet on a square of foil, skin-side down. 2. Sprinkle with garlic powder, salt, and pepper, then squeeze fresh lemon juice over each fillet. Place two lemon slices on top of each piece. Fold the foil edges to close and seal the packets. 3. Add water to the Instant Pot and insert the trivet. Place the foil packets on the trivet. 4. Secure the lid and select Steam mode, setting the cooking time to 7 minutes at Low Pressure. 5. Once done, perform a quick pressure release and carefully open the lid. 6. Use a meat thermometer to check that the internal temperature of the thickest part of each fillet has reached at least 145°F (63°C). The salmon should flake easily when fully cooked. 7. Serve immediately for best flavor.

Per Serving:

calories: 128 | fat: 5g | protein: 19g | carbs: 0g | net carbs: 0g | fiber: 0g

Classic Ahi Poke with Sesame & Scallions

Prep time: 10 minutes | Cook time: 0 minutes | Serves 6

- 3 scallions, diced
- ½ cup soy sauce
- 2 teaspoons sesame oil
- 1 tablespoon sesame seeds

- ¼ teaspoon ground ginger
- 1 teaspoon garlic powder
- 1 teaspoon salt
- 2 pounds (907 g) fresh ahi tuna, cut into ½-inch cubes

1. In a medium bowl, combine the scallions, soy sauce, sesame oil, sesame seeds, ginger, garlic powder, and salt, stirring until well mixed. 2. Add the tuna to the soy sauce mixture, tossing until the tuna is evenly coated. Serve immediately. 3. If preparing ahead, store the tuna and soy sauce mixture separately in the refrigerator and combine just before serving for optimal freshness.

Per Serving:

⅙ recipe: calories: 241 | fat: 9g | protein: 38g | carbs: 2g | net carbs: 1g | fiber: 1g

Parmesan Rosemary Haddock Bake

Prep time: 7 minutes | Cook time: 10 minutes | Serves 2

- 2 eggs, beaten
- 12 ounces (340 g) haddock fillet, chopped
- 1 tablespoon cream cheese

- ¾ teaspoon dried rosemary
- 2 ounces (57 g) Parmesan, grated
- 1 teaspoon butter

1. Whisk the beaten eggs until smooth, then add the cream cheese, dried rosemary, and dill, mixing well to combine. 2. Grease a springform pan with butter and place the haddock fillets inside. 3. Pour the egg mixture over the fish and sprinkle Parmesan cheese on top. 4. Set the Instant Pot to Manual mode on High Pressure and cook for 5 minutes. Once cooking is complete, allow a natural pressure release for an additional 5 minutes before carefully removing the lid. Serve warm.

Per Serving:

calories: 380 | fat: 16g | protein: 56g | carbs: 18g | net carbs: 18g | fiber: 0g

Sicilian Zoodles with Sardines & Bacon

Prep time: 10 minutes | Cook time: 11 minutes | Serves 2

- 4 cups zoodles (spiralled zucchini)
- 2 ounces cubed bacon
- 4 ounces canned sardines, chopped
- ½ cup canned chopped tomatoes

- 1 tablespoon capers
- 1 tablespoon parsley
- 1 teaspoon minced garlic

1. Pour a bit of the sardine oil into a pan and heat over medium. Add the garlic and sauté for 1 minute until fragrant. Add the bacon and cook for an additional 2 minutes. 2. Stir in the tomatoes and let them simmer for 5 minutes, allowing the flavors to meld. 3. Add the zoodles and sardines, cooking for 3 more minutes until the zoodles are tender. Serve warm.

Per Serving:

calories: 290 | fat: 18g | protein: 22g | carbs: 13g | net carbs: 9g | fiber: 4g

Chapter
4

Beef, Pork, and Lamb

Chapter 4 Beef, Pork, and Lamb

Ultimate Juicy Grill-Proof Burger

Prep time: 10 minutes | Cook time: 15 minutes | Serves 4

• 1 pound grass-fed ground beef	sauce
• 1 egg, lightly beaten	• 1 teaspoon dried parsley
• ½ onion, finely chopped	• ¼ teaspoon sea salt
• 1 teaspoon minced garlic	• ⅛ teaspoon freshly ground black pepper
• 1 teaspoon Worcestershire	• 1 tablespoon olive oil

1. Prepare the burger patties: In a medium bowl, mix together the ground beef, egg, onion, garlic, Worcestershire sauce, parsley, salt, and pepper until well incorporated. Shape the mixture into four equal patties, each about ¾ inch thick, then brush them lightly with olive oil for added moisture. 2. Grill the burgers: Preheat your grill to medium heat. Place the patties on the grill and cook, turning once, until the internal temperature reaches 160°F, about 8 minutes per side. 3. Rest and serve: Allow the burgers to rest for 5 minutes to retain their juices, then serve hot with your choice of toppings and sides.

Per Serving:
calories: 379 | fat: 33g | protein: 19g | carbs: 1g | net carbs: 1g | fiber: 0g

Crispy Parmesan-Crusted Pork Chops

Prep time: 15 minutes | Cook time: 9 to 14 minutes | Serves 4

• 2 large eggs	• ½ teaspoon dried oregano
• ½ cup finely grated Parmesan cheese	• ½ teaspoon garlic powder
• ½ cup finely ground blanched almond flour or finely crushed pork rinds	• Salt and freshly ground black pepper, to taste
• 1 teaspoon paprika	• 1¼ pounds (567 g) (1-inch-thick) boneless pork chops
	• Avocado oil spray

1. Crack the eggs into a shallow bowl and whisk until fully blended. In a separate bowl, mix the Parmesan cheese, almond flour, paprika, oregano, garlic powder, salt, and pepper to create a flavorful breading. 2. Dip each pork chop into the beaten eggs, ensuring they're coated, then press them into the Parmesan mixture to form a crust, gently pressing to adhere. Lightly spray each breaded pork chop with oil to help them crisp. 3. Preheat the air fryer to 400°F (204°C). Arrange the pork chops in a single layer in the air fryer basket, cooking in batches if needed. Air fry for 6 minutes, then flip each chop, spraying again with oil. Continue cooking for an additional 3 to 8 minutes until a thermometer reads 145°F (63°C). 4. Let the pork chops rest for at least 5 minutes before serving to lock in their juices.

Per Serving:
calories: 313 | fat: 14g | protein: 40g | carbs: 4g | net carbs: 3g | fiber: 1g

Savory Pork Marsala with Prosciutto & Mushrooms

Prep time: 5 minutes | Cook time: 30 minutes | Serves 4

• 4 (4-ounce / 113-g) boneless pork cutlets	• 1 garlic clove, minced
• Salt and freshly ground black pepper, to taste	• ½ cup Marsala cooking wine
• 4 tablespoons butter, divided	• ½ cup bone broth
• 8 ounces (227 g) sliced mushrooms (cremini, portabella, button, or other)	• 1 teaspoon chopped fresh thyme
	• ½ teaspoon xanthan or guar gum, to thicken (optional)
• 4 ounces (113 g) prosciutto, chopped	• Chopped fresh parsley, for garnish

1. Season the pork cutlets with salt and pepper on both sides. 2. In a large skillet over medium-high heat, melt 2 tablespoons of butter. Add the cutlets and cook for about 5 minutes per side until they're fully cooked. Remove the cutlets from the skillet and set aside. 3. Lower the heat to medium-low, add the remaining 2 tablespoons of butter, and toss in the mushrooms, prosciutto, and garlic. Stir frequently until the mushrooms are golden brown, about 5 minutes. 4. Pour in the wine, bone broth, and add thyme. Let the mixture simmer for around 15 minutes until it reduces and thickens. If you prefer a thicker sauce, add xanthan gum and stir to combine. Return the pork cutlets to the skillet, raise the heat to medium-high, and cook until warmed through. 5. Garnish with chopped parsley and serve immediately.

Per Serving:
calories: 339 | fat: 19g | protein: 36g | carbs: 6g | net carbs: 5g | fiber: 1g

Spicy Chorizo-Beef Burgers

Prep time: 10 minutes | Cook time: 15 minutes | Serves 4

♦ ¾ pound (340 g) 80/20 ground beef	♦ 5 slices pickled jalapeños, chopped
♦ ¼ pound (113 g) Mexican-style ground chorizo	♦ 2 teaspoons chili powder
♦ ¼ cup chopped onion	♦ 1 teaspoon minced garlic
	♦ ¼ teaspoon cumin

1. In a large mixing bowl, combine all ingredients until fully incorporated. Divide the mixture into four equal portions and shape each into a thick burger patty. 2. Arrange the patties in the air fryer basket, ensuring they fit in a single layer; cook in batches if needed. 3. Set the air fryer to 375°F (191°C) and cook for 15 minutes. 4. Halfway through, flip the patties to ensure even cooking. Serve the burgers warm with your favorite toppings.

Per Serving:
calories: 270 | fat: 20g | protein: 21g | carbs: 2g | net carbs: 1g | fiber: 1g

Air-Fried Herb-Crusted Lamb Chops

Prep time: 10 minutes | Cook time: 5 minutes | Serves 2

♦ 1 large egg	♦ 1 tablespoon chopped fresh rosemary leaves
♦ 2 cloves garlic, minced	♦ 1 teaspoon chopped fresh thyme leaves
♦ ¼ cup pork dust	
♦ ¼ cup powdered Parmesan cheese	♦ ½ teaspoon ground black pepper
♦ 1 tablespoon chopped fresh oregano leaves	♦ 4 (1-inch-thick) lamb chops

For Garnish/Serving (Optional):

♦ Sprigs of fresh oregano	♦ Lavender flowers
♦ Sprigs of fresh rosemary	♦ Lemon slices
♦ Sprigs of fresh thyme	

1. Lightly coat the air fryer basket with avocado oil, and preheat the air fryer to 400°F (204°C). 2. In a shallow bowl, beat the egg thoroughly, then add minced garlic and stir to incorporate. In a separate shallow bowl, combine pork dust, Parmesan, mixed herbs, and black pepper to create the coating mixture. 3. Working one at a time, dip each lamb chop in the egg mixture, letting any excess drip off, then press into the Parmesan mixture, ensuring all sides are thoroughly coated. For an extra thick crust, repeat the dipping and coating process. 4. Arrange the lamb chops in the air fryer basket, spacing them apart to allow airflow, and cook for 5 minutes or until they reach an internal temperature of 145°F (63°C) for medium doneness. Let the chops rest for 10 minutes before serving. 5. Garnish with fresh sprigs of oregano, rosemary, thyme, and a few lavender flowers if you'd like. Serve with lemon slices for a burst of citrus. 6. For best flavor, enjoy immediately. Store leftovers in an airtight container in the refrigerator for up to 4 days. Use leftovers cold over a salad, or reheat in the air fryer at 350°F (177°C) for 3 minutes until just warmed.

Per Serving:
calories: 386 | fat: 26g | protein: 31g | carbs: 4g | net carbs: 3g | fiber: 1g

Peppercorn-Sage Mascarpone Pork Chops

Prep time: 10 minutes | Cook time: 12 minutes | Serves 3

♦ 3 pork chops	peppercorns
♦ 1 tablespoon mascarpone cheese	♦ ½ teaspoon dried sage
	♦ 1 tablespoon olive oil
♦ 1 teaspoon ground	

1. In a shallow bowl, combine the crushed peppercorns, dried sage, olive oil, and mascarpone cheese, stirring until smooth and well-mixed.2. Generously brush the pork chops on all sides with the mascarpone mixture, ensuring they're fully coated, and place them in the Instant Pot.3. Set the Instant Pot to Sauté mode and cook the pork chops for 5 minutes on each side until they start to brown.4. Add any remaining mascarpone mixture over the pork chops and cook for an additional 2 minutes, allowing the flavors to meld. Serve warm for best taste.

Per Serving:
calories: 324 | fat: 18g | protein: 40g | carbs: 0g | net carbs: 0g | fiber: 0g

Apple & Pumpkin-Spiced Ham

Prep time: 10 minutes | Cook time: 10 minutes | Serves 6

♦ 1 cup apple cider vinegar	♦ 1 tablespoon avocado oil
♦ 1 pound (454 g) ham, cooked	♦ 2 tablespoons butter
♦ 2 tablespoons erythritol	♦ ½ teaspoon pumpkin pie spices

1. Pour the apple cider vinegar into the Instant Pot and place the trivet inside. 2. In a small bowl, mix erythritol, avocado oil, butter, and pumpkin pie spice until well combined. Rub this mixture evenly over the ham to coat it. 3. Place the seasoned ham on the trivet inside the Instant Pot, then close and secure the lid. 4. Select Manual mode and set to cook on High Pressure for 10 minutes. 5. Once the timer goes off, allow a natural pressure release for 5 minutes, then release any remaining pressure and carefully open the lid. 6. Slice the ham and serve warm. Enjoy!

Per Serving:
calories: 134 | fat: 5g | protein: 17g | carbs: 7g | net carbs: 7g | fiber: 0g

Creamy Almond-Infused Beef Stew

Prep time: 10 minutes | Cook time: 60 minutes | Serves 3

- 10 ounces (283 g) beef chuck roast, chopped
- ½ cup almond butter
- ½ teaspoon cayenne pepper
- ½ teaspoon salt
- 1 teaspoon dried basil
- 1 cup water

1. Add the almond butter to the Instant Pot and start preheating it on Sauté mode until the almond butter is melted and warmed. 2. In a small bowl, combine cayenne pepper, salt, and dried basil, mixing well. 3. Season the beef by sprinkling it evenly with the spice blend, then place the beef in the Instant Pot, coating it in the warm almond butter. 4. Secure and lock the Instant Pot lid. 5. Set the Instant Pot to Manual mode on Low Pressure, and cook for 60 minutes. Once done, allow the natural pressure release before opening and serving.

Per Serving:
calories: 360 | fat: 28g | protein: 25g | carbs: 1g | net carbs: 1g | fiber: 0g

Tomatillo Chile Verde Pulled Pork

Prep time: 15 minutes | Cook time: 1 hour 3 minutes | Serves 6

- 2 pounds (907 g) pork shoulder, cut into 6 equal-sized pieces
- 1 teaspoon sea salt
- ½ teaspoon ground black pepper
- 2 jalapeño peppers, deseeded and stemmed
- 1 pound (454 g) tomatillos, husks removed and quartered
- 3 garlic cloves
- 1 tablespoon lime juice
- 3 tablespoons fresh cilantro, chopped
- 1 medium white onion, chopped
- 1 teaspoon ground cumin
- ½ teaspoon dried oregano
- 1⅔ cups chicken broth
- 1½ tablespoons olive oil

1. Generously season the pork pieces with salt and pepper, rubbing the seasonings into the meat to ensure even coating. Set the pork aside. 2. In a blender, combine jalapeños, tomatillos, garlic cloves, lime juice, cilantro, onions, cumin, oregano, and chicken broth. Blend until smooth and well-combined, creating a flavorful sauce. Set aside. 3. Set the Instant Pot to Sauté mode and heat the olive oil. Once the oil is hot, add the seasoned pork pieces, searing for about 4 minutes per side until nicely browned. 4. Pour the prepared jalapeño-tomatillo sauce over the pork, gently stirring to coat the pork in the sauce. 5. Secure and lock the lid, select Manual mode, and set to High Pressure for 55 minutes. 6. Once cooking is complete, let the pressure release naturally for 10 minutes, then carefully release any remaining pressure. 7. Open the lid and transfer the pork pieces to a cutting board. Shred the pork with two forks until finely pulled. 8. Return the shredded pork to the pot, mixing it with the sauce until well combined. Transfer to a serving platter and serve warm, perfect for tacos, rice bowls, or alongside fresh tortillas.

Per Serving:
calories: 381 | fat: 25g | protein: 29g | carbs: 11g | net carbs: 8g | fiber: 3g

Aromatic Moroccan Lamb Stew

Prep time: 5 minutes | Cook time: 50 minutes | Serves 3

- ½ cup coconut milk
- 1 teaspoon butter
- ½ teaspoon dried rosemary
- ¼ teaspoon salt
- ½ teaspoon ground
- coriander
- 13 ounces (369 g) lamb shoulder, chopped
- 1 teaspoon ground anise
- ¾ cup water

1. Begin by slicing the mushrooms and placing them in the Instant Pot bowl. 2. Add all other ingredients to the pot, ensuring everything is well combined. Close the lid securely and set it to seal. 3. Select Manual mode and set the cooking time for 45 minutes. 4. Once the cooking time is complete, allow the pressure to release naturally for 10 minutes, then carefully release any remaining pressure. Open the lid and serve warm.

Per Serving:
calories: 332 | fat: 20g | protein: 35g | carbs: 3g | net carbs: 2g | fiber: 1g

Herb-Infused Cilantro Pork Shoulder

Prep time: 10 minutes | Cook time: 85 minutes | Serves 4

- 1 pound (454 g) boneless pork shoulder
- ¼ cup chopped fresh cilantro
- 1 cup water
- 1 teaspoon salt
- 1 teaspoon coconut oil
- ½ teaspoon mustard seeds

1. Pour water into the Instant Pot to create a base for steaming. 2. Add the pork shoulder, fresh cilantro, salt, coconut oil, and mustard seeds directly to the pot, ensuring the ingredients are well distributed around the meat. 3. Secure the lid and set it to seal, then select Manual mode on High Pressure and set the cooking time for 85 minutes. 4. Once cooking is complete, perform a quick pressure release, then carefully open the lid. 5. Serve the tender pork shoulder with the flavorful cooking liquid from the Instant Pot for added richness. Enjoy!

Per Serving:
calories: 343 | fat: 25g | protein: 26g | carbs: 0g | net carbs: 0g | fiber: 0g

Garlic & Herb Flank Steak Delight

Prep time: 30 minutes | Cook time: 8 to 10 minutes | Serves 6

♦ ½ cup avocado oil	♦ 1½ teaspoons sea salt
♦ ¼ cup coconut aminos	♦ 1 teaspoon freshly ground black pepper
♦ 1 shallot, minced	
♦ 1 tablespoon minced garlic	♦ ¼ teaspoon red pepper flakes
♦ 2 tablespoons chopped fresh oregano, or 2 teaspoons dried	♦ 2 pounds (907 g) flank steak

1. Prepare the marinade: In a blender, add avocado oil, coconut aminos, chopped shallot, minced garlic, oregano, salt, black pepper, and red pepper flakes. Blend until the mixture is smooth and well-combined.2. Marinate the steak: Place the steak in a zip-top bag or shallow dish, then pour the marinade over it, ensuring the steak is evenly coated. Seal the bag or cover the dish and refrigerate for at least 2 hours, or overnight, to allow the flavors to infuse deeply.3. Get ready to cook: Take the steak out of the marinade, discarding any leftover marinade.4. Air fry the steak: Preheat the air fryer to 400°F (204°C). Arrange the steak in the air fryer basket; if necessary, cut into sections and cook in batches. Air fry for 4 to 6 minutes, flip, and cook for an additional 4 minutes, or until the internal temperature reaches 120°F (49°C) for medium-rare, or to your desired doneness. Let the steak rest for a few minutes before serving.

Per Serving:

calories: 360 | fat: 20g | protein: 38g | carbs: 4g | net carbs: 4g | fiber: 0g

Sizzling Kung Pao Beef with Roasted Peppers & Peanuts

Prep time: 15 minutes | Cook time: 20 minutes | Serves 4

Sauce/Marinade:

♦ ¼ cup coconut aminos	♦ 1½ tablespoons sherry wine
♦ 1½ tablespoons white wine vinegar	♦ 1 tablespoon avocado oil
	♦ 1 teaspoon chili paste

Stir-Fry:

♦ 1 pound (454 g) flank steak, thinly sliced against the grain and cut into bite-size pieces	♦ 2 medium bell peppers (6 ounces / 170 g each), red and green, chopped into bite-size pieces
♦ 2 tablespoons avocado oil, divided into 1 tablespoon and 1 tablespoon	♦ 2 cloves garlic, minced
	♦ ¼ cup roasted peanuts

1. Prepare the sauce: In a small bowl, whisk together coconut aminos, white wine vinegar, sherry wine, avocado oil, and chili paste until smooth.2. Marinate the steak: Place sliced steak in a medium bowl and pour half of the sauce (about ¼ cup) over it, stirring to coat evenly. Cover the bowl and refrigerate for at least 30 minutes, or up to 2 hours.3. About 10 minutes before marinating time ends, heat 1 tablespoon of oil in a large wok or sauté pan over medium-high heat. Add the bell peppers and cook for 7 to 8 minutes, stirring occasionally, until they're softened and slightly browned.4. Add the minced garlic to the pan and sauté for about 1 minute, until fragrant.5. Remove the peppers and garlic from the pan, cover, and set aside to keep warm.6. Add the remaining tablespoon of oil to the pan and heat on high. Place the marinated steak in a single layer in the pan and cook undisturbed for 2 to 4 minutes per side, or until nicely browned. If additional cooking is needed, stir-fry until the steak reaches your preferred doneness. Remove from the pan and keep warm.7. Pour the reserved marinade into the pan, bringing it to a rapid simmer. Continue to cook for a few minutes until the sauce reduces and thickens slightly.8. Return the steak, peppers, and a handful of roasted peanuts to the pan. Toss everything together in the thickened sauce until well coated. Serve immediately for best flavor.

Per Serving:

calories: 341 | fat: 20g | protein: 27g | carbs: 9g | net carbs: 7g | fiber: 2g

Spiced Kheema Meatloaf with Aromatic Indian Flavors

Prep time: 10 minutes | Cook time: 15 minutes | Serves 4

♦ 1 pound (454 g) 85% lean ground beef	♦ 2 teaspoons garam masala
	♦ 1 teaspoon kosher salt
♦ 2 large eggs, lightly beaten	♦ 1 teaspoon ground turmeric
♦ 1 cup diced yellow onion	♦ 1 teaspoon cayenne pepper
♦ ¼ cup chopped fresh cilantro	♦ ½ teaspoon ground cinnamon
♦ 1 tablespoon minced fresh ginger	♦ ⅛ teaspoon ground cardamom
♦ 1 tablespoon minced garlic	

1. In a large bowl, combine the ground beef, eggs, chopped onion, cilantro, ginger, garlic, garam masala, salt, turmeric, cayenne, cinnamon, and cardamom. Gently mix until everything is thoroughly incorporated, taking care not to overmix.2. Transfer the seasoned meat mixture to a baking pan, pressing it evenly. Place the pan inside the air fryer basket. Set the air fryer to 350°F (177°C) and cook for 15 minutes. Check for doneness with a meat thermometer; the internal temperature should reach 160°F (71°C) for medium.3. Carefully drain any excess fat and liquid from the baking pan, then let the meatloaf rest for 5 minutes to retain its juices.4. Slice and serve the meatloaf while hot, enjoying the flavorful blend of spices.

Per Serving:

calories: 359 | fat: 24g | protein: 29g | carbs: 8g | net carbs: 6g | fiber: 2g

Smoky Paprika-Grilled Pork Chops

Prep time: 5 minutes | Cook time: 10 minutes | Serves 4

- 4 pork chops
- Salt and black pepper, to taste
- 3 tablespoons paprika
- ¾ cup cumin powder
- 1 teaspoon chili powder

1. In a mixing bowl, combine paprika, black pepper, cumin, salt, and chili powder. Add the pork chops to the bowl, rubbing the seasoning mixture thoroughly into each chop to coat well.2. Preheat a grill to medium heat. Place the seasoned pork chops on the grill and cook for 5 minutes on one side, then flip and cook for an additional 5 minutes on the other side, or until they reach your preferred doneness.3. Serve the grilled pork chops hot, paired with a side of freshly steamed vegetables for a balanced meal. Enjoy!

Per Serving:

calories: 355 | fat: 19g | protein: 42g | carbs: 3g | net carbs: 1g | fiber: 2g

Hearty Sausage-Stuffed Bell Peppers with Provolone Melt

Prep time: 15 minutes | Cook time: 28 to 30 minutes | Serves 6

- Avocado oil spray
- 8 ounces (227 g) Italian sausage, casings removed
- ½ cup chopped mushrooms
- ¼ cup diced onion
- 1 teaspoon Italian seasoning
- Sea salt and freshly ground
- black pepper, to taste
- 1 cup keto-friendly marinara sauce
- 3 bell peppers, halved and seeded
- 3 ounces (85 g) provolone cheese, shredded

1. Lightly spray a large skillet with oil and heat over medium-high. Add the sausage and cook for about 5 minutes, using a wooden spoon to break up the meat as it browns. Add the mushrooms, onion, and Italian seasoning, then season with salt and pepper. Continue cooking for another 5 minutes until the vegetables are softened. Stir in the marinara sauce and cook until everything is heated through.2. Spoon the sausage mixture into the halved bell peppers, filling each pepper generously.3. Preheat the air fryer to 350°F (177°C). Arrange the stuffed peppers in a single layer in the air fryer basket, cooking in batches if needed. Air fry for 15 minutes, allowing the peppers to become tender.4. Sprinkle cheese over each stuffed pepper and return to the air fryer for an additional 3 to 5 minutes, or until the cheese is melted and bubbly. Serve hot.

Per Serving:

calories: 205 | fat: 16g | protein: 10g | carbs: 6g | net carbs: 5g | fiber: 1g

Instant Pot Buttery Beef & Spinach

Prep time: 2 minutes | Cook time: 10 minutes | Serves 4

- 1 pound (454 g) 85% lean ground beef
- 1 cup water
- 4 cups fresh spinach
- ¾ teaspoon salt
- ¼ cup butter
- ¼ teaspoon pepper
- ¼ teaspoon garlic powder

1. Press the Sauté function on the Instant Pot and add the ground beef, cooking until it's fully browned. Transfer the cooked beef to a 7-cup glass bowl and set aside. Drain any remaining grease from the pot and return it to the Instant Pot. 2. Add water to the pot, then place the steam rack at the bottom. Set the glass bowl with ground beef on the steam rack, adding fresh spinach, salt, butter, pepper, and garlic powder. Cover the bowl with aluminum foil to trap the steam. Close and lock the Instant Pot lid. 3. Select Manual mode, adjusting the cooking time to 2 minutes. Once the timer goes off, perform a quick pressure release. Carefully remove the foil, stir the mixture, and serve warm.

Per Serving:

calories: 272 | fat: 19g | protein: 18g | carbs: 1g | net carbs: 0g | fiber: 1g

Apple Cider Herb-Infused Pork Tenderloin

Prep time: 15 minutes | Cook time: 18 minutes | Serves 4

- ¼ teaspoon ground cumin
- ½ teaspoon ground nutmeg
- ½ teaspoon dried thyme
- ½ teaspoon ground coriander
- 1 tablespoon sesame oil
- 1 pound (454 g) pork tenderloin
- 2 tablespoons apple cider vinegar
- 1 cup water

1. In a mixing bowl, combine ground cumin, ground nutmeg, thyme, ground coriander, and apple cider vinegar, stirring until well blended. 2. Generously rub the spice mixture over the pork tenderloin, ensuring it's evenly coated. 3. Set the Instant Pot to Sauté mode, add sesame oil, and let it heat for 2 minutes. 4. Place the pork tenderloin in the hot oil, searing for 5 minutes on each side or until lightly browned. 5. Pour in water to create steam for cooking. 6. Secure and seal the Instant Pot lid, select Manual mode, and set to High Pressure for 5 minutes. 7. Once cooking is complete, allow the pressure to release naturally for 15 minutes before carefully opening the lid. Serve the tenderloin warm.

Per Serving:

calories: 196 | fat: 7g | protein: 29g | carbs: 0g | net carbs: 0g | fiber: 0g

Mediterranean Grilled Pork Skewers

Prep time: 10 minutes | Cook time: 15 minutes | Serves 4

♦ ¼ cup good-quality olive oil	♦ 1 teaspoon dried parsley
♦ 1 tablespoon minced garlic	♦ ½ teaspoon sea salt
♦ 2 teaspoons dried oregano	♦ ¼ teaspoon freshly ground black pepper
♦ 1 teaspoon dried basil	♦ 1 (1-pound) pork tenderloin, cut into 1½-inch pieces

1. Prepare the Marinade: In a medium bowl, combine olive oil, minced garlic, dried oregano, basil, parsley, salt, and pepper. Stir until the mixture is well blended, then add the pork pieces, ensuring each piece is coated thoroughly in the marinade. Cover the bowl and refrigerate for at least 2 hours, or up to 4 hours, to let the flavors penetrate the meat. 2. Assemble the Skewers: After marinating, thread the pork pieces onto four skewers, spacing them evenly to allow heat to circulate while cooking. Avoid crowding the pieces to ensure even grilling. 3. Cook the Skewers: Preheat the grill to medium-high. Place the skewers on the grill and cook for around 12 minutes, rotating frequently to achieve an even cook on all sides. Grill until the pork is fully cooked and slightly charred on the outside. 4. Serve the Kebabs: Remove the skewers from the grill and allow them to rest for about 5 minutes to lock in the juices. Transfer each skewer to individual plates and serve immediately for the best flavor and texture. Enjoy your meal!

Per Serving:
calories: 261 | fat: 18g | protein: 24g | carbs: 1g | net carbs: 1g | fiber: 0g

Air-Fried Short Ribs with Fresh Chimichurri

Prep time: 30 minutes | Cook time: 13 minutes | Serves 4

♦ 1 pound (454 g) boneless short ribs	♦ 1 tablespoon freshly squeezed lemon juice
♦ 1½ teaspoons sea salt, divided	♦ ½ teaspoon ground cumin
♦ ½ teaspoon freshly ground black pepper, divided	♦ ¼ teaspoon red pepper flakes
♦ ½ cup fresh parsley leaves	♦ 2 tablespoons extra-virgin olive oil
♦ ½ cup fresh cilantro leaves	♦ Avocado oil spray
♦ 1 teaspoon minced garlic	

1. Begin by patting the short ribs dry with paper towels, then season them thoroughly with 1 teaspoon of salt and ¼ teaspoon of black pepper. Let the ribs rest at room temperature for 45 minutes to enhance flavor. 2. While the ribs rest, prepare the chimichurri sauce. In a blender or food processor, combine parsley, cilantro, garlic, lemon juice, cumin, red pepper flakes, the remaining ½ teaspoon of salt, and the remaining ¼ teaspoon of black pepper. With the machine running, slowly drizzle in the olive oil, blending until the sauce is smooth and emulsified, about 1 minute. 3. Preheat the air fryer to 400°F (204°C). Lightly spray both sides of the ribs with oil, then place them in the air fryer basket. Cook for 8 minutes, then flip the ribs and air fry for an additional 5 minutes, or until an instant-read thermometer registers 125°F (52°C) for medium-rare, adjusting time as needed for preferred doneness. 4. Let the ribs rest for 5 to 10 minutes before slicing to retain their juices. Serve warm, generously topped with the chimichurri sauce for a fresh, zesty finish.

Per Serving:
calories: 381 | fat: 28g | protein: 27g | carbs: 2g | net carbs: 1g | fiber: 1g

Slow-Braised Bone Broth Brisket with Rustic Tomato Sauce

Prep time: 5 minutes | Cook time: 75 minutes | Serves 4 to 5

- 2 tablespoons coconut oil
- ½ teaspoon garlic salt
- ½ teaspoon crushed red pepper
- ½ teaspoon dried basil
- ½ teaspoon kosher salt
- ½ teaspoon freshly ground black pepper
- 1 (14-ounce / 397-g) can sugar-free or low-sugar diced tomatoes
- 1 cup grass-fed bone broth
- 1 pound (454 g) beef brisket, chopped

1. Set the Instant Pot to Sauté mode and add the oil, allowing it to melt. In a medium bowl, mix together the garlic salt, red pepper flakes, basil, kosher salt, black pepper, and diced tomatoes until evenly combined.2. Pour the bone broth into the Instant Pot, then place the brisket inside and spoon the prepared tomato mixture over the top. Cancel the Sauté function by pressing Cancel, ensuring the previous program is stopped. Secure the lid, set the pressure release valve to Sealing, and select Manual mode. Set to cook on High Pressure for 75 minutes.3. Once the cooking cycle is complete, carefully switch the pressure release valve to Venting to release the steam. Open the lid and transfer the brisket to a serving dish, spooning any remaining sauce over the top, if desired. Serve hot and enjoy!

Per Serving:
calories: 240 | fat: 11g | protein: 29g | carbs: 5g | net carbs: 3g | fiber: 2g

Jerk Pulled Pork with Avocado

Prep time: 10 minutes | Cook time: 2 hours | Serves 12

- 4 pounds pork shoulder
- 1 tablespoon avocado oil
- ½ cup vegetable stock
- ¼ cup jerk seasoning
- 6 avocado, sliced

1. Generously rub the pork shoulder with jerk seasoning, then place it in a greased baking dish. Pour in the stock to keep the meat moist during cooking. Cover tightly with aluminum foil and bake at 350°F for 1 hour and 45 minutes. 2. After the initial cooking time, remove the foil and return the pork to the oven for an additional 20 minutes to allow the top to brown slightly. Let the pork rest for 30 minutes before shredding with two forks. 3. Serve the pulled pork with fresh avocado slices on top for added creaminess and flavor. Enjoy as a main dish or in sandwiches, tacos, or salads.

Per Serving:
calories: 389 | fat: 27g | protein: 30g | carbs: 9g | net carbs: 4g | fiber: 5g

Chapter

5

Poultry

Chapter 5 Poultry

Creamy Cheddar-Dill Chicken

Prep time: 15 minutes | Cook time: 20 minutes | Serves 4

♦ 1 cup chicken broth	boneless chicken breast
♦ 1 teaspoon dried dill	♦ ½ teaspoon salt
♦ 1 teaspoon dried oregano	♦ 2 tablespoons mascarpone cheese
♦ ½ teaspoon onion powder	
♦ 1 pound (454 g) skinless,	♦ 2 ounces (57 g) Cheddar cheese, shredded

1. Begin by pouring the chicken broth into the Instant Pot. 2. Add dried dill, oregano, onion powder, chicken breast, and salt to the broth, stirring to combine. 3. Secure the lid tightly and set it to seal. 4. Cook the chicken breast using Manual mode on High Pressure for 15 minutes. 5. Once the timer goes off, perform a quick pressure release and carefully transfer the cooked chicken to a bowl. 6. Use an immersion blender to blend the chicken broth mixture until smooth and well combined. 7. Stir in mascarpone cheese and Cheddar cheese, then select Sauté mode to heat the mixture for 2 minutes, allowing the cheeses to melt. 8. While the sauce heats, shred the cooked chicken into bite-sized pieces. 9. Add the shredded chicken to the cheesy broth mixture, stirring to combine, and continue to sauté for an additional 3 minutes to heat through. Serve warm and enjoy your creamy chicken dish!

Per Serving:
calories: 212 | fat: 9g | protein: 30g | carbs: 1g | net carbs: 1g | fiber: 0g

Tomato & Parmesan-Crusted Chicken Bake

Prep time: 15 minutes | Cook time: 13 minutes | Serves 2

♦ 1 tomato, sliced	♦ 1 teaspoon butter
♦ 8 ounces (227 g) chicken fillets	♦ 4 tablespoons water, for sprinkling
♦ 2 ounces (57 g) Parmesan, sliced	♦ 1 cup water, for cooking

1. Start by pouring water into the Instant Pot and inserting the steamer rack. 2. Next, grease a baking mold with butter to prevent sticking. 3. Slice the chicken fillets in half and arrange them in the prepared mold. 4. Drizzle a bit of water over the chicken, then layer with sliced tomatoes and sprinkle Parmesan cheese on top. 5. Cover the baking mold tightly with aluminum foil and place it on the steamer rack inside the Instant Pot. 6. Secure the lid and ensure it is sealed. 7. Set the Instant Pot to Manual mode and cook for 13 minutes. Once the cooking time is up, allow for a natural pressure release for 10 minutes before carefully opening the lid. Enjoy your flavorful dish!

Per Serving:
calories: 329 | fat: 16g | protein: 42g | carbs: 2g | net carbs: 2g | fiber: 0g

Golden Tandoori Spiced Chicken

Prep time: 30 minutes | Cook time: 15 minutes | Serves 4

♦ 1 pound (454 g) chicken tenders, halved crosswise	♦ 1 teaspoon ground turmeric
♦ ¼ cup plain Greek yogurt	♦ 1 teaspoon garam masala
♦ 1 tablespoon minced fresh ginger	♦ 1 teaspoon sweet smoked paprika
♦ 1 tablespoon minced garlic	♦ 1 tablespoon vegetable oil or melted ghee
♦ ¼ cup chopped fresh cilantro or parsley	♦ 2 teaspoons fresh lemon juice
♦ 1 teaspoon kosher salt	♦ 2 tablespoons chopped fresh cilantro
♦ ½ to 1 teaspoon cayenne pepper	

1. In a large glass bowl, combine the chicken pieces with yogurt, ginger, garlic, chopped cilantro, salt, cayenne pepper, turmeric, garam masala, and paprika. Mix well to coat the chicken evenly. Allow the mixture to marinate at room temperature for 30 minutes, or for enhanced flavor, cover and refrigerate for up to 24 hours. 2. Preheat your air fryer to 350°F (177°C). Arrange the marinated chicken in a single layer in the air fryer basket, discarding any leftover marinade. Lightly spray the chicken with vegetable oil. Cook for 15 minutes, shaking the basket halfway through and spraying with additional oil to ensure even cooking. 3. After 15 minutes, check for doneness; the chicken should be cooked through and golden. Transfer the cooked chicken to a serving platter, drizzle with fresh lemon juice, and toss to coat. Garnish with additional chopped cilantro before serving. Enjoy!

Per Serving:
calories: 191 | fat: 9g | protein: 24g | carbs: 3g | net carbs: 2g | fiber: 1g

Sesame-Crusted Sticky Chicken Bowls

Prep time: 10 minutes | Cook time: 30 minutes | Serves 2

Chicken:

◆ ½ cup coconut oil, for the pan	salt
◆ ½ pound boneless, skinless chicken thighs	◆ ¼ teaspoon ground black pepper
◆ ½ teaspoon pink Himalayan	◆ ⅓ cup coconut flour

Sauce:

◆ 1½ teaspoons toasted sesame oil	◆ 2½ tablespoons powdered erythritol
◆ 1 clove garlic, minced	◆ 2 tablespoons water
◆ 1 (½-inch) piece fresh ginger, grated	◆ ½ teaspoon red pepper flakes
◆ ¼ cup soy sauce	◆ ¼ teaspoon xanthan gum
◆ 2½ tablespoons unseasoned rice wine vinegar	◆ 2 cups riced cauliflower (see Tip, opposite)

For Garnish (Optional):

◆ White and/or black sesame seeds	◆ Sliced scallions

1. In a medium saucepan, heat coconut oil over medium-high heat until it reaches a temperature of 330°F to 350°F, as measured by a deep-fry thermometer. 2. While the oil heats, prepare the chicken by patting the thighs dry, cutting them into bite-sized pieces, and seasoning with salt and pepper. Dredge the chicken pieces in coconut flour until completely coated. 3. Fry the chicken in batches of 3 or 4 pieces, cooking them in the hot oil and turning occasionally until they are golden brown on the outside and cooked through, approximately 3 to 5 minutes. Use a slotted spoon to remove the chicken and place it on a paper towel-lined plate to drain while you fry the remaining pieces. 4. After all the chicken is fried, prepare the sauce: In a small saucepan, heat sesame oil over medium heat. Add minced garlic and ginger, cooking for 30 seconds until fragrant. Incorporate the remaining sauce ingredients (excluding xanthan gum) and whisk until well combined. Allow to simmer for about 3 minutes, then add xanthan gum and whisk again. Increase heat to medium-high and let the sauce reduce and thicken for 5 to 7 minutes. 5. While the sauce thickens, steam the cauliflower rice by placing it in a microwave-safe bowl and covering it with 2 or 3 damp paper towels. Microwave for 4 to 5 minutes until tender but not mushy. Divide the steamed cauliflower rice into two bowls. 6. Toss the fried chicken pieces in the saucepan with the thickened sauce, ensuring they are evenly coated, and heat for an additional 2 minutes on the stovetop. Serve the chicken and sauce over the cauliflower rice, garnishing with sesame seeds and sliced scallions if desired. Enjoy!

Per Serving:

calories: 332 | fat: 16g | protein: 35g | carbs: 13g | net carbs: 6g | fiber: 7g

Slow-Cooked Fennel & Sausage Chicken Thighs

Prep time: 10 minutes | Cook time: 8 hours | Serves 2

◆ ½ fennel bulb, cored and sliced thin	◆ 2 bone-in, skinless chicken thighs, about 8 ounces (227 g) each
◆ ½ red onion, halved and sliced thin	◆ ⅛ teaspoon sea salt
◆ 1 teaspoon extra-virgin olive oil	◆ 1 hot Italian sausage link, casing removed

1. In the slow cooker, combine fennel, onion, and olive oil, stirring gently to mix the ingredients together. 2. Season the chicken with salt and place it on top of the fennel and onion mixture. 3. Crumble the sausage around the chicken, distributing it evenly. 4. Cover the slow cooker and set it to cook on low for 8 hours, allowing the flavors to meld and the chicken to become tender. Enjoy your delicious dish!

Per Serving:

calories: 376 | fat: 15g | protein: 52g | carbs: 5g | net carbs: 3g | fiber: 2g

Cheesy Broccoli-Stuffed Chicken

Prep time: 15 minutes | Cook time: 20 minutes | Serves 4

◆ 2 ounces (57 g) cream cheese, softened	boneless, skinless chicken breasts
◆ 1 cup chopped fresh broccoli, steamed	◆ 2 tablespoons mayonnaise
◆ ½ cup shredded sharp Cheddar cheese	◆ ¼ teaspoon salt
◆ 4 (6-ounce / 170-g)	◆ ¼ teaspoon garlic powder
	◆ ⅛ teaspoon ground black pepper

1. In a medium bowl, mix together cream cheese, chopped broccoli, and shredded Cheddar cheese until well combined. Cut a 4-inch pocket into each chicken breast, being careful not to slice all the way through. Evenly divide the cream cheese mixture among the chicken breasts, stuffing each pocket generously. 2. Spread ¼ tablespoon of mayonnaise on each side of the stuffed chicken breasts, then season both sides with salt, garlic powder, and pepper to taste. 3. Place the stuffed chicken breasts in the ungreased air fryer basket with the open seams facing up. Set the air fryer temperature to 350°F (177°C) and cook for 20 minutes, turning the chicken halfway through the cooking time. The chicken should be golden brown and reach an internal temperature of at least 165°F (74°C) when done. Serve warm for a delicious meal!

Per Serving:

calories: 368 | fat: 23g | protein: 38g | carbs: 4g | net carbs: 3g | fiber: 1g

Creamy Provolone-Stuffed Chicken

Prep time: 15 minutes | Cook time: 20 minutes | Serves 4

- 12 ounces (340 g) chicken fillet
- 4 ounces (113 g) provolone cheese, sliced
- 1 tablespoon cream cheese
- ½ teaspoon dried cilantro
- ½ teaspoon smoked paprika
- 1 cup water, for cooking

1. Start by beating the chicken fillet to tenderize it, then rub it thoroughly with dried cilantro and smoked paprika for flavor. 2. Spread a generous layer of cream cheese over the chicken, then top it with slices of Provolone cheese. 3. Carefully roll the chicken fillet into a tight roll and wrap it securely in aluminum foil to hold everything in place. 4. Pour water into the Instant Pot and insert the rack to elevate the chicken. 5. Place the wrapped chicken roll on the rack inside the Instant Pot. Secure the lid and ensure it is sealed. 6. Set the Instant Pot to Manual mode and cook on High Pressure for 20 minutes. 7. Once cooking is complete, perform a quick pressure release, then carefully unwrap the foil. Slice the chicken roll into servings and enjoy!

Per Serving:
calories: 271 | fat: 15g | protein: 32g | carbs: 1g | net carbs: 1g | fiber: 0g

Air-Fried Marinated Chicken Legs with Leeks

Prep time: 30 minutes | Cook time: 18 minutes | Serves 6

- 2 leeks, sliced
- 2 large-sized tomatoes, chopped
- 3 cloves garlic, minced
- ½ teaspoon dried oregano
- 6 chicken legs, boneless and skinless
- ½ teaspoon smoked cayenne pepper
- 2 tablespoons olive oil
- A freshly ground nutmeg

1. In a mixing bowl, combine all ingredients except for the leeks, mixing thoroughly. Cover the bowl and refrigerate to allow the flavors to meld overnight. 2. Arrange the leeks in a single layer at the bottom of the air fryer basket. Place the marinated chicken legs on top of the leeks. 3. Set the air fryer to 375°F (191°C) and roast the chicken legs for 18 minutes, turning them halfway through the cooking time for even browning. Serve the chicken legs hot with hoisin sauce on the side for dipping. Enjoy your meal!

Per Serving:
calories: 275 | fat: 15g | protein: 25g | carbs: 10g | net carbs: 8g | fiber: 2g

Bacon-Wrapped Chicken Tenders

Prep time: 15 minutes | Cook time: 15 minutes | Serves 2

- 4 ounces (113 g) chicken fillet
- 2 bacon slices
- ½ teaspoon ground paprika
- ¼ teaspoon salt
- 1 teaspoon olive oil
- 1 cup water, for cooking

1. Begin by cutting the chicken fillet into two tenders, then season them with salt, ground paprika, and a drizzle of olive oil to enhance the flavor. 2. Wrap each chicken tender with bacon, ensuring they are fully covered for added richness, and transfer the wrapped tenders to the steamer rack. 3. Pour water into the Instant Pot and place the steamer rack with the chicken tenders inside. 4. Secure the lid and ensure it is sealed. Set the Instant Pot to Manual mode and cook on High Pressure for 15 minutes. 5. Once the cooking time is complete, allow the pressure to release naturally for 10 minutes before carefully opening the lid. Enjoy your delicious bacon-wrapped chicken tenders!

Per Serving:
calories: 232 | fat: 14g | protein: 23g | carbs: 1g | net carbs: 1g | fiber: 0g

Herb-Stuffed Roast Chicken with Brussels Sprouts

Prep time: 5 minutes | Cook time: 1 hour 35 minutes | Serves 8

- 5 pounds whole chicken
- 1 bunch oregano
- 1 bunch thyme
- 1 tablespoon marjoram
- 1 tablespoon parsley
- 1 tablespoon olive oil
- 2 pounds Brussels sprouts
- 1 lemon
- 4 tablespoons butter

1. Preheat your oven to 450°F (232°C) to get it nice and hot for roasting. 2. Stuff the chicken cavity with fresh oregano, thyme, and lemon slices. Place the chicken in the oven and roast for 15 minutes to start the cooking process. After 15 minutes, reduce the oven temperature to 325°F (163°C) and continue cooking for 40 minutes. Once the time is up, spread softened butter over the chicken and sprinkle with fresh parsley and marjoram for added flavor. 3. Add the Brussels sprouts around the chicken, ensuring they're well distributed. Return the dish to the oven and bake for an additional 40 minutes until everything is cooked through and golden. 4. Once done, let the chicken rest for 10 minutes before carving to allow the juices to redistribute, ensuring each slice is juicy and flavorful. Enjoy your meal!

Per Serving:
calories: 391 | fat: 21g | protein: 41g | carbs: 11g | net carbs: 7g | fiber: 4g

Savory Sun-Dried Tomato Turkey Meatballs

Prep time: 5 minutes | Cook time: 10 minutes | Serves 4

◆ 1 pound ground turkey	◆ ½ teaspoon salt
◆ 2 tablespoons chopped sun-dried tomatoes	◆ ¼ cup almond flour
	◆ 2 tablespoons olive oil
◆ 2 tablespoons chopped basil	◆ ½ cup shredded mozzarella cheese
◆ ½ teaspoon garlic powder	
◆ 1 egg	◆ ¼ teaspoon pepper

1. In a mixing bowl, combine all ingredients except for the olive oil. Use your hands to mix everything together until well combined. Shape the mixture into 16 meatballs. 2. Heat olive oil in a skillet over medium heat. Once the oil is hot, add the meatballs to the skillet and cook for 4 to 5 minutes on each side, or until they are browned and cooked through. 3. Once cooked, remove the meatballs from the skillet and serve them hot. Enjoy your delicious meatballs!

Per Serving:
calories: 343 | fat: 22g | protein: 28g | carbs: 7g | net carbs: 5g | fiber: 2g

Zesty Lemon Butter Chicken Piccata

Prep time: 5 minutes | Cook time: 25 minutes | Serves 4

◆ 4 (6-ounce / 170-g) boneless, skinless chicken breasts	◆ 2 tablespoons coconut oil
	◆ 1 cup water
	◆ 2 cloves garlic, minced
◆ ½ teaspoon salt	◆ 4 tablespoons butter
◆ ½ teaspoon garlic powder	◆ Juice of 1 lemon
◆ ¼ teaspoon pepper	◆ ¼ teaspoon xanthan gum

1. Season the chicken by generously sprinkling it with salt, garlic powder, and pepper to enhance the flavor. 2. Set your Instant Pot to Sauté mode and melt coconut oil in the pot until hot. 3. Add the chicken pieces and sear each side for about 5 to 7 minutes, or until they develop a golden brown crust. 4. Once browned, remove the chicken from the pot and place it on a plate to rest. 5. Pour water into the Instant Pot, using a wooden spoon to scrape the bottom to release any browned bits of seasoning or meat stuck to the pot. Insert the trivet and return the chicken to the pot, placing it on top of the trivet. 6. Secure the lid tightly. Select Manual mode and set the cooking time to 10 minutes on High Pressure. 7. After cooking, allow for a natural pressure release for 10 minutes, then release any remaining pressure before carefully opening the lid. 8. Remove the chicken from the pot and set it aside. Strain the broth from the Instant Pot into a large bowl, then return the liquid to the pot. 9.

Switch the Instant Pot back to Sauté mode and add the remaining ingredients. Cook for at least 5 minutes, stirring frequently, until the sauce thickens to your liking. 10. Pour the finished sauce over the chicken and serve warm, enjoying the rich flavors.

Per Serving:
calories: 338 | fat: 20g | protein: 32g | carbs: 2g | net carbs: 1g | fiber: 1g

Oven-Baked Cream of Mushroom Stuffed Chicken with Spinach

Prep time: 10 minutes | Cook time: 45 minutes | Serves 4

◆ 3 tablespoons coconut oil, avocado oil, or ghee	pepper
	◆ 1 pound (455 g) boneless, skin-on chicken breasts
◆ 7 ounces (200 g) cremini mushrooms, chopped	◆ 1 teaspoon onion powder
◆ 4 cloves garlic, minced	◆ 1 teaspoon garlic powder
◆ 3 teaspoons dried parsley, divided	◆ ½ cup (120 ml) milk (nondairy or regular)
◆ ¾ teaspoon finely ground sea salt, divided	◆ 4 cups (280 g) spinach, for serving
◆ ¼ teaspoon ground black	

1. Begin by preheating the oven to 400°F (205°C). Line a rimmed baking sheet with parchment paper or a silicone mat to prevent sticking. 2. In a large frying pan over medium heat, warm the oil. Add the sliced mushrooms, minced garlic, 2 teaspoons of parsley, ¼ teaspoon of salt, and pepper. Toss everything to coat and sauté for about 10 minutes until the mushrooms are tender and flavorful. 3. While the mushrooms are cooking, take each chicken breast and slice it horizontally, stopping about ½ inch (1.25 cm) from the opposite side so it opens like a book. Use a sharp knife and apply gentle pressure with your palm to keep the chicken steady during this process. 4. Arrange the chicken breasts on the prepared baking sheet, opening them up to create pockets. Spoon one-quarter of the sautéed mushroom mixture into the center of each opened chicken breast. If you have any leftover mushroom mixture, scatter it around the chicken on the baking sheet. 5. Fold the chicken breasts over to enclose the filling. Sprinkle the stuffed breasts with garlic powder, onion powder, the remaining 1 teaspoon of parsley, and the remaining ½ teaspoon of salt for added flavor. 6. Carefully pour milk between the chicken breasts, allowing it to fill the pan and create a creamy base. 7. Bake in the preheated oven for 30 to 35 minutes, or until the internal temperature of the chicken reaches 165°F (74°C). 8. While the chicken is baking, prepare 4 dinner plates by dividing fresh spinach among them. Once the chicken is done, place the stuffed breasts on the plates and drizzle the spinach with the creamy pan juices. Enjoy your delicious meal! (Note: If the package doesn't yield one breast half per person, cut the stuffed breasts into portions and share them equally among the plates.)

Per Serving:
calories: 388 | fat: 24g | protein: 38g | carbs: 7g | net carbs: 4g | fiber: 2g

Spicy Cajun Chicken and Sausage Gumbo

Prep time: 20 minutes | Cook time: 30 minutes | Serves 5

♦ 2 sausages, sliced	♦ 3 tablespoons dried thyme
♦ 3 chicken breasts, cubed	♦ 2 tablespoons garlic powder
♦ 1 cup celery, chopped	♦ 2 tablespoons dry mustard
♦ 2 tablespoons dried oregano	♦ 1 teaspoon cayenne powder
♦ 2 bell peppers, seeded and chopped	♦ 1 tablespoon chili powder
♦ 1 onion, peeled and chopped	♦ Salt and black pepper, to taste
♦ 2 cups tomatoes, chopped	♦ 6 tablespoons cajun seasoning
♦ 4 cups chicken broth	♦ 3 tablespoons olive oil

1. In a pot over medium heat, warm olive oil until hot. Add the sausages, chicken, chopped pepper, diced onion, dry mustard, chili, diced tomatoes, thyme, bell peppers, salt, oregano, garlic powder, cayenne, and Cajun seasoning. 2. Cook the mixture for about 10 minutes, stirring occasionally to ensure even cooking. Once the meats are browned, add the remaining ingredients and bring the pot to a boil. Reduce the heat to low, cover the pot, and let it simmer for 20 minutes to allow the flavors to meld. 3. Serve the hot dish divided between bowls, enjoying the hearty flavors and warmth of this delicious meal!

Per Serving:
calories: 376 | fat: 17g | protein: 36g | carbs: 20g | net carbs: 16g | fiber: 6g

Steph's Zesty Turkey-Stuffed Peppers

Prep time: 10 minutes | Cook time: 40 minutes | Serves 6

♦ 4 medium green bell peppers, seeded	cauliflower
♦ 1 medium red bell pepper, seeded	♦ ¾ cup no-sugar-added salsa
♦ 1 medium yellow bell pepper, seeded	♦ 1 teaspoon chili powder
	♦ 1 teaspoon ground cumin
♦ 1 pound lean ground turkey	♦ ½ teaspoon black pepper
♦ 1 cup cooked riced	♦ ¼ teaspoon salt
	♦ 1 cup shredded Cheddar cheese

1. Preheat your oven to 375°F and lightly grease a 9" × 13" baking dish to prevent sticking. 2. Prepare the bell peppers by cutting a tight circle around the stems to remove them, then slice each pepper in half vertically from top to bottom. Carefully remove the seeds and membranes, rinse gently, and pat them dry with a paper towel. 3. In a medium skillet over medium-high heat, cook the ground turkey, stirring frequently, for about 10 minutes until browned and cooked through. 4. Add the riced cauliflower to the skillet and stir in the salsa and spices, mixing until well combined. 5. Place the bell pepper halves open-side up in the prepared baking dish. Fill each half with an equal portion of the turkey mixture, dividing it into twelve portions, and top each with shredded cheese. 6. Bake in the preheated oven for 30 minutes, or until the peppers are tender and the cheese is fully melted and bubbly. Once done, remove from the oven and allow to cool slightly before serving warm. Enjoy your flavorful stuffed peppers!

Per Serving:
calories: 234 | fat: 12g | protein: 20g | carbs: 12g | net carbs: 9g | fiber: 3g

Cheesy Italian Chicken Bake

Prep time: 10 minutes | Cook time: 28 minutes | Serves 4

♦ 4 medium boneless, skinless chicken breasts (8 ounces / 227 g each)	♦ 2 tablespoons grated Parmesan cheese
♦ 2 tablespoons butter, melted	♦ ½ cup marinara sauce, no sugar added
♦ ½ teaspoon sea salt	♦ ½ cup (2 ounces / 57 g) shredded Mozzarella cheese
♦ ¼ teaspoon black pepper	♦ 2 tablespoons fresh basil, cut into ribbons
♦ ¼ cup ricotta cheese	
♦ 1 large egg	

1. Preheat your oven to 375°F (190°C) to prepare for baking. 2. Arrange the chicken breasts on a sheet pan, making sure they are at least 1 inch apart for even cooking. Brush both sides of each chicken breast with melted butter, then season generously with sea salt and black pepper. 3. In a small bowl, combine the ricotta cheese with the egg, mixing until smooth. Stir in the grated Parmesan cheese until well blended, then spread this mixture evenly over the top of each chicken breast. 4. Spoon 2 tablespoons of marinara sauce over each chicken breast, followed by a sprinkle of 2 tablespoons of Mozzarella cheese on top. 5. Bake the chicken in the preheated oven for 23 to 28 minutes, or until the chicken is fully cooked and no longer pink in the center. Once done, garnish with fresh basil leaves before serving. Enjoy your deliciously cheesy chicken dish!

Per Serving:
calories: 365 | fat: 16g | protein: 46g | carbs: 3g | net carbs: 3g | fiber: 0g

Spicy Ginger Chicken with Broccoli & Green Onions

Prep time: 10 minutes | Cook time: 25 minutes | Serves 2

◆ 2chicken thighs, skinless, boneless, cut into strips	◆ ½ teaspoon garlic powder
◆ 1 tablespoon olive oil	◆ ½ cup water
◆ 1 teaspoon red pepper flakes	◆ ½ cup erythritol
◆ 1 teaspoon onion powder	◆ ½ teaspoon xanthan gum
◆ 1 tablespoon fresh ginger, grated	◆ ½ cup green onions, chopped
◆ ¼ cup tamari sauce	◆ 1 small head broccoli, cut into florets

1. Heat oil in a pan over medium heat, then add the chicken and grated ginger. Sauté for about 4 minutes until the chicken starts to brown. 2. Stir in water, onion powder, red pepper flakes, garlic powder, tamari sauce, xanthan gum, and erythritol. Cook the mixture for 15 minutes, allowing the flavors to meld and the sauce to thicken. 3. Add chopped green onions and broccoli to the pan, cooking for an additional 6 minutes until the broccoli is tender and vibrant. Serve the dish hot, enjoying the blend of flavors and textures.

Per Serving:
calories: 386 | fat: 26g | protein: 32g | carbs: 6g | net carbs: 4g | fiber: 2g

Lemon Herb Chicken Skewers

Prep time: 10 minutes | Cook time: 12 minutes | Serves 4

◆ 3 chicken breasts, cut into cubes	◆ ½ cup lemon juice
◆ 2 tablespoons olive oil, divided	◆ Salt and black pepper to taste
◆ ⅔ jar preserved lemon, flesh removed, drained	◆ 1 teaspoon rosemary leaves to garnish
◆ 2 cloves garlic, minced	◆ 2 to 4 lemon wedges to garnish

1. Begin by threading the chicken pieces onto skewers and setting them aside for later use. 2. In a large bowl, combine half of the olive oil, minced garlic, salt, pepper, and lemon juice. Add the chicken skewers along with the lemon zest. Cover the bowl and allow the chicken to marinate in the refrigerator for a minimum of 2 hours to absorb the flavors. 3. When the marinating period is nearly complete, preheat your grill to 350ºF. Remove the chicken skewers from the marinade and place them on the grill. Cook for 6 minutes on each side, ensuring they are cooked through. 4. Once cooked, remove the skewers from the grill and serve them warm, garnished with fresh rosemary leaves and lemon wedges for an added burst of flavor. Enjoy your delicious chicken skewers!

Per Serving:
calories: 277 | fat: 11g | protein: 32g | carbs: 9g | net carbs: 7g | fiber: 2g

Layered Alfredo Chicken Bake

Prep time: 15 minutes | Cook time: 15 minutes | Serves 4

◆ 1 cup broccoli florets	◆ ¼ teaspoon pepper
◆ 1½ cups Alfredo sauce	◆ 1 pound (454 g) thin-sliced deli chicken
◆ ½ cup chopped fresh spinach	◆ 1 cup shredded whole-milk Mozzarella cheese
◆ ¼ cup whole-milk ricotta cheese	◆ 1 cup water
◆ ½ teaspoon salt	

1. Place the broccoli florets in a large mixing bowl. Add the Alfredo sauce, spinach, ricotta, salt, and pepper, stirring until everything is well combined. Use a spoon to divide the mixture into three equal portions.2. In a 7-cup glass bowl, layer the chicken at the bottom, followed by one portion of the veggie mixture, spreading it evenly. Sprinkle a layer of shredded Mozzarella on top. Repeat this layering process with the remaining veggie mix, finishing with a final layer of Mozzarella. Cover the bowl tightly with aluminum foil.3. Add water to the Instant Pot and place the trivet inside. Carefully position the covered dish on the trivet.4. Secure the Instant Pot lid, select Manual mode, and set to cook for 15 minutes at High Pressure.5. Once the timer goes off, perform a quick pressure release. Open the lid carefully to avoid steam.6. If you'd like a golden top, broil in the oven for 3 to 5 minutes until the cheese is bubbly and golden. Serve warm and enjoy!

Per Serving:
calories: 284 | fat: 13g | protein: 29g | carbs: 10g | net carbs: 9g | fiber: 1g

Instant Pot Chicken Carnitas with Crème Fraîche

Prep time: 5 minutes | Cook time: 15 minutes | Serves 8

♦ 3 pounds (1.4 kg) whole chicken, cut into pieces	♦ ½ teaspoon paprika
♦ ⅓ cup vegetable broth	♦ ⅓ teaspoon cayenne pepper
♦ 3 cloves garlic, pressed	♦ ½ teaspoon ground bay leaf
♦ 1 tablespoon avocado oil	♦ ⅓ teaspoon black pepper
♦ 1 guajillo chili, minced	♦ 2 tablespoons chopped fresh coriander, for garnish
♦ Sea salt, to taste	♦ 1 cup crème fraiche, for serving

1. In the Instant Pot, combine all the ingredients except for the coriander and crème fraîche, stirring well to mix. 2. Secure the lid tightly, ensuring it is sealed. Select the Poultry mode and set the cooking time for 15 minutes at High Pressure. 3. Once the timer goes off, perform a quick pressure release, then carefully open the lid. 4. Use two forks to shred the chicken, discarding any bones as you go. Garnish the shredded chicken with fresh coriander and serve it with a generous dollop of crème fraîche for added richness. Enjoy your meal!

Per Serving:
calories: 298 | fat: 16g | protein: 36g | carbs: 2g | net carbs: 2g | fiber: 0g

Lemon Feta Chicken Thighs

Prep time: 7 minutes | Cook time: 15 minutes | Serves 2

♦ 4 lemon slices	♦ 4 ounces (113 g) feta, crumbled
♦ 2 chicken thighs	♦ 1 teaspoon butter
♦ 1 tablespoon Greek seasoning	♦ ½ cup water

1. Begin by rubbing the chicken thighs generously with Greek seasoning to enhance their flavor. 2. Next, spread a layer of butter over each chicken thigh to keep them moist during cooking. 3. Pour water into the Instant Pot and insert the trivet to elevate the chicken above the liquid. 4. Place the seasoned chicken on a piece of foil, top it with lemon slices, and sprinkle crumbled feta cheese over the top. 5. Wrap the chicken tightly in the foil to seal in the flavors and moisture, then transfer it onto the trivet in the Instant Pot. 6. Set the Instant Pot to Sauté mode and cook for 10 minutes. Afterward, perform a quick pressure release for 5 minutes to let the steam escape. 7. Carefully remove the foil from the chicken thighs and serve them hot, enjoying the delicious flavors!

Per Serving:
calories: 341 | fat: 24g | protein: 27g | carbs: 6g | net carbs: 6g | fiber: 0g

Creamy Ranch Chicken Bake

Prep time: 5 minutes | Cook time: 0 minutes | Serves 8

♦ ½ cup chicken broth	♦ 8 ounces full-fat cream cheese, softened
♦ 1 (1-ounce) package ranch powder seasoning mix	♦ 8 slices no-sugar-added bacon, cooked and crumbled
♦ 2 pounds boneless, skinless chicken breasts	♦ ½ cup shredded Cheddar cheese

1. Pour chicken broth into the slow cooker and mix in the ranch seasoning packet until well combined. 2. Add the chicken to the slow cooker, cover with the lid, and cook on high for 2 hours and 45 minutes or on low for 5 hours and 15 minutes, allowing the flavors to meld. 3. Once cooking time is up, remove the lid and drain excess broth, leaving approximately ½ cup for moisture, depending on your preference. 4. Shred the chicken using two forks until it is fully pulled apart. 5. In a small microwave-safe bowl, heat cream cheese in the microwave for 20 to 30 seconds until softened. Combine the warmed cream cheese with crumbled bacon and Cheddar cheese until well mixed. 6. Stir the cream cheese mixture into the shredded chicken, cover, and heat on high for an additional 10 minutes, or until the cheeses have melted and everything is heated through. Serve warm for a comforting meal!

Per Serving:
calories: 362 | fat: 21g | protein: 36g | carbs: 3g | net carbs: 3g | fiber: 0g

Chapter

6

Vegetables and Sides

Chapter 6 Vegetables and Sides

Spicy Almond Butter Zoodle Stir-Fry

Prep time: 10 minutes | Cook time: 4 minutes | Serves 4

- 2 tablespoons coconut oil
- 1 yellow onion, chopped
- 2 zucchini, julienned
- 1 cup shredded Chinese cabbage
- 2 garlic cloves, minced
- 2 tablespoons almond butter
- Sea salt and freshly ground black pepper, to taste
- 1 teaspoon cayenne pepper

1. Start by pressing the Sauté button on your Instant Pot to heat it up. Add the coconut oil and sauté the chopped onion for about 2 minutes until it becomes translucent. 2. Next, add the remaining ingredients to the pot, stirring to combine everything evenly. 3. Secure the lid tightly and select Manual mode, setting it to High Pressure. Cook for 2 minutes. Once the cooking time is complete, perform a quick pressure release and carefully remove the lid to avoid steam burns. 4. Serve your dish warm and enjoy your meal! Bon appétit!

Per Serving:
calories: 145 | fat: 15g | protein: 1g | carbs: 4g | net carbs: 2g | fiber: 2g

Cheesy Cauliflower Hash Brown Bake

Prep time: 5 minutes | Cook time: 38 minutes | serves 6

- 2 tablespoons salted butter
- ¼ cup chopped onions
- ½ cup heavy whipping cream
- ½ teaspoon salt
- ½ teaspoon ground black pepper
- 1 (12-ounce) bag frozen riced cauliflower
- 1½ cups shredded cheddar cheese

TOPPING (optional):

- ¾ cup crushed pork rinds
- ¼ cup grated Parmesan cheese

1. Preheat your oven to 350°F (175°C) and grease an 11 by 8-inch or similar-sized oval baking dish to prepare for the casserole. 2. In a medium skillet over medium heat, melt the butter. Once melted, add the chopped onions and sauté until they are tender and translucent.

Lower the heat and stir in the cream, salt, and pepper. Allow the mixture to simmer for 2 minutes, then add the cauliflower and shredded cheddar cheese, mixing until well combined. 3. Pour the creamy cauliflower mixture into the prepared baking dish and spread it out evenly. Bake in the preheated oven for 25 minutes, or until the top is golden brown and bubbly around the edges. 4. If you're making a topping, combine crushed pork rinds with grated Parmesan cheese in a bowl. Sprinkle this mixture evenly over the casserole and return it to the oven for an additional 5 minutes, or until the topping is lightly browned and crispy. 5. Allow any leftovers to cool before storing them in an airtight container in the refrigerator for up to 3 days. Enjoy your delicious cauliflower casserole!

Per Serving:
calories: 278 | fat: 22g | protein: 13g | carbs: 5g | net carbs: 3g | fiber: 2g

Garlic Basil Portobello Pizzas

Prep time: 15 minutes | Cook time: 5 minutes | Serves 4

- 4 large portobello mushrooms, stems removed
- ¼ cup olive oil
- 1 teaspoon minced garlic
- 1 medium tomato, cut into 4
- slices
- 2 teaspoons chopped fresh basil
- 1 cup shredded mozzarella cheese

1. Preheat your oven to the broil setting. Line a baking sheet with aluminum foil for easy cleanup and set it aside. 2. In a small bowl, combine the mushroom caps with olive oil, tossing them gently until they are well coated. Use your fingertips to rub the oil into the mushrooms carefully, ensuring not to break them. 3. Arrange the mushrooms on the prepared baking sheet with the gill side facing down, then broil them in the oven until the tops are tender, which should take about 2 minutes. 4. Carefully flip the mushrooms over and broil for an additional minute. 5. Remove the baking sheet from the oven and spread minced garlic evenly over each mushroom. Place a slice of tomato on top of each mushroom, followed by a sprinkle of fresh basil and a generous amount of cheese. 6. Return the baking sheet to the oven and broil the mushrooms until the cheese is melted and bubbly, approximately 1 minute. 7. Serve the stuffed mushrooms warm and enjoy their delicious flavors!

Per Serving:
calories: 251 | fat: 20g | protein: 14g | carbs: 7g | net carbs: 4g | fiber: 3g

Cilantro-Lime Cauliflower Rice

Prep time: 15 minutes | Cook time: 5 minutes | Serves 4

♦ 1 medium head cauliflower, cut into florets	pepper, to taste
♦ 1 tablespoon cooking fat of choice	♦ ¼ cup finely chopped fresh cilantro leaves
♦ Sea salt and ground black	♦ Cilantro sprig, for garnish (optional)

1. Begin by shredding the cauliflower using a box grater or a food processor until it resembles rice grains. 2. In a large skillet over medium heat, melt your chosen cooking fat. Once melted, add the shredded cauliflower and season it with salt and pepper. Sauté the cauliflower for about 5 minutes, or until it becomes slightly translucent, stirring gently to ensure even cooking throughout. 3. After cooking, transfer the sautéed cauliflower to a serving bowl and toss it with the chopped cilantro for added flavor. If desired, garnish with a sprig of fresh cilantro before serving. Enjoy your delicious cauliflower rice!

Per Serving:
calories: 65 | fat: 4g | protein: 3g | carbs: 8g | net carbs: 4g | fiber: 4g

Lemon-Gremolata Asparagus with Almonds

Prep time: 15 minutes | Cook time: 2 minutes | Serves 2 to 4

Gremolata:

♦ 1 cup finely chopped fresh Italian flat-leaf parsley leaves	♦ 3 garlic cloves, peeled and grated
	♦ Zest of 2 small lemons

Asparagus:

♦ 1½ pounds (680 g) asparagus, trimmed	♦ 1 teaspoon Swerve
♦ 1 cup water	♦ 1 teaspoon Dijon mustard
♦ Lemony Vinaigrette:	♦ 2 tablespoons extra-virgin olive oil
♦ 1½ tablespoons fresh lemon juice	♦ Kosher salt and freshly ground black pepper, to taste

Garnish:

♦ 3 tablespoons slivered almonds

1. In a small bowl, mix together all the ingredients for the gremolata until well combined. 2. Pour water into the Instant Pot and place the asparagus in a steamer basket. Lower the steamer basket into the pot. 3. Secure the lid on the Instant Pot. Select the Steam mode and set the cooking time for 2 minutes on Low Pressure. 4. While the asparagus is cooking, prepare the lemony vinaigrette: In a separate bowl, whisk together the lemon juice, Swerve, and mustard. Gradually drizzle in the olive oil while whisking continuously until emulsified. Season generously with salt and pepper to taste. 5. Once the timer beeps, perform a quick pressure release and carefully open the lid. Remove the steamer basket from the Instant Pot. 6. Transfer the asparagus to a serving platter and drizzle with the vinaigrette. Top with the gremolata and sprinkle slivered almonds over the asparagus. Serve warm and enjoy!

Per Serving:
calories: 132 | fat: 9g | protein: 3g | carbs: 13g | net carbs: 8g | fiber: 5g

Garlic-Parmesan Pan-Roasted Green Beans

Prep time: 5 minutes | Cook time: 15 minutes | Serves 4

♦ 3 tablespoons extra-virgin olive oil	♦ 1 teaspoon freshly ground black pepper
♦ 1 (12-ounce / 340-g) bag frozen green beans, rinsed and patted dry	♦ ¼ cup sliced almonds
♦ 1 teaspoon garlic salt	♦ ¼ cup grated Parmesan cheese

1. In a skillet over medium heat, add the oil and let it warm up. 2. Add the green beans along with garlic salt and pepper, then cook for 10 to 12 minutes, stirring frequently to ensure they are evenly coated. 3. Increase the heat to high and continue to stir the beans until they start to brown nicely. 4. Once browned, sprinkle the sliced almonds into the skillet and stir to combine everything thoroughly. 5. Remove the skillet from the heat and top the green beans with grated Parmesan cheese before serving. Enjoy your flavorful dish!

Per Serving:
¼ recipe: calories: 193 | fat: 16g | protein: 6g | carbs: 8g | net carbs: 5g | fiber: 3g

Savory Bacon-Fried Cabbage

Prep time: 5 minutes | Cook time: 15 minutes | serves 4

♦ 4 slices bacon, chopped	♦ ½ teaspoon salt
♦ 1 medium head green cabbage, coarsely chopped	♦ ¾ teaspoon ground black pepper

1. In a medium-sized skillet over medium heat, cook the bacon until it becomes crispy. Once done, use a slotted spoon to remove the bacon from the skillet and set it aside on a plate, leaving the drippings in the pan. 2. Add the chopped cabbage to the skillet with the bacon drippings and cook, stirring frequently, for about 10 minutes until the cabbage is tender and slightly caramelized. Return the cooked bacon to the skillet, then season with salt and pepper. Continue cooking for an additional 5 minutes to allow the flavors to meld. 3. Serve the dish immediately while it's hot and enjoy!

Per Serving:
calories: 86 | fat: 5g | protein: 5g | carbs: 9g | net carbs: 5g | fiber: 4g

Sesame Scallion Zucchini Noodles

Prep time: 10 minutes | Cook time: 3 minutes | Serves 6

- 2 large zucchinis, trimmed and spiralized
- ¼ cup chicken broth
- 1 tablespoon chopped scallions
- 1 tablespoon coconut aminos
- 1 teaspoon sesame oil
- 1 teaspoon sesame seeds
- ¼ teaspoon chili flakes

1. Start by setting the Instant Pot to Sauté mode. Add the zucchini spirals to the pot, then pour in the chicken broth. Sauté the zoodles for about 3 minutes until they are slightly softened, then transfer them to serving bowls. 2. Top the zucchini noodles with chopped scallions, coconut aminos, sesame oil, sesame seeds, and chili flakes. Gently stir to combine all the ingredients. 3. Serve the dish immediately while it's warm and enjoy your flavorful zoodles!

Per Serving:
calories: 28 | fat: 2g | protein: 2g | carbs: 0g | net carbs: 0g | fiber: 0g

Ginger-Infused Braised Cabbage

Prep time: 10 minutes | Cook time: 8 minutes | Serves 6

- 1 tablespoon avocado oil
- 1 tablespoon butter or ghee (or more avocado oil)
- ½ medium onion, diced
- 1 medium bell pepper (any color), diced
- 1 teaspoon sea salt
- ½ teaspoon ground black
- pepper
- 1 clove garlic, minced
- 1-inch piece fresh ginger, grated
- 1 pound (454 g) green or red cabbage, cored and leaves chopped
- ½ cup bone broth or vegetable broth

1. Begin by setting your Instant Pot to the Sauté function, then heat the oil and butter together in the pot. Once the butter has stopped foaming, add the chopped onion, diced bell pepper, salt, and black pepper. Sauté the mixture, stirring frequently, until the vegetables are just softened, which should take about 3 minutes. Then, add the minced garlic and grated ginger, cooking for an additional minute. Incorporate the chopped cabbage and stir well to combine everything. Pour the broth into the pot. 2. Secure the lid of the Instant Pot and ensure the steam release valve is set to Sealing. Press the Manual button and adjust the cook time to 2 minutes. 3. Once the cooking time is complete and the Instant Pot beeps, carefully switch the steam release valve to Venting for a quick pressure release. After all the steam has been released, open the lid. Give the cabbage a good stir and transfer it to a serving dish. Serve warm and enjoy your delicious dish!

Per Serving:
calories: 73 | fat: 5g | protein: 2g | carbs: 7g | net carbs: 5g | fiber: 2g

Crispy Parmesan Pork Rind Green Beans

Prep time: 5 minutes | Cook time: 15 minutes | Serves 2

- ½ pound fresh green beans
- 2 tablespoons crushed pork rinds
- 2 tablespoons olive oil
- 1 tablespoon grated Parmesan cheese
- Pink Himalayan salt
- Freshly ground black pepper

1. Preheat your oven to 400°F (200°C). 2. In a medium bowl, mix together the green beans, crushed pork rinds, olive oil, and grated Parmesan cheese. Season the mixture with pink Himalayan salt and pepper, then toss until the green beans are evenly coated. 3. Spread the coated green beans in a single layer on a baking sheet and roast them in the oven for approximately 15 minutes. At the halfway mark, give the pan a shake or stir the beans to ensure even cooking. 4. Once roasted, divide the green beans between two plates and serve immediately. Enjoy your delicious dish!

Per Serving:
calories: 175 | fat: 15g | protein: 6g | carbs: 8g | net carbs: 5g | fiber: 3g

Crispy Parmesan Pork Rind Zucchini Sticks

Prep time: 5 minutes | Cook time: 25 minutes | Serves 2

- 2 medium zucchini, halved lengthwise and seeded
- ¼ cup crushed pork rinds
- ¼ cup grated Parmesan cheese
- 2 garlic cloves, minced
- 2 tablespoons melted butter
- Pink Himalayan salt
- Freshly ground black pepper
- Olive oil, for drizzling

1. Begin by preheating your oven to 400°F (200°C). Line a baking sheet with aluminum foil or a silicone baking mat to prevent sticking. 2. Place the zucchini halves on the prepared baking sheet with the cut side facing up. 3. In a medium bowl, mix together the crushed pork rinds, grated Parmesan cheese, minced garlic, and melted butter. Season the mixture with pink Himalayan salt and pepper, stirring until everything is well combined. 4. Generously spoon the pork rind mixture onto each zucchini half, ensuring they are evenly coated. Drizzle a little olive oil over each zucchini for added flavor. 5. Bake the zucchini in the preheated oven for approximately 20 minutes, or until the topping is golden brown and crispy. 6. After baking, turn on the broiler to finish browning the zucchini sticks, cooking for an additional 3 to 5 minutes. Once done, remove from the oven and serve warm. Enjoy your delicious dish!

Per Serving:
calories: 231 | fat: 20g | protein: 9g | carbs: 8g | net carbs: 6g | fiber: 2g

Creamy Garlic Mashed Cauliflower

Prep time: 10 minutes | Cook time: 15 minutes | Serves 4

◆ 8 cups water	◆ 1 garlic clove, minced
◆ 1 head cauliflower, washed and chopped	◆ ¼ cup heavy (whipping) cream, plus more as needed
◆ 2 to 3 tablespoons butter	◆ Salt and freshly ground black pepper, to taste

1. In a large saucepan, bring the water to a vigorous boil over high heat. 2. Add the cauliflower to the boiling water and cook for approximately 10 minutes, or until it is fork-tender. Once cooked, remove from the heat, drain well, and set aside. 3. Return the saucepan to medium heat and add the butter along with minced garlic. Sauté for 2 to 3 minutes, or until the garlic turns a light golden brown. 4. Add the cooked cauliflower back into the pan. Using an immersion blender, purée the mixture until smooth. If you don't have an immersion blender, carefully transfer the mixture to a traditional blender and blend until smooth. 5. Pour in the cream and continue blending until the mashed cauliflower reaches your desired consistency. Season with salt and pepper to taste. If the mixture is too thick, you can add a splash more of cream or some chicken broth to thin it out slightly. Serve immediately, or keep warm until you're ready to enjoy. Store any leftovers in an airtight container in the refrigerator for up to 5 days.

Per Serving:
calories: 180 | fat: 14g | protein: 5g | carbs: 12g | net carbs: 7g | fiber: 5g

Garlic Butter Roasted Whole Cauliflower

Prep time: 5 minutes | Cook time: 8 minutes | Serves 4

◆ 1 large cauliflower, rinsed and patted dry	◆ Pinch of sea salt
◆ 1 cup water	◆ Pinch of fresh ground black pepper
◆ 4 tablespoons melted butter	◆ 1 tablespoon chopped fresh flat leaf parsley, for garnish
◆ 2 cloves garlic, minced	

1. Start by pouring water into the Instant Pot and placing the trivet inside. Position the cauliflower on top of the trivet. 2. Secure the lid, select Manual mode, and set the cooking time for 3 minutes at High Pressure. 3. While the cauliflower is cooking, preheat the oven to 550°F (288°C) and line a baking sheet with parchment paper. 4. In a small bowl, whisk together the melted butter, minced garlic, sea salt, and black pepper, and set this mixture aside. 5. Once the timer goes off, perform a quick pressure release and carefully open the lid. 6. Move the cauliflower to the lined baking sheet and gently dab the surface dry with a clean kitchen towel. Brush the cauliflower generously with the garlic butter mixture. 7. Place the baking sheet in the preheated oven and roast the cauliflower for about 5 minutes, or until it turns golden brown. Drizzle any remaining garlic butter over the cauliflower and sprinkle with chopped parsley before serving immediately. Enjoy your dish!

Per Serving:
calories: 141 | fat: 12g | protein: 3g | carbs: 8g | net carbs: 4g | fiber: 4g

Crispy Bacon-Sautéed Green Beans

Prep time: 2 minutes | Cook time: 20 minutes | Serves 2

◆ 2 ounces (57 g) bacon, cut into ½-inch-wide crosswise strips	beans, trimmed
	◆ ½ teaspoon seasoning salt
◆ 6 ounces (170 g) green	◆ ¼ teaspoon red pepper flakes

1. Begin by heating a medium sauté pan or skillet over medium-high heat. Add the bacon to the pan and cook for 7 to 10 minutes, or until it is nearly crispy. 2. Once the bacon is cooked, reduce the heat to medium-low and add the beans, seasoning salt, and red pepper flakes to the pan. 3. Sauté the beans for an additional 7 to 10 minutes, cooking until they are tender yet still crisp. 4. Once done, transfer the mixture to a serving plate and enjoy your flavorful dish!

Per Serving:
calories: 142 | fat: 11g | protein: 5g | carbs: 6g | net carbs: 4g | fiber: 2g

Zesty Lemon-Paprika Broccoli

Prep time: 5 minutes | Cook time: 4 minutes | Serves 4

◆ 2 cups broccoli florets	zest
◆ 1 tablespoon ground paprika	◆ 1 teaspoon olive oil
◆ 1 tablespoon lemon juice	◆ ½ teaspoon chili powder
◆ 1 teaspoon grated lemon	◆ 1 cup water

1. Start by pouring water into the Instant Pot and inserting the trivet to create a steam rack. 2. In the Instant Pot's inner pan, combine the remaining ingredients, stirring well to ensure everything is evenly mixed. 3. Carefully place the inner pan on top of the trivet. 4. Secure the lid on the Instant Pot, select Manual mode, and set the cooking time to 4 minutes on High Pressure. Once the timer sounds, perform a quick pressure release by turning the valve. 5. After the pressure is fully released, carefully open the lid and serve the dish immediately. Enjoy your meal!

Per Serving:
calories: 34 | fat: 2g | protein: 2g | carbs: 4g | net carbs: 2g | fiber: 2g

Sautéed Herbed Radishes with Chives

Prep time: 10 minutes | Cook time: 15 minutes | Serves 2

♦ 3 tablespoons lard	pepper
♦ 14 ounces (400 g) radishes (about 2 bunches), quartered	♦ 2 tablespoons sliced fresh chives
♦ ⅛ teaspoon finely ground gray sea salt	♦ 1 tablespoon chopped fresh herbs, such as thyme and/or rosemary
♦ ⅛ teaspoon ground black	

1. Begin by melting the lard in a large frying pan over medium heat. Once melted, add the quartered radishes along with salt and pepper. Cover the pan and cook for about 5 minutes, or until the radishes are softened. 2. After 5 minutes, remove the lid and continue cooking for an additional 7 minutes, stirring frequently, until the radish pieces start to brown nicely. 3. Next, add the chopped chives and fresh herbs to the pan, tossing everything together to combine. Lower the heat to medium-low and cook for an extra 2 minutes to allow the flavors to meld. 4. Once done, remove the pan from the heat, divide the radish mixture among 4 small bowls, and serve immediately. Enjoy your delicious dish!

Per Serving:
calories: 223 | fat: 19g | protein: 6g | carbs: 7g | net carbs: 6g | fiber: 1g

Quick Stir-Fried Asparagus and Kale

Prep time: 5 minutes | Cook time: 3 minutes | Serves 4

♦ 8 ounces (227 g) asparagus, chopped	♦ 1 teaspoon apple cider vinegar
♦ 2 cups chopped kale	♦ ½ teaspoon minced ginger
♦ 2 bell peppers, chopped	♦ ½ cup water
♦ 1 tablespoon avocado oil	

1. Begin by pouring water into the Instant Pot to create steam. 2. In the inner pan of the Instant Pot, combine the remaining ingredients, stirring them together until well mixed. 3. Insert the trivet into the pot and carefully place the inner pan on top of it. 4. Secure the lid in place, select Manual mode, and set the cooking time for 3 minutes on High Pressure. When the timer signals the end of cooking, perform a quick pressure release. Carefully open the lid to avoid steam. 5. Serve the dish immediately while hot and enjoy!

Per Serving:
calories: 56 | fat: 4g | protein: 2g | carbs: 4g | net carbs: 2g | fiber: 2g

Spiced Whole Cauliflower Head

Prep time: 5 minutes | Cook time: 7 minutes | Serves 4

♦ 13 ounces (369 g) cauliflower head	♦ 1 teaspoon ground paprika
♦ 1 cup water	♦ 1 teaspoon ground turmeric
♦ 1 tablespoon coconut cream	♦ ½ teaspoon ground cumin
♦ 1 tablespoon avocado oil	♦ ½ teaspoon salt

1. Start by pouring water into the Instant Pot and inserting the trivet to create a steam rack. 2. In a mixing bowl, combine the coconut cream, avocado oil, paprika, turmeric, cumin, and salt, stirring until well mixed. 3. Carefully brush the cauliflower head with the coconut cream mixture, ensuring it is evenly coated. Then, sprinkle the remaining mixture over the cauliflower. 4. Place the coated cauliflower head onto the trivet in the Instant Pot. 5. Secure the lid on the pot, select Manual mode, and set the cooking time for 7 minutes on High Pressure. Once the timer goes off, allow for a natural pressure release for 10 minutes before releasing any remaining pressure. 6. After opening the lid, serve the cauliflower immediately while warm and enjoy!

Per Serving:
calories: 71 | fat: 5g | protein: 2g | carbs: 5g | net carbs: 2g | fiber: 3g

Creamy Cauliflower "Potato" Salad

Prep time: 10 minutes | Cook time: 25 minutes | Serves 2

♦ ½ head cauliflower	♦ ⅓ cup mayonnaise
♦ 1 tablespoon olive oil	♦ 1 tablespoon mustard
♦ Pink Himalayan salt	♦ ¼ cup diced dill pickles
♦ Freshly ground black pepper	♦ 1 teaspoon paprika

1. Begin by preheating the oven to 400°F (200°C) and lining a baking sheet with aluminum foil or a silicone baking mat for easy cleanup. 2. Cut the cauliflower into 1-inch pieces and place them in a large mixing bowl. 3. Drizzle the olive oil over the cauliflower, then season with pink Himalayan salt and pepper. Toss everything together until the cauliflower is evenly coated. 4. Spread the seasoned cauliflower in a single layer on the prepared baking sheet and bake for about 25 minutes, or until it starts to brown. Be sure to shake the pan or stir the cauliflower halfway through cooking to ensure even browning on all sides. 5. Once cooked, transfer the cauliflower to a large bowl and mix it with the mayonnaise, mustard, and chopped pickles. Sprinkle paprika on top, then cover and chill in the refrigerator for 3 hours before serving. Enjoy your delicious cauliflower salad!

Per Serving:
calories: 386 | fat: 37g | protein: 5g | carbs: 13g | net carbs: 8g | fiber: 5g

Crispy Balsamic Brussels Sprouts with Bacon

Prep time: 5 minutes | Cook time: 12 minutes | Serves 4

◆ 2 cups trimmed and halved fresh Brussels sprouts	pepper
◆ 2 tablespoons olive oil	◆ 2 tablespoons balsamic vinegar
◆ ¼ teaspoon salt	◆ 2 slices cooked sugar-free bacon, crumbled
◆ ¼ teaspoon ground black	

1. In a large bowl, coat the Brussels sprouts with olive oil, ensuring they are evenly covered. Sprinkle with salt and pepper to taste. Transfer the seasoned Brussels sprouts into the ungreased air fryer basket. Adjust the air fryer temperature to 375ºF (191ºC) and set the timer for 12 minutes, shaking the basket halfway through the cooking time to ensure even browning. The Brussels sprouts should be tender and golden brown when finished. 2. Once cooked, place the Brussels sprouts in a large serving dish and drizzle them with balsamic vinegar for added flavor. Top with crispy bacon for a delicious finish. Serve warm and enjoy!

Per Serving:

calories: 114| fat: 9g | protein: 4g | carbs: 6g | net carbs: 4g | fiber: 2g

Creamy Cauliflower Faux-tato Salad

Prep time: 20 minutes | Cook time: 10 minutes | Serves 4

◆ ½ head cauliflower, cut into florets	◆ 4 ounces (113 g) bacon, cooked until crisp and chopped
◆ ⅓ cup mayonnaise	◆ 1 large egg, hard-boiled, peeled, and chopped
◆ 2 tablespoons stone-ground mustard	◆ ¼ medium red onion, thinly sliced
◆ 1 tablespoon red wine vinegar	◆ 2 tablespoons grated Cheddar cheese
◆ ¼ teaspoon pink Himalayan sea salt	◆ 2 scallions, white and green parts, chopped
◆ ¼ teaspoon freshly ground black pepper	

1. Begin by placing a steamer basket in a small pot and adding a couple of inches of water. Place the cauliflower in the steamer basket, cover the pot, and steam for 7 to 10 minutes until the cauliflower is tender but still firm. Once done, let it cool. 2. In a small bowl, whisk together the mayonnaise, mustard, vinegar, salt, and pepper to create the dressing. 3. In a large mixing bowl, combine the cooled cauliflower, cooked bacon, chopped egg, red onion, cheese, and scallions, mixing them together well. 4. Drizzle the dressing over the salad and give everything a final mix to ensure it's well coated. If you prefer, you can refrigerate the salad for about 1 hour before serving to chill it. Enjoy your delicious salad!

Per Serving:

calories: 287 | fat: 27g | protein: 7g | carbs: 3g | net carbs: 2g | fiber: 1g

Walnut-Infused Sautéed Asparagus

Prep time: 10 minutes | Cook time: 5 minutes | Serves 4

◆ 1½ tablespoons olive oil	◆ Sea salt
◆ ¾ pound asparagus, woody ends trimmed	◆ Freshly ground pepper
	◆ ¼ cup chopped walnuts

1. Begin by heating a large skillet over medium-high heat and adding the olive oil. 2. Once the oil is hot, add the asparagus and sauté for about 5 minutes, or until the spears are tender and lightly browned. 3. Season the asparagus generously with salt and pepper to taste. 4. Remove the skillet from the heat and toss the cooked asparagus with the walnuts until well combined. 5. Serve the dish warm and enjoy your deliciously sautéed asparagus!

Per Serving:

calories: 124 | fat: 12g | protein: 3g | carbs: 4g | net carbs: 2g | fiber: 2g

Creamy Garlic Butter Broccoli

Prep time: 5 minutes | Cook time: 10 minutes | Serves 4

◆ 1 (12.6-ounce / 357-g) microwavable bag frozen broccoli florets	◆ 1 tablespoon cream cheese, at room temperature
◆ 3 tablespoons butter, at room temperature	◆ 2 teaspoons garlic salt
	◆ 1 teaspoon freshly ground black pepper

1. Start by microwaving the broccoli according to the package instructions until fully cooked. 2. Carefully remove the bag from the microwave and tear open a small corner to drain any excess water from the broccoli. 3. In a small bowl, combine the butter, cream cheese, garlic salt, and pepper, mashing them together until smooth. Add this mixture to the bag of drained broccoli. 4. Roll the top of the broccoli bag closed and shake it gently for about a minute until the broccoli is thoroughly coated with the buttery mixture. 5. Pour the coated broccoli into a bowl and enjoy your delicious side dish!

Per Serving:

¼ bag: calories: 111 | fat: 10g | protein: 3g | carbs: 4g | net carbs: 1g | fiber: 3g

Mediterranean Satarash with Eggs

Prep time: 10 minutes | Cook time: 5 minutes | Serves 4

♦ 2 tablespoons olive oil	♦ 1 teaspoon paprika
♦ 1 white onion, chopped	♦ ½ teaspoon dried oregano
♦ 2 cloves garlic	♦ ½ teaspoon turmeric
♦ 2 ripe tomatoes, puréed	♦ Kosher salt and ground black pepper, to taste
♦ 1 green bell pepper, deseeded and sliced	♦ 1 cup water
♦ 1 red bell pepper, deseeded and sliced	♦ 4 large eggs, lightly whisked

1. Begin by pressing the Sauté button on the Instant Pot and adding the olive oil. Once the oil is heated, add the chopped onion and minced garlic to the pot, sautéing for about 2 minutes until fragrant. Then, stir in the remaining ingredients, leaving out the eggs for now. 2. Secure the lid on the Instant Pot, select Manual mode, and set the cooking time to 3 minutes on High Pressure. When the timer finishes, perform a quick pressure release and carefully open the lid. 3. Gently fold in the eggs and stir the mixture to combine thoroughly. Lock the lid again and let it sit in the residual heat for an additional 5 minutes. 4. Serve the dish warm and enjoy!

Per Serving:
calories: 169 | fat: 12g | protein: 8g | carbs: 9g | net carbs: 7g | fiber: 2g

Coconut Flour Butter Biscuits

Prep time: 15 minutes | Cook time: 25 minutes | Serves 12

♦ ¾ cup (180 ml) water	♦ ½ cup (120 ml) full-fat coconut milk
♦ 3 tablespoons unflavored gelatin	♦ 6 tablespoons (80 g) coconut oil
♦ 1½ cups (150 g) coconut flour	♦ 1 tablespoon apple cider vinegar
♦ ¾ teaspoon baking powder	♦ ¾ cup (160 g) coconut oil, for serving
♦ ¾ teaspoon finely ground gray sea salt	

1. Preheat your oven to 375°F (190°C) and line a baking sheet with parchment paper or a silicone baking mat to prevent sticking. 2. In a small saucepan, pour the water and sprinkle gelatin on top without stirring. Let it sit for 5 minutes. Afterward, turn on the burner to medium heat and bring the mixture to a light boil, stirring occasionally until smooth. Once melted, set it aside. If the mixture begins to cool and solidify, simply reheat it to return it to liquid form. 3. In the bowl of a stand mixer fitted with the flat beater attachment, or in a mixing bowl if using a hand mixer, combine the coconut flour, baking powder, and salt. Mix until well blended. 4. Add the coconut milk, melted coconut oil, vinegar, and the prepared gelatin mixture to the dry ingredients. Mix until the batter is combined and sticky. Be careful not to overmix, as you want to maintain that sticky texture. 5. Quickly divide the batter into 12 portions, approximately ¼ cup each, and place them on a clean surface. Use the palm of your hand to flatten each portion into a biscuit shape about 1½ inches (4 cm) thick, rotating it to achieve the desired shape. 6. Arrange the shaped biscuits on the lined baking sheet, leaving about ½ inch (1.25 cm) of space between each one. 7. Bake the biscuits in the preheated oven for 20 to 25 minutes, or until the tops crack and begin to turn golden brown. 8. Once baked, allow the biscuits to cool on the baking sheet for 1 hour. Enjoy each biscuit spread with 1 tablespoon of coconut oil for added flavor!

Per Serving:
calories: 266 | fat: 24g | protein: 4g | carbs: 8g | net carbs: 3g | fiber: 5g

Garlic Butter Sautéed Spinach

Prep time: 5 minutes | Cook time: 10 minutes | Serves 4

♦ 2 tablespoons butter, or olive oil	♦ 12 ounces (340 g) fresh spinach
♦ ¼ white onion, diced	♦ Salt and freshly ground black pepper, to taste
♦ 3 garlic cloves, sliced	

1. Begin by melting the butter in a large skillet over medium heat until it is fully melted and bubbling. 2. Add the chopped onion and minced garlic to the skillet, cooking for 5 to 7 minutes until the onion becomes soft and translucent. 3. Next, add the fresh spinach to the skillet and lower the heat to medium-low. Season the mixture generously with salt and pepper to taste. Cook for an additional 3 to 4 minutes, or until the spinach has wilted and reduced in volume. Serve immediately while warm and enjoy this flavorful dish!

Per Serving:
calories: 75 | fat: 6g | protein: 3g | carbs: 4g | net carbs: 2g | fiber: 2g

Crispy Zucchini and Daikon Fritters

Prep time: 10 minutes | Cook time: 8 minutes | Serves 4

♦ 2 large zucchinis, grated	♦ 1 teaspoon ground flax meal
♦ 1 daikon, diced	♦ 1 teaspoon salt
♦ 1 egg, beaten	♦ 1 tablespoon coconut oil

1. In a mixing bowl, combine all the ingredients, leaving out the coconut oil. Mix well and form the zucchini mixture into fritters. 2. Next, press the Sauté button on the Instant Pot and add the coconut oil, allowing it to melt. 3. Once the oil is hot, carefully place the zucchini fritters in the skillet and cook for 4 minutes on each side, or until they are golden brown. 4. After cooking, transfer the fritters to a plate and serve warm. Enjoy your delicious zucchini fritters!

Per Serving:
calories: 77 | fat: 5g | protein: 4g | carbs: 6g | net carbs: 4g | fiber: 2g

Crispy Bacon and Acorn Squash Rosti

Prep time: 15 minutes | Cook time: 15 minutes | Serves 8

♦ 8 bacon slices, chopped	♦ 1 teaspoon chopped fresh thyme
♦ 1 cup shredded acorn squash	♦ Sea salt
♦ 1 cup shredded raw celeriac	♦ Freshly ground black pepper
♦ 2 tablespoons grated or shredded Parmesan cheese	♦ 2 tablespoons butter
♦ 2 teaspoons minced garlic	

1. Begin by cooking the bacon in a large skillet over medium-high heat until it becomes crispy, which should take about 5 minutes. 2. While the bacon cooks, combine the squash, celeriac, Parmesan cheese, minced garlic, and thyme in a large bowl. Season the mixture generously with salt and pepper, then set it aside. 3. Once the bacon is crispy, use a slotted spoon to transfer it to the rosti mixture, stirring to incorporate evenly. 4. Remove all but 2 tablespoons of the bacon fat from the skillet and add butter to the remaining fat. 5. Lower the heat to medium-low, then add the rosti mixture to the skillet, spreading it out evenly to form a large round patty about 1 inch thick. 6. Cook the patty until the bottom is golden brown and crisp, which should take around 5 minutes. 7. Carefully flip the rosti over and continue cooking until the other side is crispy and the center is cooked through, approximately 5 more minutes. 8. Once cooked, remove the skillet from the heat and cut the rosti into 8 pieces. 9. Serve the rosti warm and enjoy!

Per Serving:
calories: 171 | fat: 15g | protein: 5g | carbs: 3g | net carbs: 3g | fiber: 0g

Chapter
7

Vegetarian Mains

Chapter 7 Vegetarian Mains

Cream Cheese-Stuffed Portobello Mushrooms

Prep time: 10 minutes | Cook time: 8 minutes | Serves 4

- 3 ounces (85 g) cream cheese, softened
- ½ medium zucchini, trimmed and chopped
- ¼ cup seeded and chopped red bell pepper
- 1½ cups chopped fresh
- spinach leaves
- 4 large portobello mushrooms, stems removed
- 2 tablespoons coconut oil, melted
- ½ teaspoon salt

1. In a medium bowl, combine the cream cheese, zucchini, bell pepper, and spinach, mixing until well blended. 2. Drizzle the mushrooms with coconut oil and season with salt. Carefully scoop ¼ of the zucchini mixture into each mushroom cap. 3. Arrange the stuffed mushrooms in an ungreased air fryer basket. 4. Set the air fryer temperature to 400°F (204°C) and cook for 8 minutes. The portobello mushrooms should be tender and the tops golden brown when finished. 5. Serve the stuffed mushrooms warm and enjoy!

Per Serving:
calories: 157 | fat: 14g | protein: 4g | carbs: 5g | net carbs: 3g | fiber: 2g

Creamy Garlic Zucchini Rolls

Prep time: 20 minutes | Cook time: 20 minutes | Serves 4

- 2 medium zucchini
- 2 tablespoons unsalted butter
- ¼ white onion, peeled and diced
- ½ teaspoon finely minced roasted garlic
- ¼ cup heavy cream
- 2 tablespoons vegetable broth
- ⅛ teaspoon xanthan gum
- ½ cup full-fat ricotta cheese
- ¼ teaspoon salt
- ½ teaspoon garlic powder
- ¼ teaspoon dried oregano
- 2 cups spinach, chopped
- ½ cup sliced baby portobello mushrooms
- ¾ cup shredded Mozzarella cheese, divided

1. Begin by slicing the zucchini into long, thin strips using a mandoline or a sharp knife. Layer the strips between paper towels to absorb excess moisture and set aside. 2. In a medium saucepan set over medium heat, melt the butter. Once melted, add the chopped onion and sauté until fragrant. Then, add the minced garlic and sauté for an additional 30 seconds. 3. Pour in the heavy cream, broth, and xanthan gum. Turn off the heat and whisk the mixture until it starts to thicken, which should take about 3 minutes. 4. In a separate bowl, combine the ricotta cheese, salt, garlic powder, and oregano. Mix thoroughly, then fold in the spinach, mushrooms, and ½ cup of Mozzarella cheese. 5. To assemble the rolls, pour half of the prepared sauce into a round baking pan. Take two strips of zucchini and lay them flat on a work surface. Spoon 2 tablespoons of the ricotta mixture onto the strips and roll them up tightly. Place each roll seam side down on top of the sauce. Continue this process with the remaining ingredients. 6. Once all rolls are in the pan, pour the remaining sauce over the top and sprinkle with the rest of the Mozzarella cheese. Cover the dish with foil and carefully place it in the air fryer basket. 7. Set the air fryer to 350°F (177°C) and cook for 20 minutes. 8. In the last 5 minutes of cooking, remove the foil to allow the cheese to brown nicely. Serve the zucchini rolls immediately and enjoy!

Per Serving:
calories: 270 | fat: 21g | protein: 14g | carbs: 7g | net carbs: 5g | fiber: 2g

Spicy Roasted Vegetable Bowl

Prep time: 10 minutes | Cook time: 15 minutes | Serves 2

- 1 cup broccoli florets
- 1 cup quartered Brussels sprouts
- ½ cup cauliflower florets
- ¼ medium white onion, peeled and sliced ¼ inch thick
- ½ medium green bell pepper, seeded and sliced ¼ inch thick
- 1 tablespoon coconut oil
- 2 teaspoons chili powder
- ½ teaspoon garlic powder
- ½ teaspoon cumin

1. In a large bowl, combine all the ingredients and toss until the vegetables are evenly coated with oil and seasoning. 2. Transfer the coated vegetables into the air fryer basket. 3. Set the air fryer temperature to 360°F (182°C) and roast the vegetables for 15 minutes. 4. Shake the basket two or three times during the cooking process to ensure even roasting. 5. Once done, serve the vegetables warm and enjoy!

Per Serving:
calories: 168 | fat: 11g | protein: 4g | carbs: 15g | net carbs: 9g | fiber: 6g

Savory White Cheddar and Mushroom Soufflés

Prep time: 15 minutes | Cook time: 12 minutes | Serves 4

◆ 3 large eggs, whites and yolks separated	◆ ¼ teaspoon cream of tartar
◆ ½ cup sharp white Cheddar cheese	◆ ¼ teaspoon salt
	◆ ¼ teaspoon ground black pepper
◆ 3 ounces (85 g) cream cheese, softened	◆ ½ cup cremini mushrooms, sliced

1. In a large bowl, whip the egg whites until stiff peaks form, which should take about 2 minutes. In another large bowl, combine the Cheddar cheese, egg yolks, cream cheese, cream of tartar, salt, and pepper, mixing until thoroughly blended. 2. Gently fold the whipped egg whites into the cheese mixture, being careful not to over-stir. Next, fold in the mushrooms, then evenly distribute the mixture into four ungreased ramekins. 3. Place the ramekins in the air fryer basket. 4. Set the air fryer temperature to 350°F (177°C) and bake for 12 minutes. The tops should be browned, and the centers firm when done. 5. Serve the dishes warm and enjoy your delicious creation!

Per Serving:
calories: 228 | fat: 19g | protein: 13g | carbs: 2g | net carbs: 2g | fiber: 0g

Asparagus and Fennel Egg Frittata

Prep time: 10 minutes | Cook time: 30 minutes | Serves 4

◆ 1 teaspoon coconut or regular butter, plus more for greasing	◆ ½ cup full-fat regular milk or coconut milk
◆ 8 asparagus spears, diced	◆ 1 tomato, sliced
◆ ½ cup diced fennel	◆ 1 teaspoon salt
◆ ½ cup mushrooms, sliced (optional)	◆ ½ teaspoon freshly ground black pepper
◆ 8 eggs	◆ Grated cheese (optional)

1. Preheat your oven to 350°F (180°C) and grease a pie dish with butter to prepare it. 2. In a shallow skillet, melt 1 teaspoon of butter over medium-high heat. Add the asparagus, fennel, and mushrooms (if using) and sauté for about 5 minutes, until they are fork-tender. 3. Transfer the sautéed vegetables into the prepared pie dish. 4. In a mixing bowl, crack the eggs and pour in the milk. Whisk them together until well combined. 5. Pour the egg mixture over the vegetables in the pie dish, seasoning with salt and pepper. Gently mix everything together, then layer the tomato slices on top. 6. Bake the frittata in the preheated oven for about 30 minutes, or until set. 7. Once done, remove it from the oven and let it cool for

5 to 10 minutes before slicing into wedges. If desired, sprinkle with grated cheese before serving. Enjoy!

Per Serving:
calories: 188 | fat: 12g | protein: 14g | carbs: 6g | net carbs: 4g | fiber: 2g

Layered Caprese Eggplant Stacks

Prep time: 5 minutes | Cook time: 12 minutes | Serves 4

◆ 1 medium eggplant, cut into ¼-inch slices	Mozzarella, cut into ½-ounce / 14-g slices
◆ 2 large tomatoes, cut into ¼-inch slices	◆ 2 tablespoons olive oil
◆ 4 ounces (113 g) fresh	◆ ¼ cup fresh basil, sliced

1. Begin by laying four slices of eggplant at the bottom of a baking dish. On top of each eggplant slice, layer a slice of tomato, followed by a slice of Mozzarella, and then another slice of eggplant. Repeat the layering process as desired. 2. Drizzle the stacked layers with olive oil, then cover the dish with foil and place it in the air fryer basket. 3. Set the air fryer temperature to 350°F (177°C) and bake for 12 minutes. 4. Once cooked, the eggplant should be tender. Garnish with fresh basil before serving. Enjoy your delicious dish!

Per Serving:
calories: 203 | fat: 16g | protein: 8g | carbs: 10g | net carbs: 7g | fiber: 3g

Italian Vegetable and Egg Bake

Prep time: 10 minutes | Cook time: 10 minutes | Serves 2

◆ 2 tablespoons salted butter	◆ 1 medium Roma tomato, diced
◆ 1 small zucchini, sliced lengthwise and quartered	◆ 2 large eggs
◆ ½ medium green bell pepper, seeded and diced	◆ ¼ teaspoon onion powder
	◆ ¼ teaspoon garlic powder
◆ 1 cup fresh spinach, chopped	◆ ½ teaspoon dried basil
	◆ ¼ teaspoon dried oregano

1. Start by greasing two ramekins with 1 tablespoon of butter each. 2. In a large bowl, combine the zucchini, bell pepper, spinach, and tomatoes. Divide this mixture evenly between the two ramekins, placing half in each. 3. Crack an egg on top of each ramekin and season with onion powder, garlic powder, basil, and oregano. Place the ramekins in the air fryer basket. 4. Set the air fryer temperature to 330°F (166°C) and cook for 10 minutes. 5. Once done, serve the dishes immediately and enjoy your meal!

Per Serving:
calories: 260 | fat: 21g | protein: 10g | carbs: 8g | net carbs: 5g | fiber: 3g

Cheesy Cauliflower Rice-Stuffed Bell Peppers

Prep time: 10 minutes | Cook time: 15 minutes | Serves 4

- 2 cups uncooked cauliflower rice
- ¾ cup drained canned petite diced tomatoes
- 2 tablespoons olive oil
- 1 cup shredded Mozzarella cheese
- ¼ teaspoon salt
- ¼ teaspoon ground black pepper
- 4 medium green bell peppers, tops removed, seeded

1. In a large mixing bowl, combine all the ingredients except for the bell peppers. Once well mixed, scoop the filling evenly into each bell pepper. 2. Arrange the stuffed peppers in the ungreased air fryer basket. Set the temperature to 350°F (177°C) and air fry for 15 minutes. The peppers should be tender, and the cheese should be melted when finished. 3. Serve the stuffed peppers warm and enjoy!

Per Serving:
calories: 309 | fat: 23g | protein: 16g | carbs: 11g | net carbs: 7g | fiber: 4g

Creamy Cheese-Stuffed Bell Peppers

Prep time: 20 minutes | Cook time: 15 minutes | Serves 2

- 1 red bell pepper, top and seeds removed
- 1 yellow bell pepper, top and seeds removed
- Salt and pepper, to taste
- 1 cup Cottage cheese
- 4 tablespoons mayonnaise
- 2 pickles, chopped

1. Place the peppers in the air fryer basket that has been lightly greased. Cook them in the preheated air fryer at 400°F (204°C) for 15 minutes, turning them over halfway through to ensure even cooking. 2. After cooking, season the peppers with salt and pepper. In a mixing bowl, combine the cream cheese, mayonnaise, and chopped pickles. 3. Stuff each pepper with the cream cheese mixture and serve immediately. Enjoy your delicious stuffed peppers!

Per Serving:
calories: 250 | fat: 20g | protein: 11g | carbs: 8g | net carbs: 6g | fiber: 2g

Triple-Cheese Stuffed Zucchini Boats

Prep time: 15 minutes | Cook time: 20 minutes | Serves 2

- 2 medium zucchini
- 1 tablespoon avocado oil
- ¼ cup low-carb, no-sugar-added pasta sauce
- ¼ cup full-fat ricotta cheese
- ¼ cup shredded Mozzarella
- cheese
- ¼ teaspoon dried oregano
- ¼ teaspoon garlic powder
- ½ teaspoon dried parsley
- 2 tablespoons grated vegetarian Parmesan cheese

1. Start by trimming about 1 inch from both the top and bottom of each zucchini. Then, slice the zucchini in half lengthwise and use a spoon to scoop out some of the insides, creating space for the filling. Brush the zucchini shells with oil and spoon 2 tablespoons of pasta sauce into each one. 2. In a medium bowl, combine the ricotta cheese, Mozzarella cheese, oregano, garlic powder, and parsley. Mix well, then spoon this cheesy mixture into each zucchini shell. Place the filled zucchini shells in the air fryer basket. 3. Set the air fryer temperature to 350°F (177°C) and cook for 20 minutes. 4. Once done, carefully remove the stuffed zucchini from the basket using tongs or a spatula. Top each zucchini with Parmesan cheese. Serve immediately and enjoy your delicious dish!

Per Serving:
calories: 245 | fat: 18g | protein: 12g | carbs: 9g | net carbs: 7g | fiber: 2g

Spinach-Artichoke Goat Cheese Stuffed Mushrooms

Prep time: 10 minutes | Cook time: 10 to 14 minutes | Serves 4

- 2 tablespoons olive oil
- 4 large portobello mushrooms, stems removed and gills scraped out
- ½ teaspoon salt
- ¼ teaspoon freshly ground pepper
- 4 ounces (113 g) goat cheese, crumbled
- ½ cup chopped marinated artichoke hearts
- 1 cup frozen spinach, thawed and squeezed dry
- ½ cup grated Parmesan cheese
- 2 tablespoons chopped fresh parsley

1. Begin by preheating the air fryer to 400°F (204°C). 2. Coat the portobello mushrooms with olive oil, ensuring they are thoroughly covered. Season both sides with salt and black pepper, then place them top-side down on a clean surface. 3. In a small bowl, mix together the goat cheese, artichoke hearts, and spinach, mashing with a fork until well blended. Evenly distribute the cheese mixture onto the mushrooms and sprinkle Parmesan cheese on top. 4. Place the mushrooms in the air fryer and cook for 10 to 14 minutes, or until they are tender and the cheese starts to brown. Finish by garnishing with fresh parsley right before serving. Enjoy your delicious stuffed mushrooms!

Per Serving:
calories: 255 | fat: 20g | protein: 13g | carbs: 7g | net carbs: 4g | fiber: 3g

Crispy Sesame Garlic Tofu

Prep time: 30 minutes | Cook time: 15 to 20 minutes | Serves 4

- 1 (16-ounce / 454-g) block extra-firm tofu
- 2 tablespoons coconut aminos
- 1 tablespoon toasted sesame oil
- 1 tablespoon olive oil
- 1 tablespoon chili-garlic sauce
- 1½ teaspoons black sesame seeds
- 1 scallion, thinly sliced

1. Start by pressing the tofu to remove excess moisture. Wrap it in paper towels and place a heavy pan on top for at least 15 minutes. 2. Once pressed, cut the tofu into bite-sized cubes and place them in a mixing bowl. Drizzle the cubes with coconut aminos, sesame oil, olive oil, and chili-garlic sauce. Mix well, then cover the bowl and refrigerate for 1 hour, or overnight for more flavor. 3. Preheat your air fryer to 400°F (204°C). 4. Place the marinated tofu in a single layer in the air fryer basket. Cook for 15 to 20 minutes, shaking the basket halfway through to ensure even crisping. 5. After cooking, serve the tofu warm, drizzled with any juices that collected in the bottom of the air fryer. Top with sesame seeds and sliced scallions for garnish.

Per Serving:
calories: 186 | fat: 14g | protein: 12g | carbs: 4g | net carbs: 3g | fiber: 1g

Cheesy Quiche-Stuffed Bell Peppers

Prep time: 5 minutes | Cook time: 15 minutes | Serves 2

- 2 medium green bell peppers
- 3 large eggs
- ¼ cup full-fat ricotta cheese
- ¼ cup diced yellow onion
- ½ cup chopped broccoli
- ½ cup shredded medium Cheddar cheese

1. Start by cutting the tops off the peppers and carefully removing the seeds and white membranes using a small knife. 2. In a medium bowl, whisk together the eggs and ricotta until well blended. 3. Incorporate the chopped onion and broccoli into the egg mixture, ensuring everything is evenly mixed. Pour this mixture into each prepared pepper, filling them generously. Top each filled pepper with Cheddar cheese. Place the stuffed peppers into a 4-cup round baking dish and set the dish in the air fryer basket. 4. Set the air fryer temperature to 350°F (177°C) and cook for 15 minutes. 5. The eggs should be mostly firm and the peppers tender when they are fully cooked. Serve the stuffed peppers immediately for the best flavor and texture.

Per Serving:
calories: 382 | fat: 27g | protein: 24g | carbs: 11g | net carbs: 7g | fiber: 4g

Crispy Zucchini and Spinach Croquettes

Prep time: 9 minutes | Cook time: 7 minutes | Serves 6

- 4 eggs, slightly beaten
- ½ cup almond flour
- ½ cup goat cheese, crumbled
- 1 teaspoon fine sea salt
- 4 garlic cloves, minced
- 1 cup baby spinach
- ½ cup Parmesan cheese, grated
- ⅓ teaspoon red pepper flakes
- 1 pound (454 g) zucchini, peeled and grated
- ⅓ teaspoon dried dill weed

1. In a mixing bowl, thoroughly combine all ingredients until well blended. Once mixed, roll the mixture into small croquettes, shaping them to your preference. 2. Preheat the air fryer to 340°F (171°C) and place the croquettes in the basket. Air fry for about 7 minutes, or until they are golden brown and crispy. 3. Taste the croquettes and adjust the seasoning if necessary. Serve them warm for the best flavor and texture.

Per Serving:
calories: 179 | fat: 12g | protein: 11g | carbs: 6g | net carbs: 3g | fiber: 3g

Crispy Parmesan Artichokes

Prep time: 10 minutes | Cook time: 10 minutes | Serves 4

- 2 medium artichokes, trimmed and quartered, center removed
- 2 tablespoons coconut oil
- 1 large egg, beaten
- ½ cup grated vegetarian Parmesan cheese
- ¼ cup blanched finely ground almond flour
- ½ teaspoon crushed red pepper flakes

1. Begin by preparing the artichokes. In a large bowl, combine the artichokes with coconut oil, ensuring each piece is well coated. Next, dip each artichoke piece into the beaten egg until fully covered. 2. In a separate large bowl, mix together the Parmesan cheese and almond flour. Add the egg-coated artichokes to this mixture and toss thoroughly to ensure each piece is evenly coated. Sprinkle with red pepper flakes for added flavor. 3. Transfer the coated artichokes into the air fryer basket, spreading them out in a single layer. 4. Preheat the air fryer to 400°F (204°C) and air fry the artichokes for 10 minutes, making sure to toss the basket twice during the cooking process to promote even cooking. 5. Once done, remove from the air fryer and serve warm for a delicious snack or appetizer.

Per Serving:
calories: 220 | fat: 18g | protein: 10g | carbs: 9g | net carbs: 4g | fiber: 5g

Garlic Herb Roasted Spaghetti Squash

Prep time: 10 minutes | Cook time: 45 minutes | Serves 6

♦ 1 (4 pounds / 1.8 kg) spaghetti squash, halved and seeded	♦ 4 tablespoons salted butter, melted
♦ 2 tablespoons coconut oil	♦ 1 teaspoon garlic powder
	♦ 2 teaspoons dried parsley

1. Coat the outer shell of the spaghetti squash with coconut oil and brush the inside with butter. Sprinkle garlic powder and parsley inside the squash. 2. Place the squash in the air fryer basket with the skin side facing down, working in batches if necessary. Set the air fryer to 350ºF (177ºC) and cook for 30 minutes. When the timer goes off, flip the squash over and cook for an additional 15 minutes, or until it is fork-tender. 3. Once cooked, use a fork to scrape out the spaghetti strands from the shell and serve warm. Enjoy your meal!

Per Serving:

calories: 210 | fat: 19g | protein: 2g | carbs: 11g | net carbs: 8g | fiber: 3g

Crispy Eggplant Parmesan with Marinara

Prep time: 15 minutes | Cook time: 17 minutes | Serves 4

♦ 1 medium eggplant, ends trimmed, sliced into ½-inch rounds	♦ 1 ounce (28 g) 100% cheese crisps, finely crushed
♦ ¼ teaspoon salt	♦ ½ cup low-carb marinara sauce
♦ 2 tablespoons coconut oil	♦ ½ cup shredded Mozzarella cheese
♦ ½ cup grated Parmesan cheese	

1. Begin by sprinkling salt on both sides of the eggplant rounds and wrapping them in a kitchen towel. Let them sit for 30 minutes to draw out excess moisture. After the time is up, press the rounds to remove any remaining water, then drizzle coconut oil over both sides of the eggplant. 2. In a medium-sized bowl, combine Parmesan cheese and cheese crisps. Take each eggplant slice and press it into the mixture, ensuring both sides are well coated. 3. Arrange the coated eggplant rounds in the ungreased air fryer basket. Set the temperature to 350ºF (177ºC) and air fry for 15 minutes, flipping the rounds halfway through the cooking process. The edges should become crispy when they are done. 4. Once cooked, spoon marinara sauce over each eggplant round and sprinkle with Mozzarella cheese. Return the rounds to the air fryer and cook for an additional 2 minutes at 350ºF (177ºC) or until the cheese is melted. Serve the eggplant warm for a delicious treat.

Per Serving:

calories: 330 | fat: 24g | protein: 18g | carbs: 13g | net carbs: 9g | fiber: 4g

Savory Mushroom and Zucchini Vegetable Burgers

Prep time: 10 minutes | Cook time: 12 minutes | Serves 4

♦ 8 ounces (227 g) cremini mushrooms	yellow onion
♦ 2 large egg yolks	♦ 1 clove garlic, peeled and finely minced
♦ ½ medium zucchini, trimmed and chopped	♦ ½ teaspoon salt
♦ ¼ cup peeled and chopped	♦ ¼ teaspoon ground black pepper

1. Add all ingredients to a food processor and pulse about twenty times until the mixture is finely chopped and well combined. 2. Divide the mixture into four equal portions and shape each portion into a burger patty. Place the patties in the ungreased air fryer basket. 3. Preheat the air fryer to 375ºF (191ºC) and cook the burgers for 12 minutes, turning them halfway through the cooking time. The burgers should be browned and firm when finished. 4. Transfer the burgers to a large plate and allow them to cool for 5 minutes before serving.

Per Serving:

calories: 62 | fat: 3g | protein: 3g | carbs: 6g | net carbs: 4g | fiber: 2g

Spinach and Cheese Crustless Pie

Prep time: 10 minutes | Cook time: 20 minutes | Serves 4

♦ 6 large eggs	spinach, drained
♦ ¼ cup heavy whipping cream	♦ 1 cup shredded sharp Cheddar cheese
♦ 1 cup frozen chopped	♦ ¼ cup diced yellow onion

1. In a medium bowl, whisk together the eggs and cream until well combined. Stir in the remaining ingredients until evenly distributed. 2. Transfer the mixture into a round baking dish suitable for the air fryer. 3. Preheat the air fryer to 320ºF (160ºC) and place the baking dish in the air fryer basket. 4. Cook for 20 minutes, or until the eggs are firm and lightly browned on top. Serve immediately.

Per Serving:

calories: 317 | fat: 24g | protein: 21g | carbs: 4g | net carbs: 3g | fiber: 1g

Garlic Herb Roasted Broccoli with Dipping Sauce

Prep time: 19 minutes | Cook time: 15 minutes | Serves 4

♦ 2 tablespoons olive oil	♦ 2 teaspoons dried rosemary, crushed
♦ Kosher salt and freshly ground black pepper, to taste	♦ 3 garlic cloves, minced
♦ 1 pound (454 g) broccoli florets	♦ ⅓ teaspoon dried marjoram, crushed
♦ Dipping Sauce:	♦ ¼ cup sour cream
	♦ ⅓ cup mayonnaise

1. Start by lightly coating the broccoli with a thin layer of olive oil, then season it generously with salt and freshly ground black pepper. 2. Place the seasoned broccoli into the air fryer basket, ensuring they are spread out evenly. Set the air fryer to cook at 395°F (202°C) for 15 minutes, shaking the basket once or twice during cooking for even roasting. 3. While the broccoli is cooking, prepare the dipping sauce by thoroughly mixing all the sauce ingredients in a small bowl. 4. Once the broccoli is done, remove it from the air fryer and serve it warm alongside the dipping sauce. Enjoy your delicious, healthy snack!

Per Serving:
calories: 250 | fat: 23g | protein: 3g | carbs: 10g | net carbs: 9g | fiber: 1g

Herbed Cauliflower Steaks with Lemon Gremolata

Prep time: 15 minutes | Cook time: 25 minutes | Serves 4

♦ 2 tablespoons olive oil	sliced lengthwise through the core into thick "steaks"
♦ 1 tablespoon Italian seasoning	♦ Salt and freshly ground black pepper, to taste
♦ 1 large head cauliflower, outer leaves removed and Gremolata:	♦ ¼ cup Parmesan cheese
♦ 1 bunch Italian parsley (about 1 cup packed)	1 to 2 teaspoons lemon juice
♦ 2 cloves garlic	♦ ½ cup olive oil
♦ Zest of 1 small lemon, plus	♦ Salt and pepper, to taste

1. Begin by preheating your air fryer to 400°F (204°C). 2. In a small bowl, mix together the olive oil and Italian seasoning. Use a brush to generously coat both sides of each cauliflower "steak" with the oil mixture, then season them with salt and freshly ground black pepper to your liking. 3. Depending on the size of your air fryer, place the cauliflower steaks in a single layer in the basket, working in batches if necessary. Cook for 15 to 20 minutes, turning the steaks halfway through, until they are tender and the edges are starting to brown. 4. After the initial cooking time, sprinkle the Parmesan cheese over the steaks and return them to the air fryer for an additional 5 minutes to melt the cheese. 5. While the cauliflower is finishing, prepare the gremolata: In a food processor with a metal blade, combine the parsley, garlic, and lemon zest and juice. With the processor running, gradually drizzle in the olive oil until a vibrant green sauce forms. Season with salt and pepper to taste. 6. Serve the cauliflower steaks topped with the fresh gremolata, allowing the bright flavors to enhance your dish. Enjoy your meal!

Per Serving:
calories: 257 | fat: 23g | protein: 6g | carbs: 9g | net carbs: 7g | fiber: 4g

Mediterranean Stuffed Eggplant Boats

Prep time: 20 minutes | Cook time: 1 hour | Serves 2 to 4

♦ 1 small eggplant, halved lengthwise	♦ ½ block (8 ounces / 227 g) extra-firm tofu (optional)
♦ 3 tablespoons olive, avocado, or macadamia nut oil	♦ 3 tablespoons chopped fresh basil leaves
♦ 1 onion, diced	♦ Salt and freshly ground black pepper, to taste
♦ 12 asparagus spears or green beans, diced	♦ ¼ cup water
♦ 1 red bell pepper, diced	♦ 2 eggs
♦ 1 large tomato, chopped	♦ Chopped fresh parsley, for garnish (optional)
♦ 2 garlic cloves, minced	

Shredded cheese, for garnish (optional)

1. Start by preheating your oven to 350°F (180°C). 2. Carefully scoop out the flesh from the halved eggplant, chop it into small cubes, and set the eggplant skins aside. 3. In a sauté pan with a lid, heat the oil over medium-high heat, then add the chopped eggplant, onion, asparagus, bell pepper, tomato, garlic, and tofu (if you're using it). Stir to combine. Mix in the basil, and season with salt and pepper; cook for about 5 minutes. 4. Pour in the water, cover the pan, lower the heat to medium, and let it cook for another 15 minutes. 5. Arrange the eggplant skins on a baking sheet. Fill each "boat" with the cooked vegetable mixture, leaving room for the egg. Any extra filling can be roasted alongside the eggplant. 6. Crack an egg on top of each filled eggplant half, then place them in the oven and bake for about 40 minutes, or until the eggs reach your preferred level of doneness. 7. After removing the eggplant from the oven, you can sprinkle parsley and cheese over the top if desired. Allow the cheese to melt and cool for about 5 minutes before serving. Enjoy your delicious eggplant boats!

Per Serving:
calories: 380 | fat: 26g | protein: 12g | carbs: 25g | net carbs: 15g | fiber: 10g

Spicy Loaded Cauliflower Steaks

Prep time: 5 minutes | Cook time: 7 minutes | Serves 4

♦ 1 medium head cauliflower	melted
♦ ¼ cup hot sauce	♦ ¼ cup blue cheese crumbles
♦ 2 tablespoons salted butter,	♦ ¼ cup full-fat ranch dressing

1. Start by taking off the leaves from the cauliflower and cutting the head into slices that are about ½ inch thick. 2. In a separate small bowl, combine hot sauce and melted butter, mixing them together well. Use a brush to coat each cauliflower slice evenly with the spicy butter mixture. 3. Arrange the cauliflower steaks in the air fryer basket, making sure not to overcrowd them, and cook in batches if needed. 4. Set the air fryer temperature to 400ºF (204ºC) and let the cauliflower cook for 7 minutes. 5. Once cooked, the edges of the cauliflower should be darkened and caramelized, indicating a delicious crispness. 6. For serving, top each steak with crumbled blue cheese and finish with a drizzle of ranch dressing for added flavor.

Per Serving:
calories: 140 | fat: 12g | protein: 5g | carbs: 6g | net carbs: 5g | fiber: 1g

Cheesy Veggie Crustless Quiche

Prep time: 5 minutes | Cook time: 25 minutes | Serves 4

♦ 1 tablespoon grass-fed butter, divided	♦ ½ cup sliced mushrooms, chopped
♦ 6 eggs	♦ 1 scallion, white and green parts, chopped
♦ ¾ cup heavy (whipping) cream	♦ 1 cup shredded fresh spinach
♦ 3 ounces goat cheese, divided	♦ 10 cherry tomatoes, cut in half

1. Begin by preheating your oven to 350°F (175°C). Prepare a 9-inch pie plate by greasing it with ½ teaspoon of butter and setting it aside. 2. In a medium mixing bowl, whisk together the eggs, cream, and 2 ounces of cheese until thoroughly combined. Set this mixture aside for later use. 3. For the vegetables, melt the remaining butter in a small skillet over medium-high heat. Add the chopped mushrooms and scallions, sautéing them until they soften, which should take about 2 minutes. Next, incorporate the spinach and continue to sauté until it wilts, roughly 2 more minutes. 4. To assemble your quiche, spread the sautéed vegetable mixture evenly across the bottom of the prepared pie plate. Pour the egg and cream mixture over the vegetables, ensuring an even distribution. Finally, scatter the cherry tomatoes and the remaining 1 ounce of goat cheese on top. Bake in the preheated oven for 20 to 25 minutes, or until the quiche is puffed, lightly browned, and cooked through. 5. Once baked, allow the quiche to cool slightly before cutting it into wedges. Serve warm or cold on individual plates for a delightful meal.

Per Serving:
calories: 355 | fat: 30g | protein: 18g | carbs: 5g | net carbs: 4g | fiber: 1g

Creamy Cauliflower Tikka Masala

Prep time: 10 minutes | Cook time: 20 minutes | Serves 4

For The Cauliflower

♦ 1 head cauliflower, cut into small florets	♦ 1 teaspoon ground cumin
♦ 1 tablespoon coconut oil, melted	♦ ½ teaspoon ground coriander

For The Sauce

♦ 2 tablespoons coconut oil	♦ ½ teaspoon salt
♦ ½ onion, chopped	♦ 1 cup crushed tomatoes
♦ 1 tablespoon minced garlic	♦ 1 cup heavy (whipping) cream
♦ 1 tablespoon grated ginger	
♦ 2 tablespoons garam masala	♦ 1 tablespoon chopped fresh cilantro
♦ 1 tablespoon tomato paste	

1. Begin by preheating your oven to 425°F and prepare a baking sheet with aluminum foil to make cleanup easier. 2. In a spacious mixing bowl, combine the cauliflower florets with coconut oil, cumin, and coriander, ensuring each piece is well coated. 3. Spread the seasoned cauliflower evenly on the baking sheet and roast in the oven for about 20 minutes or until it becomes tender. 4. While the cauliflower is baking, heat a generous amount of coconut oil in a large skillet over medium-high heat. 5. Add chopped onion, minced garlic, and grated ginger to the pan and sauté for around 3 minutes, or until the mixture is fragrant and the onions are softened. 6. Incorporate garam masala, tomato paste, and salt into the sautéed vegetables, mixing thoroughly. 7. Pour in the crushed tomatoes and bring the mixture to a boil, then reduce the heat to low, letting it simmer for approximately 10 minutes while stirring frequently. 8. Once the sauce has thickened, remove it from the heat and stir in the cream along with freshly chopped cilantro. 9. Once the cauliflower has finished roasting, add it to the skillet with the sauce and mix everything together to ensure even distribution. 10. Serve the hearty cauliflower dish by ladling the mixture into four bowls, and enjoy it hot, perhaps with an extra sprinkle of cilantro for garnish if desired.

Per Serving:
calories: 372 | fat: 32g | protein: 8g | carbs: 17g | net carbs: 10g | fiber: 7g

Creamy Cheddar Baked Zucchini

Prep time: 10 minutes | Cook time: 8 minutes | Serves 4

- 2 tablespoons salted butter
- ¼ cup diced white onion
- ½ teaspoon minced garlic
- ½ cup heavy whipping cream

- 2 ounces (57 g) full-fat cream cheese
- 1 cup shredded sharp Cheddar cheese
- 2 medium zucchini, spiralized

1. In a large saucepan set over medium heat, melt the butter until it's bubbly. Add the chopped onion and sauté for about 1 to 3 minutes, until it starts to soften. Stir in the minced garlic and sauté for an additional 30 seconds before adding the cream and cream cheese to the pan. 2. Once combined, remove the saucepan from the heat and stir in the shredded Cheddar cheese until melted. Fold in the zucchini, ensuring it's well coated in the creamy sauce, then transfer the mixture into a round baking dish. Cover the dish tightly with foil before placing it in the air fryer basket. 3. Set the air fryer to a temperature of 370°F (188°C) and program it to cook for 8 minutes. 4. After 6 minutes, carefully remove the foil to allow the top to brown during the final cooking time. Once finished, give the dish a good stir before serving. Enjoy your creamy zucchini dish!

Per Serving:

calories: 346 | fat: 32g | protein: 11g | carbs: 6g | net carbs: 5g | fiber: 1g

Lemon Herb Whole Roasted Cauliflower

Prep time: 5 minutes | Cook time: 15 minutes | Serves 4

- 1 medium head cauliflower
- 2 tablespoons salted butter, melted
- 1 medium lemon

- ½ teaspoon garlic powder
- 1 teaspoon dried parsley

1. Start by removing the leaves from the cauliflower head and brush it generously with melted butter. Zest one half of the lemon directly onto the cauliflower, then squeeze the juice from that zested half over the entire head. 2. Next, sprinkle the cauliflower with garlic powder and fresh parsley for added flavor. Place the prepared cauliflower head into the air fryer basket. 3. Set the air fryer temperature to 350°F (177°C) and cook for 15 minutes. 4. During cooking, check the cauliflower every 5 minutes to ensure it doesn't overcook; it should become fork-tender. 5. Once done, squeeze the juice from the remaining lemon half over the cauliflower before serving. Enjoy immediately for the best flavor and texture.

Per Serving:

calories: 90 | fat: 7g | protein: 3g | carbs: 6g | net carbs: 4g | fiber: 2g

Mediterranean Cheese Pan Pizza

Prep time: 5 minutes | Cook time: 8 minutes | Serves 2

- 1 cup shredded Mozzarella cheese
- ¼ medium red bell pepper, seeded and chopped
- ½ cup chopped fresh spinach leaves

- 2 tablespoons chopped black olives
- 2 tablespoons crumbled feta cheese

1. Evenly sprinkle Mozzarella cheese in an ungreased round nonstick baking dish. Layer the remaining ingredients on top of the cheese. 2. Place the dish into the air fryer basket and set the temperature to 350°F (177°C). Bake for 8 minutes, checking halfway through to prevent burning. The pizza should be golden brown on top with melted cheese when finished. 3. Carefully remove the dish from the air fryer and allow it to cool for 5 minutes before slicing and serving. Enjoy your delicious pizza!

Per Serving:

calories: 239 | fat: 17g | protein: 17g | carbs: 6g | net carbs: 5g | fiber: 1g

Spicy Vegetarian Chili with Avocado and Sour Cream

Prep time: 10 minutes | Cook time: 25 minutes | Serves 8

- 2 tablespoons good-quality olive oil
- ½ onion, finely chopped
- 1 red bell pepper, diced
- 2 jalapeño peppers, chopped
- 1 tablespoon minced garlic
- 2 tablespoons chili powder
- 1 teaspoon ground cumin
- 4 cups canned diced tomatoes
- 2 cups pecans, chopped
- 1 cup sour cream
- 1 avocado, diced
- 2 tablespoons chopped fresh cilantro

1. Start by sautéing the vegetables. In a large pot set over medium-high heat, add the olive oil and allow it to warm. Incorporate the onion, red bell pepper, jalapeño peppers, and garlic, cooking them until softened, which should take around 4 minutes. Add the chili powder and cumin, stirring well to coat the vegetables evenly with the spices. 2. Next, prepare the chili. Mix in the tomatoes and pecans, bringing the mixture to a boil. Once boiling, reduce the heat to low and let it simmer, allowing the vegetables to become tender and the flavors to blend, for approximately 20 minutes. 3. Finally, serve the chili. Use a ladle to pour the chili into bowls and garnish each serving with sour cream, avocado, and fresh cilantro for added flavor and presentation. Enjoy your delicious chili!

Per Serving:
calories: 332 | fat: 32g | protein: 5g | carbs: 11g | net carbs: 5g | fiber: 6g

Crispy Almond-Cauliflower Gnocchi

Prep time: 5 minutes | Cook time: 25 to 30 minutes | Serves 4

- 5 cups cauliflower florets
- ⅔ cup almond flour
- ½ teaspoon salt
- ¼ cup unsalted butter, melted
- ¼ cup grated Parmesan cheese

1. Begin by processing the cauliflower. Use a food processor fitted with a metal blade to pulse the cauliflower until it's finely chopped. Transfer the processed cauliflower to a large microwave-safe bowl and cover it with a paper towel. Microwave for 5 minutes. After microwaving, spread the cauliflower on a towel to cool down. 2. Once the cauliflower is cool enough to handle, gather the sides of the towel and squeeze tightly over the sink to eliminate excess moisture. Return the cauliflower to the food processor and blend until creamy. Add the flour and salt, pulsing until a sticky dough forms. 3. Move the dough to a lightly floured surface using almond flour. Shape it into a ball, then divide it into 4 equal parts. Roll each part into a rope about 1 inch thick, and cut the dough into squares using a sharp knife. 4. Preheat the air fryer to 400°F (204°C). 5. In batches if necessary, place the gnocchi in a single layer in the air fryer basket and spray them generously with olive oil. Air fry for 25 to 30 minutes, turning the gnocchi halfway through, until they are golden brown and crispy around the edges. Once cooked, transfer the gnocchi to a large bowl and toss them with melted butter and Parmesan cheese for added flavor.

Per Serving:
calories: 220 | fat: 20g | protein: 7g | carbs: 8g | net carbs: 5g | fiber: 3g

Chapter

8

Snacks and Appetizers

Chapter 8 Snacks and Appetizers

Crispy Parmesan Zucchini Fries

Prep time: 15 minutes | Cook time: 5 minutes | Serves 4

- 1 zucchini
- 1 ounce (28 g) Parmesan, grated
- 1 tablespoon almond flour
- ½ teaspoon Italian seasoning
- 1 tablespoon coconut oil

1. Start by trimming the ends of the zucchini and then slicing it into fry-shaped pieces. 2. Next, toss the zucchini fries in a mixture of grated Parmesan, almond flour, and Italian seasoning until they are well coated. 3. Set the Instant Pot to Sauté mode and add the coconut oil, allowing it to melt completely. 4. Once the oil is hot, carefully place the zucchini fries in a single layer in the pot and cook for 2 minutes on each side, or until they achieve a golden brown color. 5. After cooking, transfer the zucchini fries to a plate and use paper towels to pat them dry and remove any excess oil.

Per Serving:

calories: 102 | fat: 9g | protein: 4g | carbs: 3g | net carbs: 2g | fiber: 1g

Cheesy Bacon-Stuffed Portobello Bites

Prep time: 10 minutes | Cook time: 35 minutes | Serves 12

- 24 ounces (680 g) baby portobello mushrooms
- 2 tablespoons avocado oil
- 3 ounces (85 g) cream cheese
- ¼ cup sour cream
- 2 cloves garlic, minced
- 1 tablespoon chopped fresh
- dill
- 1 tablespoon chopped fresh parsley
- ¾ cup (3 ounces / 85 g) shredded Cheddar cheese
- ⅓ cup cooked bacon bits
- 3 tablespoons sliced green onions

1. Begin by preheating your oven to 400ºF (205ºC) and prepare a sheet pan by lining it with foil or parchment paper, then lightly greasing it. 2. Remove the stems from the mushrooms and position the caps cavity side up on the baking sheet. Drizzle avocado oil over the mushrooms for flavor. 3. Place the mushrooms in the oven and roast them for 15 to 20 minutes, until they become soft. 4. While the mushrooms are roasting, melt the cream cheese in a microwave-safe bowl or saucepan until it becomes soft and easily stirrable. Remove from heat. 5. To the melted cream cheese, add sour cream, garlic, dill, and parsley, stirring well to combine. Next, incorporate the Cheddar cheese, bacon, and green onions into the mixture. 6. Once the mushrooms are soft, take them out of the oven, keeping the oven on. Drain any excess liquid from the pan and the mushrooms, then use paper towels to pat the cavities dry. Fill each mushroom with the prepared dip mixture using a small cookie scoop or spoon. 7. Return the stuffed mushrooms to the oven and bake for an additional 10 to 15 minutes, until they are hot and bubbling.

Per Serving:

calories: 107 | fat: 8g | protein: 4g | carbs: 3g | net carbs: 3g | fiber: 0g

Mediterranean Olive Tapenade

Prep time: 5 minutes | Cook time: 0 minutes | Serves 2

- 1 cup pitted black olives
- 1 cup pitted green olives
- ¼ cup sun-dried tomatoes in oil, drained
- 6 fresh basil leaves
- 1 tablespoon capers
- 1 tablespoon fresh parsley leaves
- 2 teaspoons fresh thyme leaves
- Leaves from 1 sprig fresh oregano
- 1 clove garlic
- 1 anchovy fillet
- ¼ cup olive oil
- 6 medium celery stalks, cut into sticks, for serving

1. Begin by adding all the ingredients, omitting the olive oil and celery sticks, into a blender or food processor. 2. Pulse the mixture until it's roughly chopped to your desired consistency. 3. Next, incorporate the olive oil and pulse a few more times to blend everything together. 4. Once combined, transfer the mixture to a serving dish that holds at least 16 ounces (475 ml). 5. Serve with celery sticks for dipping and enjoy! 6. For storage, keep the dip in an airtight container in the refrigerator for up to 5 days.

Per Serving:

calories: 167 | fat: 16g | protein: 1g | carbs: 4g | net carbs: 3g | fiber: 1g

Sweet and Spicy Georgia Pecans

Prep time: 10 minutes | Cook time: 1 hour | Serves 12

♦ 12 ounces raw pecan halves	liquid stevia
♦ 1 large egg white	♦ 1 teaspoon ground cinnamon
♦ 1 teaspoon water	
♦ 2 teaspoons vanilla extract	♦ 1 teaspoon pink Himalayan salt
♦ ½ teaspoon plus 10 drops of	

1. Start by preheating your oven to 250°F and lining a rimmed baking sheet with parchment paper. 2. Evenly spread the pecan halves on the prepared baking sheet. 3. In a small bowl, whisk together the egg white, water, vanilla extract, stevia, cinnamon, and salt until well combined. Pour this mixture over the pecans, tossing with your hands or a spoon until all the pecans are evenly coated. 4. Arrange the pecans in a single layer and bake them in the oven for 45 to 60 minutes, stirring every 15 minutes to ensure even cooking. The pecans are ready when they are completely dried out and have a golden-brown color.

Per Serving:
calories: 202 | fat: 24g | protein: 3g | carbs: 4g | net carbs: 3g | fiber: 3g

Cinnamon-Spiced Roasted Nut Mix

Prep time: 10 minutes | Cook time: 10 minutes | Serves 8

♦ 1 teaspoon vanilla extract	♦ 1 teaspoon liquid stevia (optional)
♦ 1 teaspoon ground cinnamon	♦ 4 tablespoons butter
♦ 1 teaspoon ground allspice	♦ 1 cup pecans
♦ ½ teaspoon ground ginger	♦ ½ cup almonds
♦ ½ teaspoon ground nutmeg	♦ ½ cup macadamia nuts

1. Begin by preheating your oven to 375°F (190°C). 2. In a small bowl, mix together the vanilla, cinnamon, allspice, ginger, nutmeg, and stevia (if using) and set it aside. 3. In a large nonstick skillet over medium-low heat, melt the butter until it's fully melted and bubbling. 4. Add the pecans, almonds, and macadamias to the skillet. Sprinkle the prepared spice mixture over the nuts, stirring well to ensure they are completely coated in the buttery spice blend. Cook for about 10 minutes, or until the nuts are golden brown, stirring occasionally. Remove the skillet from the heat and allow the nuts to cool slightly before serving. 5. Store the spiced nuts in an airtight container on the counter for a few days or refrigerate them for up to 1 week for optimal freshness.

Per Serving:
¼ cup: calories: 279 | fat: 27g | protein: 4g | carbs: 5g | net carbs: 2g | fiber: 3g

Bacon-Infused Pimento Cheese Dip

Prep time: 10 minutes | Cook time: 5 minutes | Serves 6

♦ 2 ounces (57 g) bacon (about 4 thick slices)	♦ ¼ teaspoon cayenne pepper (optional)
♦ 4 ounces (113 g) cream cheese, room temperature	♦ 1 cup thick-shredded extra-sharp Cheddar cheese
♦ ¼ cup mayonnaise	♦ 2 ounces (57 g) jarred diced pimentos, drained
♦ ¼ teaspoon onion powder	

1. Begin by cutting the raw bacon into pieces about ½ inch thick. Place the chopped bacon in a small skillet over medium heat and cook until it reaches a crispy texture, which should take around 3 to 4 minutes. Once crispy, use a slotted spoon to transfer the bacon to a plate lined with paper towels to absorb any excess grease, making sure to save the rendered fat for later use. 2. In a large mixing bowl, combine the cream cheese, mayonnaise, onion powder, and cayenne pepper (if you choose to include it). Using an electric mixer or mixing by hand, blend the ingredients until the mixture is smooth and creamy. 3. Incorporate the reserved bacon fat into the mixture along with the Cheddar cheese and pimentos, mixing thoroughly until all ingredients are well combined. 4. For optimal flavor, refrigerate the mixture for at least 30 minutes before serving. This allows the flavors to meld beautifully. When ready to serve, enjoy it cold with an assortment of raw vegetables.

Per Serving:
calories: 216 | fat: 20g | protein: 8g | carbs: 2g | net carbs: 0g | fiber: 2

Loaded Pickle Cuban Sandwich

Prep time: 5 minutes | Cook time: 5 minutes | Serves 2

♦ 2 deli ham slices	♦ 2 jumbo dill pickles, halved lengthwise
♦ 2 deli pork tenderloin slices	
♦ 4 Swiss cheese slices	♦ 1 tablespoon yellow mustard

1. Begin by warming the ham and tenderloin slices in a small sauté pan or skillet over medium heat until heated through. 2. Once warm, use a spatula to carefully roll the deli meats into loose rolls. Layer Swiss cheese slices on top of the rolls, allowing them to melt slightly. 3. Next, place the rolled meats onto two pickle halves, creating a base for your sandwich. 4. Add a dollop of mustard on top of the cheese, then finish by placing the other pickle halves on top to close the sandwiches. 5. Secure the sandwiches with toothpicks, slice them in half crosswise, and serve immediately.

Per Serving:
calories: 256 | fat: 16g | protein: 23g | carbs: 5g | net carbs: 1g | fiber: 4g

Mackerel and Goat Cheese Fat Bombs with Herb Crust

Prep time: 10 minutes | Cook time: 0 minutes | Makes 10 fat bombs

◆ 2 smoked or cooked mackerel fillets, boneless, skin removed	◆ mustard
	◆ 1 small red onion, finely diced
◆ 4.4 ounces (125 g) soft goat's cheese	◆ 2 tablespoons chopped fresh chives or herbs of choice
◆ 1 tablespoon fresh lemon juice	◆ ¾ cup pecans, crushed
◆ 1 teaspoon Dijon or yellow	◆ 10 leaves baby gem lettuce

1. Begin by placing the mackerel, goat's cheese, lemon juice, and mustard into a food processor. Pulse the mixture until it becomes smooth and well-combined. Transfer the blended mixture to a bowl, then add the chopped onion and herbs, mixing everything thoroughly with a spoon. Refrigerate the mixture for 20 to 30 minutes, allowing it to set. 2. Once the mixture is chilled, use a large spoon or an ice cream scoop to portion it into 10 equal balls, each weighing approximately 40 g (1.4 ounces). Roll each ball in the crushed pecans until fully coated. Finally, place each coated ball on a small lettuce leaf for serving. These fat bombs can be stored in a sealed container in the refrigerator for up to 5 days.

Per Serving:
1 fat bomb: calories: 150 | fat: 13g | protein: 7g | carbs: 3g | net carbs: 2g | fiber: 1g

Almond Flour Blueberry Crumble with Coconut Cream

Prep time: 5 minutes | Cook time: 25 minutes | Serves 6

◆ 18 ounces (510 g) fresh or frozen blueberries	◆ 2 tablespoons coconut flour
◆ 1 cup (110 g) blanched almond flour	◆ 1 teaspoon ground cinnamon
◆ ⅓ cup (70 g) coconut oil or ghee, room temperature	◆ 1 cup (250 g) coconut cream, or 1 cup (240 ml) full-fat coconut milk, for serving
◆ ⅓ cup (65 g) erythritol	

1. Begin by preheating your oven to 350°F (177°C) to prepare for baking. 2. Take an 8-inch (20-cm) square baking pan and add the blueberries, spreading them evenly in the bottom of the pan. 3. In a medium bowl, combine almond flour, oil, erythritol, coconut flour, and cinnamon, mixing thoroughly with a fork until you achieve a crumbly texture. Spread this crumbly mixture evenly over the blueberries in the pan. 4. Place the pan in the oven and bake for about 22 to 25 minutes, or until the topping turns a beautiful golden brown. 5. Once baked, remove the dish from the oven and allow it to cool for 10 minutes before serving. 6. Divide the baked blueberry mixture into 6 bowls and generously top each with 2 to 3 tablespoons of rich coconut cream.

Per Serving:
calories: 388 | fat: 33g | protein: 5g | carbs: 17g | net carbs: 13g | fiber: 4g

Curried Coconut Broccoli Skewers

Prep time: 15 minutes | Cook time: 1 minute | Serves 2

◆ 1 cup broccoli florets	◆ 2 tablespoons coconut cream
◆ ½ teaspoon curry paste	
	◆ 1 cup water, for cooking

1. In a shallow bowl, combine the curry paste with coconut cream until well mixed. 2. Next, coat the broccoli florets with the curry paste mixture, ensuring they are evenly covered, and then thread them onto skewers. 3. Pour water into the Instant Pot and place the steamer rack inside. 4. Arrange the broccoli skewers on the rack above the water. Close and securely seal the lid. 5. Set the Instant Pot to Manual mode (High Pressure) and cook for 1 minute. 6. Once the cooking time is complete, perform a quick pressure release to release the steam.

Per Serving:
calories: 58 | fat: 4g | protein: 2g | carbs: 4g | net carbs: 2g | fiber: 2g

Spicy Cayenne Beef Bites

Prep time: 5 minutes | Cook time: 23 minutes | Serves 6

◆ 2 tablespoons olive oil	◆ 1 teaspoon cayenne pepper
◆ 1 pound (454 g) beef steak, cut into cubes	◆ ½ teaspoon dried marjoram
◆ 1 cup beef bone broth	◆ Sea salt and ground black pepper, to taste
◆ ¼ cup dry white wine	

1. Begin by setting your Instant Pot to the Sauté function and adding the olive oil to heat. 2. Next, add the beef and sauté it for 2 to 3 minutes, stirring occasionally until browned. 3. Incorporate the remaining ingredients into the Instant Pot, mixing everything together thoroughly. 4. Secure the lid on the Instant Pot. Select Manual mode and adjust the cooking time to 20 minutes at High Pressure. 5. Once the timer signals that cooking is complete, allow for a natural pressure release for 10 minutes before releasing any remaining pressure. Carefully lift the lid. 6. Transfer the beef to a serving platter and enjoy while warm.

Per Serving:
calories: 173 | fat: 10g | protein: 19g | carbs: 1g | net carbs: 1g | fiber: 0g

Chive-Infused Parmesan Chicken Bites

Prep time: 10 minutes | Cook time: 15 minutes | Serves 4

- 1 teaspoon coconut oil, softened
- 1 cup ground chicken
- ¼ cup chicken broth
- 1 tablespoon chopped chives
- 1 teaspoon cayenne pepper
- 3 ounces (85 g) Parmesan cheese, grated

1. Begin by setting your Instant Pot to Sauté and warming the coconut oil. 2. Next, add all the ingredients except the cheese into the pot and stir well to combine everything. 3. Secure the lid on the Instant Pot, then select Manual mode and set the cooking time for 15 minutes at High Pressure. 4. Once the cooking time is up, perform a quick pressure release and carefully open the lid. 5. Stir in the grated cheese until it's fully melted and incorporated. Form the mixture into balls and let them cool for 10 minutes before serving.
Per Serving:
calories: 154 | fat: 9g | protein: 18g | carbs: 1g | net carbs: 1g | fiber: 0g

Garlic-Sautéed Cabbage Wedges with Green Goddess Dip

Prep time: 5 minutes | Cook time: 15 minutes | Serves 6

- 1 large head green or red cabbage (about 2½ lbs/1.2 kg)
- 2 tablespoons coconut oil or avocado oil
- 2 teaspoons garlic powder
- ½ teaspoon finely ground
- sea salt
- ¾ cup (180 ml) green goddess dressing
- Special Equipment:
- 12 (4-in/10-cm) bamboo skewers

1. Start by slicing the cabbage in half from top to bottom through the core. Take each half and carefully remove the core by cutting a triangle around it and pulling it out. Next, lay the half with the cut side down and slice it into 6 wedges. To keep the leaves intact, press a bamboo skewer into each wedge. Repeat this process with the other half of the cabbage. 2. In a large frying pan, heat the oil over medium-low heat. 3. Once the oil is hot, add the cabbage wedges to the pan and sprinkle them with garlic powder and salt. Cook the wedges for 10 minutes on one side until they are lightly browned, then flip them over and cook for an additional 5 minutes on the other side. 4. Serve the cabbage wedges warm with the dressing on the side.
Per Serving:
calories: 252 | fat: 20g | protein: 3g | carbs: 12g | net carbs: 7g | fiber: 5g

Buffalo Chicken Dip with Salami Crisps

Prep time: 10 minutes | Cook time: 10 minutes | Serves 6

- 8 ounces (227 g) salami, cut crosswise into 24 slices
- Buffalo Chicken Dip:
- 1 cup full-fat coconut milk
- ¾ cup shredded cooked chicken
- ⅓ cup nutritional yeast
- 1 tablespoon coconut aminos
- 1 tablespoon hot sauce
- 2 teaspoons onion powder
- 1½ teaspoons garlic powder
- 1 teaspoon turmeric powder
- ½ teaspoon finely ground sea salt
- ¼ teaspoon ground black pepper
- ¼ cup roughly chopped fresh parsley

1. Start by preheating your oven to 400ºF (205ºC) and prepare two rimmed baking sheets by lining them with parchment paper or silicone baking mats. 2. Arrange the salami slices on the prepared baking sheets, ensuring they are evenly spaced. Bake for 8 to 10 minutes until the centers appear crisp and the edges slightly curl up. While the salami is baking, prepare the dip: 1. In a small saucepan, combine all the dip ingredients. Heat over medium-high heat until the mixture begins to simmer, then reduce the heat to medium-low. Cook uncovered for 6 minutes, stirring frequently, until the dip thickens. 2. Once the salami chips are done, transfer them to a serving plate and the dip to a separate serving bowl. Stir the chopped parsley into the dip for added flavor and freshness. Enjoy your snack! Storage: Keep any leftovers in an airtight container in the refrigerator for up to 3 days, or freeze for up to 3 months.
Per Serving:
calories: 294 | fat: 21g | protein: 20g | carbs: 7g | net carbs: 5g | fiber: 2g

Cheesy Taco Beef Bites

Prep time: 10 minutes | Cook time: 15 minutes | Serves 6

- 10 ounces (283 g) ground beef
- 3 eggs, beaten
- ⅓ cup shredded Mozzarella
- cheese
- 1 teaspoon taco seasoning
- 1 teaspoon sesame oil

1. In a mixing bowl, combine the ground beef, eggs, Mozzarella cheese, and taco seasoning until well blended. 2. Shape the mixture into small meat bites, forming them into bite-sized pieces. 3. Turn on the Instant Pot and heat sesame oil using the Sauté mode until hot. 4. Add the meat bites to the hot oil and cook for 5 minutes on each side until browned and cooked through.
Per Serving:
calories: 132 | fat: 6g | protein: 17g | carbs: 1g | net carbs: 1g | fiber: 0g

Savory BLT Salad with Creamy Dressing

Prep time: 15 minutes | Cook time: 0 minutes | Serves 4

- 2 tablespoons melted bacon fat
- 2 tablespoons red wine vinegar
- Freshly ground black pepper
- 4 cups shredded lettuce
- 1 tomato, chopped
- 6 bacon slices, cooked and chopped
- 2 hardboiled eggs, chopped
- 1 tablespoon roasted unsalted sunflower seeds
- 1 teaspoon toasted sesame seeds
- 1 cooked chicken breast, sliced (optional)

1. In a medium-sized bowl, combine the bacon fat and vinegar, whisking until the mixture is well emulsified. Season with black pepper to taste. 2. Add the lettuce and tomato to the bowl, tossing the vegetables thoroughly with the dressing to ensure they are evenly coated. 3. Portion the salad onto 4 individual plates, topping each with equal amounts of bacon, egg, sunflower seeds, sesame seeds, and chicken (if desired). Serve immediately.

Per Serving:

calories: 228 | fat: 18g | protein: 1g | carbs: 4 | net carbs: 2g | fiber: 2g

Zesty Lemon-Pepper Chicken Drumsticks

Prep time: 30 minutes | Cook time: 30 minutes | Serves 2

- 2 teaspoons freshly ground coarse black pepper
- 1 teaspoon baking powder
- ½ teaspoon garlic powder
- 4 chicken drumsticks (4 ounces / 113 g each)
- Kosher salt, to taste
- 1 lemon

1. In a small bowl, combine the pepper, baking powder, and garlic powder. Arrange the drumsticks on a plate and generously sprinkle the baking powder mixture over them, ensuring they are thoroughly coated. Allow the drumsticks to rest in the refrigerator for a minimum of 1 hour or up to overnight for better flavor. 2. After resting, season the drumsticks with salt, then carefully place them in the air fryer, positioning them bone-end up and leaning against the sides of the basket. Set the air fryer to 375°F (191°C) and cook until the drumsticks are fully cooked and the exterior is crispy, which should take around 30 minutes. 3. Once cooked, transfer the drumsticks to a serving platter and immediately grate the lemon zest over them while they're still hot. Cut the lemon into wedges and serve alongside the warm drumsticks.

Per Serving:

calories: 200 | fat: 9g | protein: 28g | carbs: 5g | net carbs: 4g | fiber: 1g

Creamy Peanut Butter Keto Fudge Squares

Prep time: 5 minutes | Cook time: 10 minutes | Serves 12

- ½ cup (1 stick) butter
- 8 ounces (227 g) cream cheese
- 1 cup unsweetened peanut butter
- 1 teaspoon vanilla extract (or the seeds from 1 vanilla bean)
- 1 teaspoon liquid stevia (optional)

1. Begin by lining an 8 or 9-inch square baking dish, or a 9-by-13-inch rectangular baking dish, with parchment paper and set it aside. 2. In a medium saucepan over medium heat, combine the butter and cream cheese, melting them together while stirring frequently for about 5 minutes. 3. Next, add the peanut butter to the mixture and stir continuously until it becomes smooth. Once well combined, remove the saucepan from heat. 4. Incorporate the vanilla extract and, if desired, stevia into the mixture. Pour it into the prepared baking dish, spreading it out evenly. 5. Refrigerate for approximately 1 hour, or until the mixture has thickened and set sufficiently for cutting. Once set, cut into small squares and enjoy! Store any leftovers in a covered container in the refrigerator for up to 1 week.

Per Serving:

1 fudge square: calories: 261 | fat: 24g | protein: 8g | carbs: 5g | net carbs: 4g | fiber: 1g

Pecan-Crusted Ranch Cheese Ball

Prep time: 15 minutes | Cook time: 0 minutes | serves 8

- 2 (8 ounces) packages cream cheese, softened
- 1 cup shredded sharp cheddar cheese
- 2 tablespoons ranch seasoning
- 1 cup chopped raw pecans

Serving Suggestions:

- Celery sticks
- Mini sweet peppers
- Pork rinds

1. In a medium-sized bowl, combine the cream cheese, cheddar cheese, and ranch seasoning. Use a spoon to thoroughly mix the ingredients until they are well blended. 2. Form the mixture into a ball or disc shape, then roll it in the crushed pecans to coat it evenly. Wrap the cheese ball tightly and refrigerate it overnight to allow the flavors to meld. 3. When ready to serve, present it alongside your choice of scoopers. Any leftovers can be stored in an airtight container in the refrigerator for up to 5 days.

Per Serving:

calories: 303 | fat: 27g | protein: 9g | carbs: 11g | net carbs: 5g | fiber: 2g

Cheesy Cauliflower Rice Medley

Prep time: 3 minutes | Cook time: 1 minute | Serves 4

◆ 1 head fresh cauliflower, chopped into florets	◆ 1 cup shredded sharp Cheddar cheese
◆ 1 cup water	◆ ½ teaspoon salt
◆ 3 tablespoons butter	◆ ¼ teaspoon pepper
◆ 1 tablespoon heavy cream	◆ ¼ teaspoon garlic powder

1. Begin by placing the cauliflower in a steamer basket. Pour water into the Instant Pot and carefully lower the steamer basket into the pot. Close the lid securely. 2. Select the Steam function and set the cooking time to 1 minute. Once the timer goes off, perform a quick release of the pressure. 3. After releasing the pressure, carefully remove the steamer basket and transfer the cauliflower to a food processor. Pulse until the cauliflower is broken down into small pearl-like pieces. 4. Transfer the processed cauliflower to a large bowl, then add the remaining ingredients. Gently fold everything together until well combined.

Per Serving:

calories: 241 | fat: 18g | protein: 10g | carbs: 8g | net carbs: 5g | fiber: 3g

Crispy Prosciutto-Wrapped Paleo Egg Rolls

Prep time: 20 minutes | Cook time: 10 minutes | Makes 10 egg rolls

◆ 1 cup coconut oil, duck fat, or avocado oil, for frying	◆ Sliced radishes, for serving (optional)
◆ 20 slices prosciutto	

Filling:

◆ 1 pound (454 g) ground pork	◆ 1 clove garlic, minced
◆ 2 cups shredded cabbage	◆ 1 teaspoon grated fresh ginger
◆ 1 green onion, chopped	◆ ½ teaspoon five-spice powder
◆ 3 tablespoons coconut aminos	◆ ½ teaspoon fine sea salt

Sweet 'n' Sour Sauce:

◆ ½ cup Swerve confectioners'-style sweetener or equivalent amount of liquid or powdered sweetener	aminos
	◆ 1 tablespoon tomato paste
	◆ ½ teaspoon minced garlic
◆ ½ cup coconut vinegar	◆ 1 teaspoon grated fresh ginger
◆ 2 tablespoons coconut	◆ ¼ teaspoon guar gum (optional)

1. Begin by heating the oil in a deep-fryer or a 4-inch-deep cast-iron skillet over medium heat until it reaches 350ºF (180ºC). Ensure the oil depth is at least 3 inches; add more oil if necessary. 2. While the oil heats up, prepare the filling. In a large skillet over medium heat, brown the ground pork along with the cabbage, green onion, coconut aminos, garlic, ginger, five-spice, and salt.

Stir frequently to break up the meat, cooking until the pork is done and the cabbage is tender, about 5 minutes. Once cooked, remove the filling from the pan and set it aside to cool. 3. Next, prepare the sauce by heating the ingredients (except for the guar gum) in a small saucepan until they begin to simmer. Whisk the mixture until smooth. If you desire a thicker sauce, sift in the guar gum; it will thicken over a few minutes. 4. To assemble the egg rolls, lay one slice of prosciutto on a sushi mat or a sheet of parchment paper, ensuring a short end is facing you. Place a second slice of prosciutto on top, positioned across the center at a right angle, creating a cross. Spoon 3 to 4 tablespoons of the filling into the center of this cross. 5. Fold the sides of the bottom slice of prosciutto up and over the filling to create the ends of the roll. Then, tightly roll the long piece of prosciutto starting from the edge closest to you into a tight egg roll shape, overlapping by about an inch. If the prosciutto rips, don't worry; it will seal when fried. Repeat this process until all prosciutto and filling have been used. 6. In batches, fry the egg rolls by placing them seam side down in the hot oil for about 2 minutes, or until they become crisp on the outside. Remove from the oil and serve immediately, optionally with sliced radishes on the side. 7. Store any leftovers in an airtight container for up to 3 days. To reheat, place them in a skillet over medium heat and sauté for about 3 minutes on all sides, or until heated through.

Per Serving:

calories: 190 | fat: 13g | protein: 15g | carbs: 3g | net carbs: 1g | fiber: 2g

Bacon-Infused Crispy Brussels Sprouts

Prep time: 5 minutes | Cook time: 10 minutes | Serves 4

◆ ½ pound (227 g) bacon	◆ 1 teaspoon salt
◆ 1 pound (454 g) Brussels sprouts	◆ ½ teaspoon pepper
◆ 4 tablespoons butter	◆ ½ cup water

1 Start by pressing the Sauté button on the Instant Pot and use the Adjust button to lower the heat to Less. Add the bacon and cook for 3 to 5 minutes, or until the fat starts to render. Then, press the Cancel button to stop the cooking process. 2. Next, re-activate the Sauté function, setting the heat to Normal, and continue frying the bacon until it becomes crispy. While the bacon cooks, wash the Brussels sprouts, removing any damaged outer leaves, and cut them in half or quarters. 3. Once the bacon is crispy, remove it from the pot and set aside. In the remaining bacon grease, add the Brussels sprouts along with the butter. Season with salt and pepper. Sauté the Brussels sprouts for 8 to 10 minutes until they are caramelized and crispy, adding a few tablespoons of water as necessary to deglaze the pan. Serve warm.

Per Serving:

calories: 387 | fat: 32g | protein: 11g | carbs: 11g | net carbs: 7g | fiber: 4g

Sautéed Cabbage and Broccoli Slaw

Prep time: 5 minutes | Cook time: 10 minutes | Serves 6

- ◆ 2 cups broccoli slaw
- ◆ ½ head cabbage, thinly sliced
- ◆ ¼ cup chopped kale
- ◆ 4 tablespoons butter
- ◆ 1 teaspoon salt
- ◆ ¼ teaspoon pepper

1. Start by pressing the Sauté button on your Instant Pot and add all the ingredients to the pot. 2. Stir the mixture well and cook for 7 to 10 minutes, allowing the cabbage to soften to your desired consistency. 3. Once cooked, serve the dish warm.

Per Serving:
calories: 97 | fat: 7g | protein: 2g | carbs: 6g | net carbs: 3g | fiber: 3g

Savory Roasted Garlic Bulbs

Prep time: 2 minutes | Cook time: 25 minutes | Serves 4

- ◆ 4 bulbs garlic
- ◆ 1 tablespoon avocado oil
- ◆ 1 teaspoon salt
- ◆ Pinch of black pepper
- ◆ 1 cup water

1. Begin by trimming the pointed tops off the garlic bulbs to reveal the cloves inside. 2. Drizzle the exposed cloves with avocado oil and season with salt and pepper to taste. 3. Position the garlic bulbs in the steamer basket with the cut sides facing up. Alternatively, you can wrap them in aluminum foil, creating a small pouch, and place it on the trivet. Set the steamer basket in the Instant Pot. 4. Close the lid securely and ensure the vent is sealed. Set the pot to cook on High Pressure for 25 minutes. Once the timer goes off, perform a quick release of the steam. 5. Allow the garlic to cool completely before taking the bulbs out of the pot. 6. Finally, grip the bottom stem of the bulb and gently squeeze to extract all the garlic cloves. Use a fork to mash the cloves into a smooth paste.

Per Serving:
calories: 44 | fat: 5g | protein: 0g | carbs: 1g | net carbs: 1g | fiber: 0g

Crispy Cheddar Cheese Chips

Prep time: 10 minutes | Cook time: 5 minutes | Serves 4

- ◆ 1 cup shredded Cheddar cheese
- ◆ 1 tablespoon almond flour

1. Begin by combining the Cheddar cheese and almond flour in a bowl until well mixed. 2. Next, set the Instant Pot to Sauté mode to preheat. 3. Line the bowl of the Instant Pot with baking paper to prevent sticking. 4. Form small rounds of the cheese mixture and place them on the baking paper in the pot. Close the lid securely. 5. Cook the cheese rounds on Sauté mode for about 5 minutes or until the cheese has melted. 6. After cooking, turn off the Instant Pot and carefully lift the baking paper with the cheese rounds out of the pot. 7. Allow the chips to cool completely before gently removing them from the baking paper.

Per Serving:
calories: 154 | fat: 13g | protein: 9g | carbs: 2g | net carbs: 1g | fiber: 1g

Golden Cauliflower Fritters

Prep time: 10 minutes | Cook time: 10 minutes | Makes 10 patties

- ◆ 1 medium head cauliflower (about 1½ pounds/680 g), or 3 cups (375 g) pre-riced cauliflower
- ◆ 2 large eggs
- ◆ ⅔ cup (75 g) blanched almond flour
- ◆ ¼ cup (17 g) nutritional yeast
- ◆ 1 tablespoon dried chives
- ◆ 1 teaspoon finely ground sea salt
- ◆ 1 teaspoon garlic powder
- ◆ ½ teaspoon turmeric powder
- ◆ ¼ teaspoon ground black pepper
- ◆ 3 tablespoons coconut oil or ghee, for the pan

1. If you're using pre-riced cauliflower, feel free to skip to Step 2. For fresh cauliflower, start by cutting off the base and removing the florets. Place the florets in a food processor or blender and pulse them 3 to 4 times until they are broken down into small pieces, roughly ¼-inch (6 mm) in size. 2. Next, transfer the riced cauliflower to a medium saucepan and cover it with enough water to fully submerge the cauliflower. Cover the pot with a lid and bring the water to a boil over medium heat. Once boiling, let it cook, covered, for 3½ minutes. 3. While the cauliflower is boiling, set a fine-mesh strainer over a bowl to catch the water. 4. Carefully pour the hot cauliflower into the strainer, allowing the boiling water to drain into the bowl. Use a spoon to press down on the cauliflower, extracting as much water as possible. 5. Discard the cooking water, then return the drained cauliflower to the bowl. Add in the eggs, almond flour, nutritional yeast, chives, salt, and spices. Mix everything together until well combined. 6. Heat a large frying pan over medium-low heat and add the oil, allowing it to melt completely. 7. Using a ¼-cup (60 ml) scoop, take a portion of the mixture and roll it into a ball about 1¾ inches (4.5 cm) in diameter. Place it in the hot oil and flatten it with the back of a fork to create a patty that is about ½ inch (1.25 cm) thick. Repeat this process until all of the cauliflower mixture is used, yielding a total of 10 patties. 8. Cook each patty for 5 minutes on each side, or until they are golden brown. Once cooked, transfer the patties to a serving plate and enjoy!

Per Serving:
calories: 164 | fat: 12g | protein: 7g | carbs: 7g | net carbs: 3g | fiber: 4g

Crispy Almond Flour Hushpuppies

Prep time: 10 minutes | Cook time: 15 minutes | Makes 10 hushpuppies

◆ High-quality oil, for frying	◆ ½ teaspoon salt
◆ 1 cup finely ground blanched almond flour	◆ ¼ cup finely chopped onions
◆ 1 tablespoon coconut flour	◆ ¼ cup heavy whipping cream
◆ 1 teaspoon baking powder	◆ 1 large egg, beaten

1. Attach a candy thermometer to a Dutch oven or other large heavy pot, then pour in 3 inches of oil and set over medium-high heat. Heat the oil to 375°F. 2. In a medium-sized bowl, stir together the almond flour, coconut flour, baking powder, and salt. Stir in the rest of the ingredients and mix until blended. Do not overmix. 3. Use a tablespoon-sized cookie scoop to gently drop the batter into the hot oil. Don't overcrowd the hushpuppies; cook them in two batches. Fry for 3 minutes, then use a mesh skimmer or slotted spoon to turn and fry them for 3 more minutes or until golden brown on all sides. 4. Use the skimmer or slotted spoon to remove the hushpuppies from the oil and place on a paper towel–lined plate to drain. They are best served immediately.

Per Serving:
calories: 172 | fat: 14g | protein: 6g | carbs: 5g | net carbs: 3g | fiber: 3g

Citrus-Infused Marinated Olives

Prep time: 10 minutes | Cook time: 0 minutes | Makes 2 cups

◆ 2 cups mixed green olives with pits	clementines or 1 large orange
◆ ¼ cup red wine vinegar	◆ 1 teaspoon red pepper flakes
◆ ¼ cup extra-virgin olive oil	◆ 2 bay leaves
◆ 4 garlic cloves, finely minced	◆ ½ teaspoon ground cumin
◆ Zest and juice of 2	◆ ½ teaspoon ground allspice

1. Start by gathering a large glass bowl or jar and add the olives along with the vinegar, oil, and minced garlic. 2. Next, incorporate the orange zest and juice, red pepper flakes, bay leaves, cumin, and allspice into the mixture. Stir everything thoroughly to combine well. 3. Once mixed, cover the bowl or jar securely and place it in the refrigerator. 4. Allow the olives to marinate for a minimum of 4 hours, or up to a week for enhanced flavor. 5. Before serving, remember to toss the marinated olives again to evenly distribute the flavors.

Per Serving:
¼ cup: calories: 100 | fat: 10g | protein: 1g | carbs: 3g | net carbs: 2g | fiber: 1g

Savory Bone Broth Gelatin Fat Bombs

Prep time: 5 minutes | Cook time: 0 minutes | Makes 12 fat bombs

◆ 1 tablespoon grass-fed powdered gelatin	◆ Special Equipment:
◆ 2 cups homemade bone broth, any type, warmed	◆ Silicone mold with 12 (1⅞ ounces / 53 g) cavities

1. Begin by sprinkling the gelatin over the broth, then whisk the mixture until well combined. 2. Position the silicone mold on a rimmed sheet pan to facilitate easy transport. Pour the prepared broth into the mold and place it in the refrigerator or freezer until the gelatin has fully set, which will take about 2 hours. To remove the fat bombs from the mold, gently press on the sides to pop them out. 3. Store the fat bombs in an airtight container in the refrigerator for up to 5 days, or freeze them for several months for longer storage.

Per Serving:
calories: 27 | fat: 5g | protein: 2g | carbs: 2g | net carbs: 2g | fiber: 0g

Coconut Strawberry Bliss Ice

Prep time: 5 minutes | Cook time: 0 minutes | Serves 5

◆ 9 hulled strawberries (fresh or frozen and defrosted)	vinegar
◆ ⅓ cup (85 g) coconut cream	◆ 2 drops liquid stevia, or 2 teaspoons erythritol
◆ 1 tablespoon apple cider	◆ 3 cups (420 g) ice cubes

1. Start by adding the strawberries, coconut cream, vinegar, and sweetener into a blender or food processor. Blend the mixture until it reaches a smooth consistency. 2. Next, incorporate the ice and pulse the blender until the ice is crushed and well mixed into the strawberry mixture. 3. Finally, distribute the blend into four bowls that are at least ¾-cup (180 ml) in capacity and serve immediately.

Per Serving:
calories: 61 | fat: 5g | protein: 0g | carbs: 3g | net carbs: 2g | fiber: 1g

Chapter

9

Stews and Soups

Chapter 9 Stews and Soups

Creamy Blue Cheese Mushroom Soup

Prep time: 15 minutes | Cook time: 20 minutes | Serves 4

- 2 cups chopped white mushrooms
- 3 tablespoons cream cheese
- 4 ounces (113 g) scallions, diced
- 4 cups chicken broth
- 1 teaspoon olive oil
- ½ teaspoon ground cumin
- 1 teaspoon salt
- 2 ounces (57 g) blue cheese, crumbled

1. In the Instant Pot, combine the mushrooms, cream cheese, scallions, chicken broth, olive oil, and ground cumin. 2. Close and seal the lid, then select Manual mode and set the cooking time to 20 minutes at High Pressure. 3. Once the timer beeps, perform a quick pressure release and carefully open the lid. 4. Stir in the salt and use an immersion blender to puree the soup until smooth. 5. Ladle the soup into bowls and garnish with crumbled blue cheese. Serve warm.

Per Serving:
calories: 142 | fat: 9g | protein: 10g | carbs: 5g | net carbs: 4g | fiber: 1g

Vibrant Green Garden Soup

Prep time: 20 minutes | Cook time: 29 minutes | Serves 5

- 1 tablespoon olive oil
- 1 garlic clove, diced
- ½ cup cauliflower florets
- 1 cup kale, chopped
- 2 tablespoons chives, chopped
- 1 teaspoon sea salt
- 6 cups beef broth

1. In the Instant Pot, heat olive oil on Sauté mode for 2 minutes, then add the garlic and sauté for an additional 2 minutes until fragrant. 2. Stir in the cauliflower, kale, chives, sea salt, and beef broth. 3. Close the lid and select Manual mode, setting the cooking time for 5 minutes at High Pressure. 4. Once the timer beeps, perform a quick pressure release and carefully open the lid. 5. Ladle the soup into bowls and serve warm.

Per Serving:
calories: 80 | fat: 5g | protein: 7g | carbs: 2g | net carbs: 2g | fiber: 1g

Cheesy Broccoli Delight Soup

Prep time: 5 minutes | Cook time: 10 minutes | Serves 4

- 2 tablespoons butter
- ⅛ cup onion, diced
- ½ teaspoon garlic powder
- ½ teaspoon salt
- ¼ teaspoon pepper
- 2 cups chicken broth
- 1 cup chopped broccoli
- 1 tablespoon cream cheese, softened
- ¼ cup heavy cream
- 1 cup shredded Cheddar cheese

1. Select the Sauté function on the Instant Pot and melt the butter. Once melted, add the onion and sauté until it becomes translucent. After that, press the Cancel button. 2. Add garlic powder, salt, pepper, broth, and broccoli to the pot, stirring to combine. 3. Close the lid securely. Press the Soup button and set the timer for 5 minutes. When the timer goes off, open the lid and stir in the heavy cream, cream cheese, and Cheddar cheese until well blended.

Per Serving:
calories: 250 | fat: 20g | protein: 9g | carbs: 4g | net carbs: 3g | fiber: 1g

Spicy Buffalo Chicken Soup

Prep time: 7 minutes | Cook time: 10 minutes | Serves 2

- 1 ounce (28 g) celery stalk, chopped
- 4 tablespoons coconut milk
- ¾ teaspoon salt
- ¼ teaspoon white pepper
- 1 cup water
- 2 ounces (57 g) Mozzarella, shredded
- 6 ounces (170 g) cooked chicken, shredded
- 2 tablespoons keto-friendly Buffalo sauce

1. Begin by placing the chopped celery stalks, coconut milk, salt, white pepper, water, and Mozzarella cheese into the Instant Pot. Stir everything together until well combined. 2. Activate the Manual mode and set the timer for 7 minutes at High Pressure. 3. Once the timer beeps, perform a quick pressure release and carefully open the lid. 4. Pour the soup into bowls and stir in the cooked chicken along with the Buffalo sauce. Serve warm for a delicious meal.

Per Serving:
calories: 287 | fat: 15g | protein: 33g | carbs: 4g | net carbs: 3g | fiber: 1g

Coconut Cauliflower Shrimp Curry Soup

Prep time: 5 minutes | Cook time: 2 hours 15 minutes | Serves 4

◆ 8 ounces water	◆ 2 tablespoons chopped fresh cilantro leaves, divided
◆ 1 (13½ounces) can unsweetened full-fat coconut milk	◆ Pink Himalayan salt
	◆ Freshly ground black pepper
◆ 2 cups riced/shredded cauliflower (I buy it pre-riced at Trader Joe's)	◆ 1 cup shrimp (I use defrosted Trader Joe's Frozen Medium Cooked Shrimp, which are peeled and deveined, with tail off)
◆ 2 tablespoons red curry paste	

1. Begin by placing the crock insert into the slow cooker and preheating it to the high setting. 2. In the insert, combine the water, coconut milk, riced cauliflower, red curry paste, and 1 tablespoon of chopped cilantro. Season the mixture with pink Himalayan salt and pepper, then stir well to incorporate all the ingredients. 3. Cover the slow cooker and allow the mixture to cook on high for 2 hours. 4. After the initial cooking time, season the shrimp with pink Himalayan salt and pepper, then add them to the slow cooker. Stir the shrimp into the soup and cook for an additional 15 minutes. 5. Once finished, ladle the soup into four bowls, garnishing each with half of the remaining 1 tablespoon of chopped cilantro before serving.

Per Serving:
calories: 269 | fat: 21g | protein: 16g | carbs: 8g | net carbs: 5g | fiber: 3g

Cheesy Mushroom Pizza Soup

Prep time: 10 minutes | Cook time: 22 minutes | Serves 3

◆ 1 teaspoon coconut oil	◆ ½ teaspoon Italian seasoning
◆ ¼ cup cremini mushrooms, sliced	
	◆ 1 teaspoon unsweetened tomato purée
◆ 5 ounces (142 g) Italian sausages, chopped	◆ 1 cup water
◆ ½ jalapeño pepper, sliced	◆ 4 ounces (113 g) Mozzarella, shredded

1. Begin by melting the coconut oil in the Instant Pot while it is set to Sauté mode. 2. Once the oil is heated, add the mushrooms and sauté them for 10 minutes until they are nicely cooked. 3. Next, incorporate the chopped sausages, sliced jalapeño, Italian seasoning, and unsweetened tomato purée. Pour in the water and stir the mixture well to ensure everything is combined. 4. Secure the lid on the Instant Pot and select Manual mode, setting the cooking time for 12 minutes on High Pressure. 5. After the timer beeps, perform a quick pressure release and carefully open the lid. 6. Serve the soup by ladling it into bowls and topping each with Mozzarella cheese. Enjoy warm!

Per Serving:
calories: 289 | fat: 23g | protein: 18g | carbs: 3g | net carbs: 2g | fiber: 0g

Spaghetti Squash Ramen Delight

Prep time: 15 minutes | Cook time: 1 hour | Serves 4

Spaghetti Squash:

◆ 1 medium (2-pound / 907-g) spaghetti squash	◆ 2 tablespoons avocado oil
	◆ Sea salt, to taste

Soup:

◆ 1 tablespoon avocado oil	◆ 8 cups chicken broth
◆ 4 cloves garlic, minced	◆ ⅓ cup coconut aminos
◆ 1 tablespoon minced fresh ginger	◆ 1 tablespoon fish sauce (optional)
◆ 2 cups (5 ounces / 142 g) shiitake mushrooms, sliced	◆ 1½ teaspoons sea salt, or to taste

Garnishes:

◆ ¼ cup (0.9 ounce / 26 g) chopped green onions	◆ 4 large eggs, soft-boiled, peeled, and cut in half

1. Begin by preheating your oven to 425°F (220°C) and lining a baking sheet with foil, lightly greasing it for easy cleanup. 2. Prepare the spaghetti squash by carefully slicing it in half using a sharp chef's knife. For easier cutting, score along the intended cut lines first before slicing. Decide whether you want longer noodles by cutting crosswise or shorter ones by cutting lengthwise, then scoop out the seeds. 3. Drizzle the inside of each squash half with avocado oil and sprinkle lightly with sea salt for flavor enhancement. 4. Place the squash halves on the lined baking sheet with the cut side facing down. Roast in the oven for 25 to 35 minutes, or until the skin can be pierced easily with a knife, indicating doneness. 5. After roasting, allow the squash to rest on the pan (cut side down, without moving) for 10 minutes. Once rested, use a fork to scrape out the strands inside the squash and set them aside. 6. While the squash is resting, start on the soup: In a large soup pot, heat oil over medium heat. 7. Add minced garlic and ginger to the pot, sautéing for about 1 minute until they become fragrant. 8. Incorporate the shiitake mushrooms, continuing to sauté for about 5 minutes, or until they soften. 9. Pour in the chicken broth, coconut aminos, and fish sauce (if using). Season with salt to taste, starting with 1 teaspoon and adjusting as needed, up to 1½ teaspoons. Bring the mixture to a boil, then lower the heat and let it simmer for 10 minutes. 10. Finally, stir in the spaghetti squash noodles and allow the soup to simmer for an additional 10 to 15 minutes, until heated through and the flavors meld together. 11. Serve the soup in bowls, garnishing with chopped green onions and soft-boiled eggs for added texture and flavor.

Per Serving:
calories: 238 | fat: 16g | protein: 10g | carbs: 10g | net carbs: 10g | fiber: 0g

Coconut Ginger Tum Yum Soup

Prep time: 10 minutes | Cook time: 20 minutes | serves 8

- 8 cups vegetable broth
- 1-inch knob fresh ginger, peeled and diced
- 2 garlic cloves, diced
- 1 teaspoon galangal
- 2 kefir lime leaves
- 1 cup coconut cream
- 1 cup sliced mushrooms
- 1 Roma tomato, coarsely chopped
- ½ yellow onion, coarsely chopped
- 1 cup coarsely chopped broccoli
- 1 cup coarsely chopped cauliflower
- 1 cup chopped fresh cilantro, for garnish
- 1 lime, cut into wedges, for garnish

1. In a large stockpot, heat the broth over medium heat until it reaches a simmer. Add the ginger, garlic, galangal, and lime leaves to infuse the flavors. 2. Stir in the coconut cream, then add the mushrooms, tomato, onion, broccoli, and cauliflower. Continue to simmer the mixture until all the vegetables are tender. 3. Once cooked, remove the pot from the heat and ladle the soup into bowls. Garnish each serving with fresh cilantro and a slice of lime before serving.

Per Serving:
calories: 97 | fat: 7g | protein: 1g | carbs: 9g | net carbs: 6g | fiber: 3g

Bone Marrow Keto Chili Delight

Prep time: 12 minutes | Cook time: 2 hours | Serves 12

- 4 slices bacon, diced
- 1 pound (454 g) 80% lean ground beef
- 1 pound (454 g) Mexican-style fresh (raw) chorizo, removed from casings
- 1 (26½ ounce / 751-g) box diced tomatoes with juices
- 1 cup tomato sauce
- ¼ cup chopped onions
- 1 red bell pepper, chopped
- 2 green chiles, chopped
- ½ cup beef bone broth, Bone Marrow:
- 8 (2-inch) cross-cut beef or veal marrow bones, split lengthwise
- 1 teaspoon fine sea salt
- homemade or store-bought
- 2 tablespoons chili powder
- 2 teaspoons minced garlic
- 2 teaspoons dried oregano leaves
- 1 teaspoon ground cumin
- ½ teaspoon cayenne pepper
- ½ teaspoon paprika
- ½ teaspoon fine sea salt
- ½ teaspoon freshly ground black pepper
- 2 bay leaves
- ½ teaspoon freshly ground black pepper
- For Garnish:
- Chopped fresh cilantro

1. In a large stockpot over medium-high heat, cook the bacon until it's crisp, then remove it from the pot and set it aside, leaving the rendered fat in the pan. Crumble the ground beef and chorizo into the hot bacon fat and cook until evenly browned, about 5 minutes. 2. Add the diced tomatoes and tomato sauce to the pot. Then, incorporate the onions, bell pepper, chiles, beef broth, and half of the reserved bacon. Season the mixture with chili powder, garlic, oregano, cumin, cayenne, paprika, salt, and pepper. Toss in the bay leaves and stir well to combine. Cover the pot and let it simmer on low heat for at least 2 hours, stirring occasionally. 3. After 2 hours, taste the chili and adjust the seasoning with additional salt, pepper, or chili powder if needed. The flavors will develop more as it simmers, so feel free to let it cook longer. Before serving, make sure to remove the bay leaves. 4. While the chili is simmering, prepare the bone marrow. Preheat your oven to 450°F (235°C). Rinse and drain the bones, patting them dry, and then season with salt and pepper. 5. Place the bones cut side up in a roasting pan and roast for 15 to 25 minutes, until the marrow has puffed slightly and is warm in the center. The timing will vary depending on the thickness of the bones; bones that are 2 inches in diameter will take closer to 15 minutes. 6. To check for doneness, insert a metal skewer into the center of a bone; it should slide in easily, and some marrow should begin to ooze out. Use a small spoon to scoop the warm marrow into each bowl of chili, and garnish with chopped cilantro before serving.

Per Serving:
calories: 366 | fat: 32g | protein: 13g | carbs: 6g | net carbs: 4g | fiber: 2g

Creamy Power Greens Soup

Prep time: 10 minutes | Cook time: 15 minutes | Serves 6

- 1 broccoli head, chopped
- 1 cup spinach
- 1 onion, chopped
- 2 garlic cloves, minced
- ½ cup watercress
- 5 cups veggie stock
- 1 cup coconut milk
- 1 tablespoon ghee
- 1 bay leaf
- Salt and black pepper, to taste

1. Start by melting the ghee in a large pot set over medium heat. Once melted, add the chopped onion and minced garlic, cooking them for about 3 minutes until fragrant. 2. Next, add the broccoli and continue cooking for an additional 5 minutes. Then, pour the stock into the pot and add the bay leaf. Close the lid, bring the mixture to a boil, and then reduce the heat to a simmer for approximately 3 minutes. 3. After simmering, incorporate the spinach and watercress, cooking for another 3 minutes until the greens are wilted. Stir in the coconut cream along with salt and black pepper to taste. Finally, discard the bay leaf and blend the soup until smooth using a hand blender.

Per Serving:
calories: 392 | fat: 38g | protein: 5g | carbs: 7g | net carbs: 6g | fiber: 1g

Creamy Cheddar Cauliflower Soup

Prep time: 5 minutes | Cook time: 20 minutes | Serves 4

◆ 1 tablespoon butter	◆ 1 cup heavy (whipping) cream
◆ ½ onion, chopped	◆ Pink Himalayan salt
◆ 2 cups riced/shredded cauliflower (I buy it pre-riced at Trader Joe's)	◆ Freshly ground pepper
◆ 1 cup chicken broth	◆ ½ cup shredded Cheddar cheese (I use sharp Cheddar)
◆ 2 ounces cream cheese	

1. In a medium saucepan over medium heat, melt the butter. Once melted, add the onion and cook, stirring occasionally, until it softens, which should take about 5 minutes. 2. Next, add the cauliflower and chicken broth, allowing the mixture to come to a boil while stirring occasionally. 3. Reduce the heat to medium-low and let it simmer until the cauliflower is tender enough to mash, approximately 10 minutes. 4. Stir in the cream cheese and mash the mixture until combined. 5. Add the cream and purée the soup using an immersion blender, or carefully transfer it to a blender, blend, and then return it to the pan to heat. 6. Season the soup with pink Himalayan salt and pepper to taste. 7. Serve the soup in four bowls, topping each with shredded Cheddar cheese before serving.

Per Serving:
calories: 372 | fat: 35g | protein: 9g | carbs: 9g | net carbs: 6g | fiber: 3g

Creamy Summer Vegetable Soup

Prep time: 10 minutes | Cook time: 6 minutes | Serves 6

◆ 3 cups finely sliced leeks	black pepper
◆ 6 cups chopped rainbow chard, stems and leaves separated	◆ 3 cups chicken broth, plus more as needed
◆ 1 cup chopped celery	◆ 2 cups sliced yellow summer squash, ½-inch slices
◆ 2 tablespoons minced garlic, divided	◆ ¼ cup chopped fresh parsley
◆ 1 teaspoon dried oregano	◆ ¾ cup heavy (whipping) cream
◆ 1 teaspoon salt	
◆ 2 teaspoons freshly ground	◆ 4 to 6 tablespoons grated Parmesan cheese

1. Place the leeks, chard, celery, 1 tablespoon of garlic, oregano, salt, pepper, and broth into the inner pot of the Instant Pot. 2. Secure the lid and select the Manual setting, adjusting the pressure to High. Cook for 3 minutes. Once cooking is complete, perform a quick release to release the pressure and unlock the lid. 3. If necessary, add more broth to achieve your desired consistency. 4. Switch the pot to the Sauté mode, setting the heat to high. Add the yellow squash, parsley, and the remaining 1 tablespoon of garlic. 5. Cook for an additional 2 to 3 minutes, allowing the squash to soften and cook through. 6. Stir in the cream, then ladle the soup into bowls. Finish by sprinkling with Parmesan cheese before serving.

Per Serving:
calories: 210 | fat: 14g | protein: 10g | carbs: 12g | net carbs: 8g | fiber: 4g

Thai Coconut Shrimp Soup with Mushrooms

Prep time: 15 minutes | Cook time: 10 minutes | Serves 6

◆ 2 tablespoons unsalted butter, divided	paste
	◆ 2 tablespoons lime juice
◆ ½ pound (227 g) medium uncooked shrimp, shelled and deveined	◆ 1 stalk lemongrass, outer stalk removed, crushed, and finely chopped
◆ ½ medium yellow onion, diced	◆ 2 tablespoons coconut aminos
◆ 2 cloves garlic, minced	◆ 1 teaspoon sea salt
◆ 1 cup sliced fresh white mushrooms	◆ ½ teaspoon ground black pepper
◆ 1 tablespoon freshly grated ginger root	◆ 13½ ounces (383 g) can unsweetened, full-fat coconut milk
◆ 4 cups chicken broth	
◆ 2 tablespoons fish sauce	◆ 3 tablespoons chopped fresh cilantro
◆ 2½ teaspoons red curry	

1. Start by selecting the Instant Pot and setting it to Sauté mode. Add 1 tablespoon of butter to the pot. 2. Once the butter has melted, toss in the shrimp and sauté for approximately 3 minutes or until they become opaque. Remove the shrimp and transfer them to a medium bowl. Set aside. 3. Next, add the remaining butter to the pot. Once melted, incorporate the onions and garlic, sautéing for about 2 minutes until the garlic is fragrant and the onions have softened. 4. Add the mushrooms, ginger root, chicken broth, fish sauce, red curry paste, lime juice, lemongrass, coconut aminos, sea salt, and black pepper into the pot. Stir well to combine all the ingredients. 5. Lock the lid in place, select Manual mode, and set the cooking time for 5 minutes on High Pressure. 6. After cooking, allow the pressure to release naturally for 5 minutes before releasing any remaining pressure. 7. Carefully open the lid and stir in the cooked shrimp and coconut milk. 8. Select Sauté mode again, bringing the soup to a boil, then press Keep Warm / Cancel. Let the soup rest in the pot for 2 minutes. 9. Finally, ladle the soup into bowls and garnish with cilantro on top. Serve hot for a delightful meal.

Per Serving:
calories: 237 | fat: 20g | protein: 9g | carbs: 9g | net carbs: 6g | fiber: 2g

Spicy Pancetta and Jalapeño Cream Soup

Prep time: 10 minutes | Cook time: 10 minutes | Serves 4

- 3 ounces (85 g) pancetta, chopped
- 1 teaspoon coconut oil
- 2 jalapeño peppers, sliced
- ½ teaspoon garlic powder
- ½ teaspoon smoked paprika
- ½ cup heavy cream
- 2 cups water
- ½ cup Monterey Jack cheese, shredded

1. Start by placing the pancetta in the Instant Pot, then add coconut oil and set to Sauté mode. Cook for 4 minutes, stirring continuously to ensure even cooking. 2. Next, incorporate the sliced jalapeños, garlic powder, and smoked paprika, sautéing for an additional minute. 3. Pour in the heavy cream and water, then add the Monterey Jack cheese, stirring thoroughly to combine all the ingredients. 4. Secure the lid on the Instant Pot, select Manual mode, and set the cooking time to High Pressure. 5. Once the timer signals completion, perform a quick pressure release before carefully opening the lid. 6. Ladle the warm soup into bowls and serve immediately.

Per Serving:
calories: 234 | fat: 20g | protein: 12g | carbs: 2g | net carbs: 1g | fiber: 0g

Creamy Chicken Thigh and Cauliflower Rice Soup

Prep time: 15 minutes | Cook time: 13 minutes | Serves 5

- 2 cups cauliflower florets
- 1 pound (454 g) boneless, skinless chicken thighs
- 4½ cups chicken broth
- ½ yellow onion, chopped
- 2 garlic cloves, minced
- 1 tablespoon unflavored gelatin powder
- 2 teaspoons sea salt
- ½ teaspoon ground black
- pepper
- ½ cup sliced zucchini
- ⅓ cup sliced turnips
- 1 teaspoon dried parsley
- 3 celery stalks, chopped
- 1 teaspoon ground turmeric
- ½ teaspoon dried marjoram
- 1 teaspoon dried thyme
- ½ teaspoon dried oregano

1. Begin by placing the cauliflower florets in a food processor and pulsing until they achieve a rice-like consistency. Set this aside for later use. 2. In the Instant Pot, combine chicken thighs, chicken broth, onions, garlic, gelatin powder, sea salt, and black pepper. Gently mix everything together. 3. Secure the lid on the Instant Pot, select Manual mode, and set the cooking time to 10 minutes on High Pressure. 4. After cooking, perform a quick pressure release and carefully open the lid. 5. Transfer the chicken thighs to a cutting board, chop them into bite-sized pieces, and return the chopped chicken to the pot. 6. Add the cauliflower rice, zucchini, turnips, parsley, celery, turmeric, marjoram, thyme, and oregano to the mixture. Stir everything to combine well. 7. Lock the lid again, select Manual mode, and set the cooking time for 3 minutes on High Pressure. 8. Once finished, quick release the pressure once more. 9. Open the lid and ladle the soup into serving bowls. Enjoy hot!

Per Serving:
calories: 247 | fat: 10g | protein: 30g | carbs: 8g | net carbs: 6g | fiber: 2g

Silky Bacon and Mushroom Soup with Egg

Prep time: 10 minutes | Cook time: 30 minutes | Serves 4

- 2 slices bacon, cut into ¼-inch dice
- 2 tablespoons minced shallots or onions
- 1 teaspoon minced garlic
- 1 pound (454 g) button mushrooms, cleaned and quartered or sliced
- 1 teaspoon dried thyme

For Garnish:
- Fresh thyme leaves
- leaves
- 2 cups chicken bone broth, homemade or store-bought
- 1 teaspoon fine sea salt
- ½ teaspoon freshly ground black pepper
- 2 large eggs
- 2 tablespoons lemon juice
- MCT oil or extra-virgin olive oil, for drizzling

1. Start by placing the diced bacon in a stockpot and sautéing it over medium heat until it turns crispy, which should take about 3 minutes. Afterward, remove the bacon from the pan but retain the drippings. 2. In the same pan with the bacon drippings, add the shallots and garlic. Sauté them over medium heat for approximately 3 minutes, or until they become softened and aromatic. 3. Next, introduce the mushrooms and dried thyme into the pan. Continue to sauté over medium heat until the mushrooms are golden brown, which should take about 10 minutes. Pour in the broth, and season with salt and pepper, then bring the mixture to a boil. 4. In a medium bowl, whisk together the eggs and lemon juice. While whisking, very gradually pour in ½ cup of the hot soup; this step is crucial to prevent the eggs from curdling. Follow up by whisking in another cup of the hot soup slowly. 5. Now, while stirring, pour the hot egg mixture back into the pot. Add the cooked bacon, then reduce the heat and let it simmer for 10 minutes, stirring constantly. The soup will thicken slightly as it cooks. Once done, remove it from the heat. Garnish the soup with fresh thyme and drizzle with MCT oil before serving. 6. This soup is best enjoyed fresh but can be stored in an airtight container in the fridge for up to 3 days. When reheating, place the soup in a saucepan over medium-low heat and stir constantly to prevent the eggs from curdling.

Per Serving:
calories: 185 | fat: 13g | protein: 11g | carbs: 6g | net carbs: 4g | fiber: 2g

Creamy Salsa Verde Chicken Soup

Prep time: 5 minutes | Cook time: 10 minutes | Serves 4

♦ ½ cup salsa verde	♦ ½ teaspoon chili powder
♦ 2 cups cooked and shredded chicken	♦ ½ teaspoon ground cumin
♦ 2 cups chicken broth	♦ ½ teaspoon fresh cilantro, chopped
♦ 1 cup shredded cheddar cheese	♦ Salt and black pepper, to taste
♦ 4 ounces cream cheese	

1. In a food processor, combine the cream cheese, salsa verde, and broth, then pulse until the mixture is smooth. Transfer this mixture to a pot and place it over medium heat. Cook until it is hot, being careful not to let it boil. 2. Add the chicken, chili powder, and cumin to the pot, cooking for about 3 to 5 minutes until everything is heated through. 3. Stir in the cheddar cheese and adjust the seasoning with salt and pepper to your liking. If the mixture is too thick, add a few tablespoons of water and continue to heat for an additional 1 to 3 minutes. Serve hot in bowls, garnished with fresh cilantro.

Per Serving:
calories: 346 | fat: 23g | protein: 25g | carbs: 4g | net carbs: 3g | fiber: 1g

Hearty Venison and Vegetable Stew

Prep time: 12 minutes | Cook time: 42 minutes | Serves 8

♦ 1 tablespoon unsalted butter	diced tomatoes
♦ 1 cup diced onions	♦ 1 teaspoon fine sea salt
♦ 2 cups button mushrooms, sliced in half	♦ 1 teaspoon ground black pepper
♦ 2 large stalks celery, cut into ¼-inch pieces	♦ ½ teaspoon dried rosemary, or 1 teaspoon fresh rosemary, finely chopped
♦ Cloves squeezed from 2 heads roasted garlic or 4 cloves garlic, minced	♦ ½ teaspoon dried thyme leaves, or 1 teaspoon fresh thyme leaves, finely chopped
♦ 2 pounds (907 g) boneless venison or beef roast, cut into 4 large pieces	♦ ½ head cauliflower, cut into large florets
♦ 5 cups beef broth	♦ Fresh thyme leaves, for garnish
♦ 1 (14½-ounce / 411-g) can	

1. Begin by placing the butter in the Instant Pot and pressing the Sauté button. Once the butter has melted, add the chopped onions and sauté for about 4 minutes, or until they become soft. 2. Next, introduce the mushrooms, celery, and garlic to the pot, sautéing

for an additional 3 minutes until the mushrooms are golden brown. After this, press Cancel to stop the Sauté function. Add the roast, broth, diced tomatoes, salt, pepper, rosemary, and thyme to the mixture. 3. Seal the lid securely, select Manual mode, and set the timer for 30 minutes. Once cooking is complete, turn the valve to venting for a quick pressure release. 4. After the initial release, add the cauliflower florets to the pot. Seal the lid again, press Manual, and set the timer for 5 minutes. Once finished, allow the pressure to release naturally. 5. Carefully remove the lid and use two forks to shred the meat in the pot. Taste the broth and adjust the seasoning with more salt if necessary. Serve the stew in bowls and garnish with fresh thyme leaves for added flavor.

Per Serving:
calories: 359 | fat: 21g | protein: 32g | carbs: 9g | net carbs: 6g | fiber: 3g

Velvety Turmeric Butternut Squash Soup

Prep time: 5 minutes | Cook time: 35 minutes | serves 8

♦ 1 small butternut squash	coarsely chopped
♦ 3 tablespoons coconut oil	♦ ½ cup dry Marsala wine (optional)
♦ 3 shallots, coarsely chopped	♦ 8 cups miso broth
♦ 1-inch knob fresh ginger, peeled and coarsely chopped	♦ 1 cup coconut cream
♦ 1-inch knob fresh turmeric root, peeled and coarsely chopped	♦ Cold-pressed olive oil, for drizzling
♦ 1 fresh lemongrass stalk,	♦ Handful toasted pumpkin seeds, for garnish (optional)

1. Begin by preheating your oven to 365°F (185°C). 2. Carefully poke the skin of the squash several times with a fork to create air vents. Place the whole squash in a baking dish and bake for about 30 minutes, or until it becomes very tender. 3. While the squash is baking, heat oil in a large stockpot over medium heat. Add shallots, ginger, turmeric, and lemongrass, sautéing until the spices are aromatic and the shallots are soft. 4. To deglaze the pot, pour in the Marsala wine (if using), stirring and scraping the bottom of the pot to release any stuck bits. Once the alcohol has reduced, add the miso broth and lower the heat. 5. Once the squash is done baking, check for tenderness by poking it with a fork. Carefully cut it in half lengthwise, allowing any liquid to drain. 6. After the squash has cooled enough to handle, scoop out the seeds and use a paring knife to remove the skin. Roughly chop the squash and add it to the stockpot. 7. Stir in the coconut cream, bring the mixture to a simmer, and then remove it from the heat. 8. Blend the soup using an immersion blender until it reaches a smooth and velvety consistency. Drizzle with olive oil and, if desired, sprinkle with toasted pumpkin seeds before serving warm.

Per Serving:
calories: 149 | fat: 13g | protein: 2g | carbs: 10g | net carbs: 9g | fiber: 1g

Creamy Broccoli and Brie Soup

Prep time: 5 minutes | Cook time: 14 minutes | Serves 6

◆ 1 tablespoon coconut oil or unsalted butter	into chunks
◆ 1 cup finely diced onions	◆ 1 cup unsweetened almond milk or heavy cream, plus more for drizzling
◆ 1 head broccoli, cut into small florets	◆ Fine sea salt and ground black pepper, to taste
◆ 2½ cups chicken broth or vegetable broth	◆ Extra-virgin olive oil, for drizzling
◆ 8 ounces (227 g) Brie cheese, cut off rind and cut	◆ Coarse sea salt, for garnish

1. Begin by adding coconut oil to the Instant Pot and selecting the Sauté function. Once the oil is hot, incorporate the onions and sauté for about 4 minutes, or until they are tender. Press Cancel to stop the Sauté function. 2. Next, mix in the broccoli and broth. Seal the lid securely, select the Manual mode, and set the timer for 10 minutes. Once cooking is complete, allow the pressure to release naturally. 3. After removing the lid, add the Brie and almond milk to the pot. Use a food processor or blender to purée the soup until smooth, or opt for a stick blender to blend it directly in the pot. 4. Adjust the seasoning with salt and pepper to taste. Serve the soup in bowls, drizzling with almond milk and olive oil, and finish with a sprinkle of coarse sea salt and freshly ground pepper.

Per Serving:
calories: 210 | fat: 16g | protein: 9g | carbs: 7g | net carbs: 6g | fiber: 1g

Creamy Chicken and Garden Vegetable Delight

Prep time: 5 minutes | Cook time: 2 minutes | Serves 4

◆ 1 pound (454 g) boneless, skinless chicken thighs, diced small	◆ 1 tablespoon powdered chicken broth base
◆ 1 (10-ounce / 283-g) bag frozen vegetables	◆ 1 teaspoon salt
◆ 2 cups water	◆ 1 teaspoon freshly ground black pepper
◆ 1 teaspoon poultry seasoning	◆ 1 cup heavy (whipping) cream

1. Place the chicken, vegetables, water, poultry seasoning, chicken broth base, salt, and pepper into the inner pot of your Instant Pot. 2. Secure the lid tightly. Select the Manual setting and set the pressure to High. Cook for 2 minutes. Once the cooking cycle is complete, perform a quick release of the pressure (you might want to release it in short bursts to prevent the soup from splattering). Carefully unlock the lid. 3. Stir in the cream and serve the soup warm. If desired, you can shred the chicken by mashing it with the back of a wooden spoon before incorporating the cream for a heartier texture.

Per Serving:
calories: 327 | fat: 19g | protein: 26g | carbs: 13g | net carbs: 10g | fiber: 3g

Savory Beef and Eggplant Tagine

Prep time: 15 minutes | Cook time: 25 minutes | Serves 6

◆ 1 pound (454 g) beef fillet, chopped	◆ 4 cups beef broth
◆ 1 eggplant, chopped	◆ 1 teaspoon ground allspices
◆ 6 ounces (170 g) scallions, chopped	◆ 1 teaspoon erythritol
	◆ 1 teaspoon coconut oil

1. Place all the ingredients into the Instant Pot and stir thoroughly to combine. 2. Secure the lid tightly. Choose Manual mode and set the cooking time for 25 minutes at High Pressure. 3. Once the timer goes off, allow for a natural pressure release for 15 minutes, then carefully release any remaining pressure. Open the lid. 4. Serve the dish warm.

Per Serving:
calories: 158 | fat: 5g | protein: 21g | carbs: 8g | net carbs: 5g | fiber: 4g

Cheesy Broccoli Bliss Soup

Prep time: 25 minutes | Cook time: 25 minutes | Serves 8

◆ 8 cups chicken broth	◆ ¼ cup heavy whipping cream
◆ 2 large heads broccoli, chopped into bite-sized florets	◆ ¼ cup shredded Cheddar cheese
◆ 1 clove garlic, peeled and minced	◆ ⅛ teaspoon salt
	◆ ⅛ teaspoon black pepper

1. In a medium pot over medium heat, pour in the broth and bring it to a boil, which should take about 5 minutes. Once boiling, add the broccoli and garlic. Reduce the heat to low, cover the pot, and let it simmer until the vegetables are completely softened, approximately 15 minutes. 2. After cooking, remove the pot from heat and use an immersion blender to blend the soup to your desired consistency, leaving some chunks for texture. 3. Place the pot back on medium heat and stir in the cream and cheese. Continue stirring for 3 to 5 minutes until everything is fully blended. Season with salt and pepper to taste. 4. Once mixed, remove the pot from the heat and allow it to cool for about 10 minutes before serving.

Per Serving:
calories: 82 | fat: 4g | protein: 5g | carbs: 8g | net carbs: 5g | fiber: 3g

Spicy Lamb and Cabbage Soup

Prep time: 5 minutes | Cook time: 25 minutes | Serves 6

♦ 1 tablespoon coconut oil	♦ 2 cups coconut milk
♦ ¾ pound ground lamb	♦ 1½ tablespoons red chili paste or as much as you want
♦ 2 cups shredded cabbage	
♦ ½ onion, chopped	
♦ 2 teaspoons minced garlic	♦ Zest and juice of 1 lime
♦ 4 cups chicken broth	♦ 1 cup shredded kale

1. Start by cooking the lamb. In a medium stockpot over medium-high heat, melt the coconut oil. Once hot, add the lamb and sauté, stirring frequently, until browned, which should take about 6 minutes. 2. Next, incorporate the vegetables. Add the cabbage, onion, and garlic to the pot, sautéing until they become tender, approximately 5 minutes. 3. Proceed to simmer the soup. Pour in the chicken broth, coconut milk, red chili paste, lime zest, and lime juice. Bring the mixture to a boil, then lower the heat and let it simmer until the cabbage is soft, about 10 minutes. 4. Introduce the kale. Stir in the kale and allow the soup to simmer for an additional 3 minutes. 5. Finally, serve the soup. Ladle it into six bowls and enjoy!

Per Serving:
calories: 380 | fat: 32g | protein: 17g | carbs: 7g | net carbs: 6g | fiber: 1g

Hearty Chicken and Zucchini Noodle Soup

Prep time: 8 minutes | Cook time: 14 minutes | Serves 6

♦ ¼ cup coconut oil or unsalted butter	♦ 6 cups chicken broth
♦ 1 cup chopped celery	♦ 1 tablespoon dried parsley
♦ ¼ cup chopped onions	♦ 1 teaspoon fine sea salt
♦ 2 cloves garlic, minced	♦ ½ teaspoon dried marjoram
♦ 1 pound (454 g) boneless, skinless chicken breasts, cut into 1-inch cubes	♦ ½ teaspoon ground black pepper
	♦ 1 bay leaf
	♦ 2 cups zucchini noodles

1. Begin by adding coconut oil to the Instant Pot and selecting the Sauté function. Once the oil has melted, incorporate the celery, onions, and garlic, cooking while stirring occasionally for about 4 minutes, or until the onions become tender. Press Cancel to stop the Sauté process. 2. Next, add cubed chicken, broth, parsley, salt, marjoram, pepper, and a bay leaf into the pot. Secure the lid, choose the Manual setting, and set the timer for 10 minutes. After cooking, allow the pressure to release naturally. 3. Once the lid is removed, stir the contents well. Portion out ⅓ cup of noodles into bowls and ladle the soup over the noodles. Serve immediately, as letting it sit too long will cause the noodles to become overly soft.

Per Serving:
calories: 253 | fat: 15g | protein: 21g | carbs: 11g | net carbs: 10g | fiber: 1g

Savory Beef Meatball Minestrone

Prep time: 5 minutes | Cook time: 35 minutes | Serves 6

♦ 1 pound (454 g) ground beef	♦ 2 garlic cloves, minced
♦ 1 large egg	♦ ½ medium yellow onion, minced
♦ 1½ tablespoons golden flaxseed meal	
♦ ⅓ cup shredded Mozzarella cheese	♦ ¼ cup pancetta, diced
	♦ 1 cup sliced yellow squash
♦ ¼ cup unsweetened tomato purée	♦ 1 cup sliced zucchini
	♦ ½ cup sliced turnips
♦ 1½ tablespoons Italian seasoning, divided	♦ 4 cups beef broth
♦ 1½ teaspoons garlic powder, divided	♦ 14 ounces (397 g) can diced tomatoes
	♦ ½ teaspoon ground black pepper
♦ 1½ teaspoons sea salt, divided	♦ 3 tablespoons shredded Parmesan cheese
♦ 1 tablespoon olive oil	

1. Start by preheating your oven to 400°F (205°C) and prepare a large baking sheet by lining it with aluminum foil. 2. In a sizable mixing bowl, combine ground beef, egg, flaxseed meal, Mozzarella cheese, unsweetened tomato purée, ½ tablespoon of Italian seasoning, ½ teaspoon of garlic powder, and ½ teaspoon of sea salt. Mix thoroughly until all ingredients are well incorporated. 3. Form the mixture into meatballs, using about 1 heaping tablespoon of the mixture for each. Place the formed meatballs onto the prepared baking sheet. 4. Bake the meatballs in the preheated oven for 15 minutes, then remove them and set aside. 5. Next, set the Instant Pot to Sauté mode. Once it's hot, pour in the olive oil and add the garlic, onion, and pancetta. Sauté for about 2 minutes until the garlic is fragrant and the onions are starting to soften. 6. Introduce the yellow squash, zucchini, and turnips to the pot, continuing to sauté for another 3 minutes. 7. Pour in the beef broth, diced tomatoes, black pepper, and the remaining garlic powder, sea salt, and Italian seasoning. Stir everything together, then gently place the meatballs into the mixture. 8. Secure the lid on the Instant Pot. Select Manual mode and set the timer for 15 minutes on High Pressure. 9. Once cooking is finished, let the pressure release naturally for 10 minutes before releasing any remaining pressure. 10. Carefully open the lid and stir the soup gently. Serve the soup hot in bowls, topped with Parmesan cheese.

Per Serving:
calories: 373 | fat: 19g | protein: 35g | carbs: 15g | net carbs: 11g | fiber: 4g

Creamy Chicken Cauliflower Soup

Prep time: 5 minutes | Cook time: 20 minutes | Serves 4

◆ 4 tablespoons butter	◆ ¼ teaspoon dried parsley
◆ ¼ cup diced onion	◆ 1 bay leaf
◆ 2 stalks celery, chopped	◆ 2 cups chicken broth
◆ ½ cup fresh spinach	◆ 2 cups diced cooked chicken
◆ ½ teaspoon salt	◆ ¾ cup uncooked cauliflower rice
◆ ¼ teaspoon pepper	
◆ ¼ teaspoon dried thyme	◆ ½ teaspoon xanthan gum (optional)

1. Begin by pressing the Sauté button on the Instant Pot and melting the butter. Once melted, add the onions and sauté until they turn translucent. Next, incorporate the celery and spinach, cooking for 2 to 3 minutes until the spinach wilts. Press the Cancel button to stop the sautéing process. 2. Next, sprinkle the seasoning into the pot along with the bay leaf, broth, and the previously cooked chicken. Secure the lid and close it tightly. Press the Soup button and set the cooking time for 10 minutes. 3. When the timer beeps, perform a quick pressure release and then add the cauliflower rice. Keep the Instant Pot on the Keep Warm setting for an additional 10 minutes to fully cook the cauliflower rice. Serve the soup warm. 4. If you desire a thicker consistency, stir in some xanthan gum before serving.

Per Serving:

calories: 228 | fat: 14g | protein: 22g | carbs: 3g | net carbs: 2g | fiber: 1g

Spicy Chicken Enchilada Soup

Prep time: 10 minutes | Cook time: 40 minutes | Serves 6

◆ 2 (6-ounce / 170-g) boneless, skinless chicken breasts	◆ 2 cups chicken broth
	◆ ⅛ cup pickled jalapeños
◆ ½ tablespoon chili powder	◆ 4 ounces (113 g) cream cheese
◆ ½ teaspoon salt	
◆ ½ teaspoon garlic powder	◆ 1 cup uncooked cauliflower rice
◆ ¼ teaspoon pepper	◆ 1 avocado, diced
◆ ½ cup red enchilada sauce	◆ 1 cup shredded mild Cheddar cheese
◆ ½ medium onion, diced	
◆ 1 (4-ounce / 113-g) can green chilies	◆ ½ cup sour cream

1. Season the chicken breasts with the seasoning blend and set them aside. Pour the enchilada sauce into the Instant Pot, then place the seasoned chicken on top of the sauce. 2. Add the onion, chilies, broth, and jalapeños to the pot, and place the cream cheese on top of the chicken breasts. Close the lid securely. Set the cooking time to 25 minutes. When the timer goes off, perform a quick release of the pressure and shred the chicken using forks. 3. Stir the mixture well and add the cauliflower rice while the pot is set to Keep Warm. Cover the pot again and let it sit for 15 minutes on the Keep Warm setting to cook the cauliflower rice. Serve with toppings of avocado, Cheddar cheese, and sour cream.

Per Serving:

calories: 318 | fat: 19g | protein: 21g | carbs: 10g | net carbs: 7g | fiber: 3g

Mediterranean Cioppino Seafood Stew

Prep time: 10 minutes | Cook time: 30 minutes | Serves 6

◆ 2 tablespoons olive oil	◆ 2 teaspoons chopped fresh oregano
◆ ½ onion, chopped	
◆ 2 celery stalks, sliced	◆ ½ teaspoon sea salt
◆ 1 red bell pepper, chopped	◆ ½ teaspoon freshly ground black pepper
◆ 1 tablespoon minced garlic	
◆ 2 cups fish stock	◆ ¼ teaspoon red pepper flakes
◆ 1 (15-ounce) can coconut milk	◆ 10 ounces salmon, cut into 1-inch pieces
◆ 1 cup crushed tomatoes	◆ ½ pound shrimp, peeled and deveined
◆ 2 tablespoons tomato paste	
◆ 1 tablespoon chopped fresh basil	◆ 12 clams or mussels, cleaned and debearded but in the shell

1. Begin by sautéing the vegetables. In a large stockpot over medium-high heat, add the olive oil. Once hot, toss in the onion, celery, red bell pepper, and garlic, sautéing for about 4 minutes until the vegetables have softened. 2. Next, prepare the soup base. Pour in the fish stock, coconut milk, crushed tomatoes, and tomato paste. Season with basil, oregano, salt, pepper, and red pepper flakes. Bring the mixture to a boil, then lower the heat to a simmer and cook for 10 minutes. 3. Now, incorporate the seafood. Add the salmon and allow it to simmer until it becomes opaque, approximately 5 minutes. Then, introduce the shrimp, cooking until they are nearly done, about 3 minutes. Finally, add the mussels and let them simmer until they open up, which should take about 3 minutes. Discard any mussels that remain closed. 4. To finish, ladle the soup into bowls and serve it hot.

Per Serving:

calories: 377 | fat: 29g | protein: 24g | carbs: 9g | net carbs: 7g | fiber: 2g

Savory Sausage Zoodle Broth

Prep time: 10 minutes | Cook time: 25 minutes | Serves 8

◆ 1 tablespoon olive oil	◆ 3 cups regular beef broth
◆ 4 cloves garlic, minced	◆ 3 cups beef bone broth
◆ 1 pound (454 g) pork sausage (no sugar added)	◆ 2 medium zucchini (6 ounces / 170 g each), spiralized
◆ ½ tablespoon Italian seasoning	

1. Start by heating the oil in a large soup pot over medium heat. Once the oil is warm, add the garlic and sauté for about 1 minute until it becomes fragrant. 2. Next, add the sausage to the pot and raise the heat to medium-high. Cook for approximately 10 minutes, stirring occasionally and breaking the sausage into small pieces until it is nicely browned. 3. After browning the sausage, incorporate the seasoning along with both the regular broth and bone broth. Allow the mixture to simmer for 10 minutes. 4. Finally, add the zucchini to the pot. Bring the soup back to a simmer and let it cook for about 2 minutes, or until the zucchini is tender. Be careful not to overcook the zoodles, as they can become mushy.

Per Serving:

calories: 216 | fat: 17g | protein: 12g | carbs: 2g | net carbs: 2g | fiber: 0g

Zesty Avocado-Lime Vegetable Soup

Prep time: 5 minutes | Cook time: 20 minutes | serves 8

◆ 2 tablespoons cold-pressed olive oil	◆ ½ cup chopped fresh cilantro
◆ ½ yellow onion, chopped	◆ ½ cup chopped celery
◆ 1 teaspoon ground cumin	◆ ½ jalapeño pepper, chopped
◆ 1 teaspoon ground coriander	◆ 8 cups vegetable broth
◆ 1 teaspoon chili powder	◆ Juice of 2 limes
◆ ¼ cup hemp hearts	◆ 1 avocado, peeled, pitted, and cut into cubes
◆ 1 medium tomato, chopped	
◆ 1 cup chopped cabbage (set some aside for garnish)	◆ 3 flax crackers

1. Begin by heating olive oil in a large stockpot over medium heat. Once hot, add the onion along with cumin, coriander, and chili powder. Sauté while stirring occasionally for about 5 minutes until the onion softens. 2. Next, incorporate the hemp hearts, tomato, cabbage, cilantro, celery, and jalapeño into the pot. Stir well to ensure the spices coat the vegetables, allowing them to cook for an additional 4 minutes. 3. Pour the broth into the pot, then reduce the heat and let the mixture simmer on low for 20 minutes. 4. After simmering, remove the pot from the heat and mix in the lime juice for added flavor. 5. Distribute the diced avocado evenly among four serving bowls. 6. Ladle the hot soup over the avocado in each bowl, and finish by garnishing with extra cabbage and cilantro. 7. For a "tortilla soup" feel, break the flax crackers over the top of each bowl before serving.

Per Serving:

calories: 130 | fat: 9g | protein: 3g | carbs: 9g | net carbs: 5g | fiber: 4g

Hearty Vegetable & Cabbage Soup

Prep time: 20 minutes | Cook time: 30 minutes | Serves 6

◆ 1 tablespoon olive oil	◆ 2 tablespoons tomato paste
◆ 3 garlic cloves, minced	◆ 2 (32-ounce / 907-g) cartons chicken broth
◆ 1 onion, diced	
◆ 3 carrots, diced	◆ 1 large head cabbage, chopped
◆ 1 celery stalk, diced	
◆ ½ green bell pepper, diced	◆ 1 teaspoon dried oregano
◆ Salt and freshly ground black pepper, to taste	◆ 1 teaspoon dried thyme
	◆ Grated Parmesan cheese, for topping
◆ 1 cup chopped kale	

1. Begin by heating olive oil in a large saucepan over medium heat. 2. Once the oil is hot, add the minced garlic and chopped onion. Sauté them together for about 5 minutes until they become fragrant and the onion softens. 3. Next, incorporate the diced carrots and celery into the pan. Cook for an additional 5 to 7 minutes until these vegetables are tender. 4. Stir in the chopped bell pepper and mix well. Continue cooking for another 5 to 7 minutes until the pepper softens. Season the mixture with salt and pepper, then add the chopped kale. 5. Mix in the tomato paste, ensuring everything is well combined. 6. Gradually pour in the chicken broth and bring the soup to a gentle boil. 7. Add the shredded cabbage, dried oregano, and thyme. Adjust the seasoning with more salt and pepper to taste. Lower the heat to a simmer, cover the pan, and allow the soup to cook for 15 minutes, or longer if you have extra time. 8. Once ready, ladle the soup into bowls and sprinkle with freshly grated Parmesan cheese before serving.

Per Serving:

calories: 156 | fat: 5g | protein: 10g | carbs: 23g | net carbs: 16g | fiber: 7g

Creamy Tomato-Basil Parmesan Bliss

Prep time: 5 minutes | Cook time: 12 minutes | Serves 12

- 2 tablespoons unsalted butter or coconut oil
- ½ cup finely diced onions
- Cloves squeezed from 1 head roasted garlic , or 2 cloves garlic, minced
- 1 tablespoon dried basil leaves
- 1 teaspoon dried oregano leaves
- 1 (8 ounces / 227 g) package cream cheese, softened
- 4 cups chicken broth
- 2 (14½ ounces / 411 g) cans diced tomatoes
- 1 cup shredded Parmesan cheese, plus more for garnish
- 1 teaspoon fine sea salt
- ¼ teaspoon ground black pepper
- Fresh basil leaves, for garnish

1. Begin by adding butter to the Instant Pot and selecting the Sauté function. Once the butter is melted, incorporate the onions, garlic, basil, and oregano, cooking for about 4 minutes or until the onions become soft, stirring frequently. Press Cancel to stop the Sauté process. 2. Introduce cream cheese into the pot, using a whisk to break it up and incorporate it smoothly. This step is crucial to avoid clumps in your soup. Gradually whisk in the broth, followed by the tomatoes, Parmesan cheese, salt, and pepper, stirring until everything is well combined. 3. Secure the lid on the Instant Pot, select Manual mode, and set the timer for 8 minutes. Once the cooking time is complete, carefully turn the valve to venting for a quick release of pressure. 4. After removing the lid, purée the soup using an immersion blender until smooth. Alternatively, you can transfer the soup in batches to a regular blender or food processor to achieve a silky texture. Be cautious not to overfill the blender, as this could hinder the puréeing process. 5. Taste the soup and adjust the seasoning with additional salt and pepper if needed. Serve the soup in bowls, garnishing with extra Parmesan cheese and fresh basil leaves for added flavor and presentation.

Per Serving:
calories: 146 | fat: 10g | protein: 8g | carbs: 4g | net carbs: 3g | fiber: 1g

Coconut Curry Broccoli Bliss Soup

Prep time: 10 minutes | Cook time: 20 minutes | Serves 4

- 4 tablespoons butter
- 1 celery stalk, diced
- 1 carrot, diced
- ½ onion, diced
- 1 garlic clove, minced
- 2 tablespoons curry powder
- 1 teaspoon red pepper flakes
- 3 cups chicken broth
- 2 cups broccoli florets
- 1 cup canned coconut cream
- Salt and freshly ground black pepper, to taste

1. In a large saucepan over medium heat, begin by melting the butter until it's fully liquefied. 2. Next, add the celery, carrot, onion, garlic, curry powder, and red pepper flakes to the pot. Stir everything together and sauté for about 5 to 7 minutes, or until the vegetables have softened significantly. 3. Pour in the chicken broth and bring the mixture to a gentle simmer, allowing the flavors to meld. 4. Once simmering, add the broccoli and continue to simmer for another 5 to 7 minutes until the broccoli is tender. 5. Finally, stir in the coconut cream and let it simmer for an additional 5 to 10 minutes until everything is thoroughly heated and the broccoli is fully cooked. Season generously with salt and pepper to taste before serving hot. Store any leftovers in an airtight container in the refrigerator for up to 1 week.

Per Serving:
calories: 274 | fat: 25g | protein: 7g | carbs: 11g | net carbs: 8g | fiber: 3g

Chapter

10

Desserts

Chapter 10 Desserts

Decadent Cocoa Coconut Muffins

Prep time: 5 minutes | Cook time: 25 minutes | Serves 5

- ½ cup coconut flour
- 2 tablespoons cocoa powder
- 3 tablespoons erythritol
- 1 teaspoon baking powder
- 2 tablespoons coconut oil
- 2 eggs, beaten
- ½ cup coconut shred

1. In a mixing bowl, combine all the ingredients thoroughly until well blended. 2. Pour the mixture into the muffin molds and place them in the air fryer basket. 3. Set the air fryer to cook the muffins at 350°F (177°C) for 25 minutes.

Per Serving:
calories: 182 | fat: 14g | protein: 6g | carbs: 12g | net carbs: 5g | fiber: 7g

Decadent Keto Birthday Cheesecake

Prep time: 30 minutes | Cook time: 1 hour | Serves 16

Crust

- 2 cups blanched almond flour
- ⅓ cup unsalted butter, melted

Cheesecake Filling

- 32 ounces full-fat cream cheese, softened
- ¾ cup full-fat sour cream
- 1¼ cups 0g net carb sweetener
- 3 tablespoons 0g net carb sweetener
- 1 teaspoon pure vanilla extract
- 3 large eggs, room temperature
- 1 tablespoon lemon juice
- 1½ teaspoons pure vanilla extract

1. Begin by preheating your oven to 350°F. 2. Generously coat the sides of a 9-inch springform pan with cooking spray. Cut a piece of parchment paper to fit the bottom and grease it lightly as well. 3. For the crust, combine almond flour, melted butter, sweetener, and vanilla in a medium bowl. The mixture should appear crumbly. Evenly spread and firmly press the crust into the bottom of the prepared pan. Bake for 10 to 15 minutes or until it turns a golden brown color. 4. In a large mixing bowl, use an electric mixer to combine softened cream cheese, sour cream, and sweetener at a low speed, minimizing bubbles in the mixture. Add the eggs one by one, stopping occasionally to scrape down the sides of the bowl to ensure everything is fully blended. Finally, mix in lemon juice and vanilla extract until smooth. 5. Carefully pour the cream cheese batter over the baked crust and smooth out the top. Bake for 50 to 60 minutes, or until the center is nearly set. 6. Once baked, take the cheesecake out of the oven and run a sharp knife around the edges to loosen it. Allow it to cool for 10 minutes before refrigerating it in the pan for at least 4 hours. When you are ready to serve, carefully remove the cheesecake from the pan.

Per Serving:
calories: 343 | fat: 28g | protein: 9g | carbs: 8g | net carbs: 7g | fiber: 1g

Cinnamon Hazelnut Bliss Cookies

Prep time: 30 minutes | Cook time: 20 minutes | Serves 10

- 4 tablespoons liquid monk fruit
- ½ cup hazelnuts, ground
- 1 stick butter, room temperature
- 2 cups almond flour
- 1 cup coconut flour
- 2 ounces (57 g) granulated Swerve
- 2 teaspoons ground cinnamon

1. Begin by creaming the liquid monk fruit and butter together until the mixture is light and fluffy. Sift both types of flour into the bowl. 2. Next, fold in the hazelnuts. Knead the mixture until it forms a cohesive dough, then wrap it in plastic and refrigerate for approximately 35 minutes. 3. Once chilled, portion the dough into small balls and place them on a baking sheet. Use the back of a spoon to gently flatten each ball. 4. Combine granulated Swerve with ground cinnamon in a small bowl. Roll each cookie in the cinnamon mixture until fully coated. 5. Bake the cookies for 20 minutes at a temperature of 310°F (154°C). 6. Allow the cookies to cool on the baking sheet for about 10 minutes before transferring them to a wire rack to cool completely. Enjoy your delicious treats!

Per Serving:
calories: 244 | fat: 24g | protein: 5g | carbs: 6g | net carbs: 2g | fiber: 4g

Low-Carb Cream Cheese Delight

Prep time: 10 minutes | Cook time: 40 minutes | Serves 4

Crust:

♦ ⅔ cup almond flour	♦ ⅛ teaspoon ground cinnamon
♦ 2 teaspoons granulated erythritol	♦ 2 tablespoons butter, melted
♦ ¼ teaspoon psyllium husk powder	♦ 1½ teaspoons heavy (whipping) cream

Filling:

♦ 8 ounces (227 g) full-fat cream cheese, at room temperature	♦ 2 tablespoons sour cream
	♦ ¼ teaspoon freshly squeezed lemon juice
♦ 1 large egg	♦ ½ teaspoon liquid stevia
♦ 2 tablespoons granulated erythritol	♦ Pinch of pink Himalayan sea salt

1. Start by preheating your oven to 325ºF (163ºC). 2. To prepare the crust, mix almond flour, erythritol, psyllium husk powder, and cinnamon in a small bowl until well combined. 3. Incorporate the butter and cream into the dry mixture using a fork until fully blended. 4. Press the mixture into the bottom of a 7-inch springform pan, spreading it evenly. 5. Use a fork or your fingers to firmly pack the crust without extending it up the sides of the pan. 6. For the filling, in a large mixing bowl, use a whisk or a hand mixer on medium-high speed to combine cream cheese, egg, erythritol, sour cream, lemon juice, stevia, and salt until smooth. 7. Carefully pour the filling mixture directly over the crust. 8. Bake in the preheated oven for 38 to 40 minutes, or until the edges are slightly golden. 9. After baking, remove the cheesecake from the oven and allow it to cool for 1 hour. Release the springform pan and place the cheesecake in the refrigerator to chill for at least 1 hour. 10. Once chilled, slice the cheesecake into 4 pieces and serve.

Per Serving:

calories: 373 | fat: 36g | protein: 9g | carbs: 6g | net carbs: 4g | fiber: 2g

Zesty Olive Oil Orange Cupcakes

Prep time: 15 minutes | Cook time: 20 minutes | Makes 6 cupcakes

♦ 1 large egg	♦ Zest of 1 orange
♦ 2 tablespoons powdered sugar-free sweetener (such as stevia or monk fruit extract)	♦ 1 cup almond flour
	♦ ¾ teaspoon baking powder
	♦ ⅛ teaspoon salt
♦ ½ cup extra-virgin olive oil	♦ 1 tablespoon freshly squeezed orange juice
♦ 1 teaspoon almond extract	

1. Begin by preheating your oven to 350ºF (180ºC). Line 6 cups of a muffin tin with muffin liners. 2. In a large mixing bowl, whisk together the egg and powdered sweetener until well combined. Add olive oil, almond extract, and orange zest, and whisk until the mixture is smooth. 3. In a separate small bowl, mix almond flour, baking powder, and salt. Gradually add this dry mixture to the wet ingredients, along with the orange juice, stirring gently until just combined. 4. Evenly distribute the batter into the 6 muffin cups and bake for 15 to 18 minutes, or until a toothpick inserted into the center comes out clean. 5. Once baked, remove the muffins from the oven and let them cool in the tin for 5 minutes before transferring them to a wire rack to cool completely.

Per Serving:

1 cup cake: calories: 305 | fat: 28g | protein: 6g | carbs: 10g | net carbs: 4g | fiber: 6g

Fluffy Toasted Coconut Marshmallows

Prep time: 15 minutes | Cook time: 15 minutes | Serves 16

♦ ½ cup (50 g) toasted unsweetened shredded coconut, divided	♦ 1 cup (160 g) confectioners'-style erythritol
♦ 1 cup (240 ml) water, divided	♦ 2 teaspoons vanilla extract
♦ 3 tablespoons unflavored gelatin	♦ ¼ teaspoon finely ground gray sea salt

1. Start by lining an 8-inch (20-cm) square pan with parchment paper, allowing the ends to hang over the sides for easy removal. Evenly sprinkle ¼ cup (25 g) of toasted coconut into the pan. 2. Attach the whisk attachment to your hand mixer or stand mixer. 3. In the mixing bowl, pour ½ cup (120 ml) of water and sprinkle the gelatin on top. Allow it to sit undisturbed while you prepare the other ingredients. 4. In a small saucepan, combine the remaining ½ cup (120 ml) of water, erythritol, vanilla extract, and salt. Heat the mixture over medium heat, stirring occasionally until it reaches a rapid boil, then immediately remove it from the heat to prevent overflow. Lower the heat and maintain a gentle boil for 5 minutes. 5. Carefully pour the hot liquid into the bowl with the gelatin. Increase the mixer speed to high and whip for 6 to 7 minutes until the mixture becomes thick and fluffy, resembling marshmallow fluff. Be cautious not to overbeat, as it may become too stiff. 6. Once thickened, pour the mixture into the prepared pan and top with the remaining ¼ cup (25 g) of toasted coconut. 7. Use the back of a spatula to smooth the marshmallow fluff. Alternatively, grease your hands with a little coconut oil and spread the fluff with your palms. 8. Allow the marshmallows to set at room temperature for 1 to 2 hours until firm. Once set, cut into 1-inch (2.5-cm) squares and enjoy!

Per Serving:

calories: 30 | fat: 2g | protein: 2g | carbs: 1g | net carbs: 0g | fiber: 1g

Refreshing Electrolyte Gelatin Bites

Prep time: 5 minutes | Cook time: 0 minutes | Makes 10 gummies

- 1 cup cold water
- 2 tablespoons unflavored gelatin
- 2 packets/scoops flavored electrolyte powder

Stovetop Instructions 1. In a small pot, combine water and gelatin, stirring until fully blended. Place over medium heat and allow to warm for approximately 5 minutes until it starts to bubble gently. Incorporate your desired flavoring and mix thoroughly until smooth. 2. Transfer the liquid into silicone molds and place them in the refrigerator for 30 to 40 minutes, or until the mixture is firm. 3. Carefully remove the gummies from the molds and savor the treat! Microwave Instructions 1. Pour the water into a microwave-safe bowl or measuring cup with a pouring spout. 2. Add the gelatin and mix until it dissolves, then microwave for 2 minutes or until it begins to steam. 3. Stir in your chosen flavoring and mix until thoroughly combined. 4. Pour the resulting mixture into silicone molds and chill in the refrigerator for 30 to 40 minutes, or until set. 5. Remove the gummies from the molds and enjoy! Keep in an airtight container in the fridge for up to 3 weeks.

Per Serving:
1 gummy: calories: 4 | fat: 0g | protein: 1g | carbs: 0g | net carbs: 0g | fiber: 0g

Light and Fluffy Coconut Flour Delight

Prep time: 10 minutes | Cook time: 25 minutes | Serves 6

- 2 tablespoons salted butter, melted
- ⅓ cup coconut flour
- 2 large eggs, whisked
- ½ cup granular erythritol
- 1 teaspoon baking powder
- 1 teaspoon vanilla extract
- ½ cup sour cream

1. In a large bowl, combine all the ingredients until well mixed. Pour the batter into a round nonstick baking dish that hasn't been greased. 2. Carefully place the baking dish into the air fryer basket. Set the temperature to 300°F (149°C) and cook for 25 minutes. The top of the cake should turn a dark golden color, and a toothpick inserted into the center should come out clean when it's finished baking. 3. Allow the cake to cool in the dish for 15 minutes before slicing and serving.

Per Serving:
calories: 142 | fat: 10g | protein: 4g | carbs: 8g | net carbs: 4g | fiber: 4g

Coconut-Chocolate Almond Bliss Bites

Prep time: 5 minutes | Cook time: 10 minutes | Makes 10 balls

- 1 cup almond butter
- 1 large egg
- 1 teaspoon vanilla extract
- ¼ cup low-carb protein powder
- ¼ cup powdered erythritol
- ¼ cup shredded unsweetened coconut
- ¼ cup low-carb, sugar-free chocolate chips
- ½ teaspoon ground cinnamon

1. In a spacious bowl, combine almond butter and egg, mixing until well blended. Then, add vanilla extract, protein powder, and erythritol to the mixture. 2. Gently fold in shredded coconut, chocolate chips, and cinnamon until evenly incorporated. Roll the mixture into 1-inch balls and arrange them in a round baking pan, which can then be placed in the air fryer basket. 3. Set the air fryer to 320°F (160°C) and cook the balls for 10 minutes. 4. Once done, let them cool completely before storing in an airtight container in the refrigerator, where they will stay fresh for up to 4 days.

Per Serving:
calories: 199 | fat: 16g | protein: 7g | carbs: 7g | net carbs: 3g | fiber: 4g

Almond Flour Egg Custard Tarts

Prep time: 10 minutes | Cook time: 20 minutes | Serves 2

- ¼ cup almond flour
- 1 tablespoon coconut oil
- 2 egg yolks
- ¼ cup coconut milk
- 1 tablespoon erythritol
- 1 teaspoon vanilla extract
- 1 cup water, for cooking

1. Begin by preparing the dough: combine almond flour and coconut oil in a mixing bowl until well blended. 2. Next, press the dough firmly into 2 mini tart molds, shaping them into cup-like forms. 3. Add water to the Instant Pot and insert the steamer rack. 4. Carefully place the filled tart molds onto the steamer rack in the Instant Pot. Securely close and seal the lid. 5. Set the Instant Pot to Manual mode and cook for 3 minutes at High Pressure, followed by a quick release of the pressure. 6. In a separate bowl, whisk together vanilla extract, erythritol, coconut milk, and egg yolks until fully combined. 7. Pour the mixture into the tart molds, ensuring they are filled evenly, then close the lid again. 8. Cook the dessert for an additional 7 minutes on Manual mode at High Pressure. 9. Once the cooking time is complete, allow for a natural pressure release for an extra 10 minutes before opening the lid.

Per Serving:
calories: 208 | fat: 20g | protein: 4g | carbs: 3g | net carbs: 2g | fiber: 1g

Easy Almond Butter Bliss Cookies

Prep time: 5 minutes | Cook time: 14 minutes | Makes 12 cookies

- ½ cup (1 stick) salted butter, softened
- 1½ cups finely ground blanched almond flour
- ¼ teaspoon salt
- ½ cup granular erythritol
- ½ teaspoon vanilla extract
- 1 large egg
- ⅛ teaspoon liquid stevia

1. Begin by preheating your oven to 350°F (175°C) and lining a baking sheet with parchment paper. 2. In a medium mixing bowl, combine all the ingredients. Using a hand mixer, start blending on low speed, then gradually increase to medium speed, mixing until everything is thoroughly combined. 3. With a small cookie scoop, portion the dough onto the prepared baking sheet, leaving 2 inches of space between each cookie. Use the back of a fork to create crisscross patterns on top of each cookie. 4. Bake in the preheated oven for 12 to 14 minutes, or until the edges of the cookies begin to turn light brown. Allow the cookies to cool completely on the baking sheet before removing them, as they will continue to firm up as they cool. Store any leftovers in an airtight container at room temperature for up to a week.

Per Serving:
calories: 297 | fat: 29g | protein: 3g | carbs: 4g | net carbs: 2g | fiber: 3g

Pecan Bourbon Delight Bites

Prep time: 20 minutes | Cook time: 3 minutes | Makes 12 balls

- ½ cup (1 stick) salted butter, softened
- 1 cup confectioners'-style erythritol
- 3 tablespoons bourbon
- ½ teaspoon vanilla extract
- ¼ cup chopped raw pecans
- ¾ cup sugar-free chocolate chips
- 1 tablespoon avocado oil
- 12 raw pecan halves, for garnish

1. In a mixing bowl, use a hand mixer on medium speed to cream together the butter and erythritol until the mixture is pale yellow and fluffy. Stir in the bourbon, vanilla extract, and pecans until well incorporated. Transfer the mixture to the refrigerator for 30 minutes to chill, making it easier to shape. 2. In a small microwave-safe bowl, combine the chocolate chips and oil. Microwave in 30-second intervals, stirring after each interval, until melted and smooth. 3. Prepare 12 foil candy cups or line a tray with parchment paper. Remove the chilled pecan mixture from the refrigerator and roll 1-tablespoon scoops into 1-inch balls. Using a spoon, dip each ball into the melted chocolate to coat, then place them in the candy cups or on the lined tray. Garnish each ball with a pecan half on top. 4. Refrigerate the chocolate-covered balls for at least 1 hour before serving. Allow them to sit at room temperature for 10 minutes to soften before enjoying. Store any leftovers in an airtight container in the refrigerator for up to 2 weeks.

Per Serving:
calories: 117 | fat: 11g | protein: 0g | carbs: 3g | net carbs: 1g | fiber: 2g

Creamy Cheesecake Poppers

Prep time: 30 minutes | Cook time: 2 minutes | Makes 16 bites

- 8 ounces (227 g) cream cheese, softened
- ½ cup plus 2 tablespoons Swerve, divided
- 4 tablespoons heavy cream, divided
- ½ teaspoon vanilla extract
- ½ cup almond flour

1. In a stand mixer fitted with a paddle attachment, combine the cream cheese, ½ cup of Swerve, 2 tablespoons of heavy cream, and vanilla extract. Beat until the mixture is smooth. Use a small ice cream scoop to portion the mixture into 16 balls and place them on a rimmed baking sheet lined with parchment paper. Freeze for 45 minutes until they are firm. 2. While the cheesecake balls are freezing, line the air fryer basket with parchment paper and preheat the air fryer to 350°F (177°C). 3. In a small shallow bowl, mix the almond flour with the remaining 2 tablespoons of Swerve. 4. In another small shallow bowl, pour in the remaining 2 tablespoons of cream. 5. Take each frozen cheesecake ball and dip it into the cream, then roll it in the almond flour mixture, pressing gently to create an even coating. Arrange the coated balls in a single layer in the air fryer basket, ensuring there is space between them. Air fry for 2 minutes, or until the coating is lightly browned.

Per Serving:
calories: 99 | fat: 9g | protein: 2g | carbs: 3g | net carbs: 2g | fiber: 1g

Decadent Almond Cocoa Fat Bombs

Prep time: 3 minutes | Cook time: 3 minutes | Serves 6

- ¼ cup coconut oil
- ¼ cup no-sugar-added almond butter
- 2 tablespoons cacao powder
- ¼ cup powdered erythritol

1. Press the Sauté button on the Instant Pot and add coconut oil. Allow the coconut oil to melt completely, then press the Cancel button. Stir in the remaining ingredients; the mixture will be liquid. 2. Carefully pour the mixture into 6 silicone molds and place them in the freezer for 30 minutes, or until set. Once firm, store the molds in the refrigerator.

Per Serving:
calories: 142 | fat: 14g | protein: 3g | carbs: 9g | net carbs: 7g | fiber: 2g

Decadent Chocolate Walnut Delight

Prep time: 10 minutes | Cook time: 20 minutes | Serves 6

◆ 1 cup almond flour	◆ 3 eggs
◆ ⅔ cup Swerve	◆ ⅓ cup heavy (whipping) cream
◆ ¼ cup unsweetened cocoa powder	◆ ¼ cup coconut oil
◆ ¼ cup chopped walnuts	◆ Nonstick cooking spray
◆ 1 teaspoon baking powder	

1. In a large bowl, combine flour, Swerve, cocoa powder, walnuts, baking powder, eggs, cream, and coconut oil. Use a hand mixer on high speed to mix the ingredients until fluffy and well incorporated, ensuring the cake remains light and not too dense. 2. Grease a heatproof pan, such as a 3-cup Bundt pan, that fits inside your Instant Pot with cooking spray. Pour the cake batter into the pan and cover it with aluminum foil. 3. Add 2 cups of water to the inner cooking pot of the Instant Pot, then place a trivet inside. Position the pan on top of the trivet. 4. Secure the lid of the Instant Pot and select the Manual setting, adjusting the pressure to High. Cook for 20 minutes. Once cooking is complete, allow the pressure to release naturally for 10 minutes before performing a quick release for any remaining pressure. 5. Carefully remove the pan from the Instant Pot and let it cool for 15 to 20 minutes. Invert the cake onto a serving plate. It can be enjoyed hot or at room temperature, and you may serve it with a dollop of whipped cream if desired.

Per Serving:
calories: 240 | fat: 20g | protein: 5g | carbs: 10g | net carbs: 5g | fiber: 5g

Creamy Cardamom Bliss Rolls

Prep time: 20 minutes | Cook time: 18 minutes | Serves 5

◆ ½ cup coconut flour	◆ ¼ cup almond milk
◆ 1 tablespoon ground cardamom	◆ 1 tablespoon butter, softened
◆ 2 tablespoon Swerve	◆ 1 tablespoon cream cheese
◆ 1 egg, whisked	◆ ⅓ cup water

1. In a mixing bowl, combine coconut flour, almond milk, and softened butter until well blended. 2. Knead the mixture until it forms a smooth dough. 3. Use a rolling pin to roll out the dough evenly. 4. In a separate bowl, mix together Swerve and ground cardamom. 5. Sprinkle the cardamom mixture generously over the surface of the rolled-out dough. 6. Roll the dough into a large log and slice it into individual servings. 7. Place the cut rolls into the round mold designed for the Instant Pot. 8. Pour ⅓ cup of water into the Instant Pot and insert the mold with the rolls inside. 9. Select Manual mode and set it to High Pressure for 18 minutes. 10. After cooking, allow the pressure to release naturally for 15 minutes. 11. Let the rolls cool to room temperature before spreading cream cheese on top.

Per Serving:
calories: 128 | fat: 6g | protein: 5g | carbs: 12g | net carbs: 8g | fiber: 4g

Decadent Cocoa Delight Mousse

Prep time: 10 minutes | Cook time: 4 minutes | Serves 1

◆ 1 egg yolk	◆ 2 tablespoons coconut milk
◆ 1 teaspoon erythritol	◆ 1 tablespoon cream cheese
◆ 1 teaspoon cocoa powder	◆ 1 cup water, for cooking

1. Begin by pouring water into the Instant Pot and inserting the steamer rack. 2. In a bowl, whisk the egg yolk together with erythritol until well combined. 3. Once the mixture turns a lemon color, add coconut milk, cream cheese, and cocoa powder. Whisk until the mixture is smooth and fully incorporated. 4. Pour the mixture into a glass jar and place it on the steamer rack inside the Instant Pot. 5. Securely close and seal the lid of the Instant Pot. 6. Set the cooking mode to Manual (High Pressure) for 4 minutes, then perform a quick pressure release when the cooking time is complete.

Per Serving:
calories: 162 | fat: 15g | protein: 4g | carbs: 3g | net carbs: 2g | fiber: 1g

Zesty Lime Delight Muffins

Prep time: 10 minutes | Cook time: 15 minutes | Serves 6

◆ 1 teaspoon lime zest	◆ 2 eggs, beaten
◆ 1 tablespoon lemon juice	◆ 1 tablespoon Swerve
◆ 1 teaspoon baking powder	◆ ¼ cup heavy cream
◆ 1 cup almond flour	◆ 1 cup water, for cooking

1. In a mixing bowl, combine lemon juice, baking powder, almond flour, eggs, Swerve, and heavy cream, mixing until well blended. 2. Once the batter is smooth, stir in lime zest until evenly distributed. 3. Pour the batter into the muffin molds, filling each one. 4. Add water to the Instant Pot and insert the rack. 5. Carefully place the muffin molds on the rack inside the Instant Pot. Securely close and seal the lid. 6. Set the Instant Pot to cook on Manual (High Pressure) for 15 minutes. 7. After cooking, allow the pressure to release naturally.

Per Serving:
calories: 153 | fat: 12g | protein: 6g | carbs: 5g | net carbs: 3g | fiber: 2g

Creamy Coconut Almond Popsicles

Prep time: 10 minutes | Cook time: 5 minutes | Makes 8 ice pops

- 2 cups almond milk
- 1 cup heavy (whipping) cream
- 1 vanilla bean, halved lengthwise
- 1 cup shredded unsweetened coconut

1. In a medium saucepan, combine almond milk, heavy cream, and the vanilla bean over medium heat. 2. Bring the mixture to a gentle simmer, then reduce the heat to low and let it simmer for an additional 5 minutes. 3. Remove the saucepan from the heat and allow the liquid to cool. 4. Carefully extract the vanilla bean from the liquid, using a knife to scrape the seeds into the mixture. 5. Stir in the coconut, ensuring it is well combined, then pour the liquid into ice pop molds. 6. Freeze the molds until solid, which will take about 4 hours, then enjoy your homemade pops!

Per Serving:

1 ice pop: calories: 166 | fat: 15g | protein: 3g | carbs: 4g | net carbs: 2g | fiber: 2g

Refreshing Lemon Tea Gummies

Prep time: 10 minutes | Cook time: 5 minutes | Serves 4

- ¾ cup (180 ml) boiling water
- 3 tea bags
- ¼ cup (40 g) unflavored gelatin
- ¾ cup (180 ml) fresh lemon juice
- 2 tablespoons confectioners'-style erythritol or granulated xylitol
- Special Equipment:
- Silicone mold(s) with 36 (½ ounce/15 ml) cavities

1. Place the silicone mold(s) on a rimmed baking sheet to catch any spills. 2. In a heat-safe mug, pour boiling water and steep the tea according to the package instructions, removing the tea bags once steeped and squeezing out any excess liquid. Sprinkle gelatin over the brewed tea and set it aside to dissolve. 3. In a small saucepan, combine the lemon juice and erythritol, bringing it to a light simmer over medium heat for about 5 minutes. 4. After reaching a light simmer, take the saucepan off the heat. Whisk the tea mixture until the gelatin is completely dissolved, then add it to the hot lemon juice mixture, whisking to combine. 5. Carefully pour the hot mixture into the mold(s), then transfer the baking sheet to the refrigerator and allow it to set for at least 1 hour. Once firm, remove the gummies from the mold(s) and enjoy!

Per Serving:

calories: 48 | fat: 0g | protein: 10g | carbs: 1g | net carbs: 1g | fiber: 0g

Decadent Almond Chocolate Lava Cups

Prep time: 5 minutes | Cook time: 15 minutes | Serves 2

- 2 large eggs, whisked
- ¼ cup blanched finely ground almond flour
- ½ teaspoon vanilla extract
- 2 ounces (57 g) low-carb chocolate chips, melted

1. In a medium bowl, combine the eggs, flour, and vanilla extract. Gently fold in the chocolate until the mixture is fully combined. 2. Grease two ramekins with cooking spray and pour the batter evenly into each. Place the ramekins in the air fryer basket. 3. Set the temperature to 320ºF (160ºC) and air fry for 15 minutes. The cakes should have set edges and a firm center when done. 4. Allow the cakes to cool for 5 minutes before serving.

Per Serving:

calories: 300 | fat: 22g | protein: 10g | carbs: 9g | net carbs: 5g | fiber: 4g

Zesty Cashew Lemon Bliss Bars

Prep time: 5 minutes | Cook time: 35 minutes | Makes 12 bars

- 2 tablespoons butter, melted, plus 2 tablespoons, at room temperature, plus more for the baking dish
- 1 cup finely crushed cashews
- 1 cup almond flour
- ½ cup Swerve
- Zest of 2 lemons
- ½ cup freshly squeezed lemon juice
- 6 egg yolks
- 2 tablespoons gelatin

1. Begin by preheating the oven to 375ºF (190ºC). 2. Lightly grease an 8- or 9-inch square baking dish with butter. 3. In a large mixing bowl, combine cashews and almond flour. Drizzle the melted butter over the mixture and stir until the nuts are evenly coated and crumbly. Press the mixture firmly into the bottom of the prepared baking dish. Bake for about 15 minutes or until the crust starts to brown. Once baked, remove from the oven and allow to cool completely. 4. Lower the oven temperature to 350ºF (180ºC). 5. In a small saucepan, melt 2 tablespoons of room-temperature butter over low heat. 6. Add Swerve, lemon zest, and lemon juice, stirring to combine. 7. Gradually incorporate the egg yolks one at a time, whisking continuously as the filling thickens. Cook for an additional 2 to 3 minutes while whisking. 8. Remove from heat and whisk in the gelatin until the mixture is smooth. Pour the lemon filling over the cooled crust, spreading it evenly. Bake for 10 to 12 minutes, then remove from the oven and allow to cool. Cut into 12 squares and serve. Store in the refrigerator, covered, for up to 1 week.

Per Serving:

1 bar: calories: 144 | fat: 13g | protein: 4g | carbs: 4g | net carbs: 4g | fiber: 0g

Coconut Pistachio Dream Fudge

Prep time: 10 minutes | Cook time: 0 minutes | Makes 16 pieces

◆ ½ cup coconut oil, melted	liquid stevia
◆ 4 ounces cream cheese (½ cup), room temperature	◆ ½ cup shelled raw pistachios, roughly chopped, divided
◆ 1 teaspoon vanilla extract	
◆ ¼ teaspoon plus 10 drops of	◆ ½ cup unsweetened shredded coconut, divided

1. In a medium bowl, use a hand mixer to beat together the coconut oil and cream cheese until the mixture is smooth and creamy. Add the vanilla extract and stevia, mixing until fully combined. 2. Gently fold in one-third of the pistachios and one-third of the coconut flakes using a rubber spatula. Pour the fudge mixture into a 5-inch square dish or pan, then sprinkle the remaining pistachios and shredded coconut on top. 3. Chill the mixture in the refrigerator for at least 2 hours before serving. Once set, cut into 16 pieces. 4. Store any leftovers in a sealed container in the refrigerator for up to one week.

Per Serving:

calories: 123 | fat: 13g | protein: 1g | carbs: 2g | net carbs: 1g | fiber: 1g

Frozen Strawberry Cream Cheesecake

Prep time: 20 minutes | Cook time: 10 minutes | Serves 2

◆ 1 tablespoon gelatin	◆ 1 strawberry, chopped
◆ 4 tablespoon water (for gelatin)	◆ ¼ cup coconut milk
	◆ 1 tablespoon Swerve
◆ 4 tablespoon cream cheese	

1. In a small bowl, combine gelatin and water, allowing the mixture to sit for 10 minutes to bloom. 2. Meanwhile, pour coconut milk into the Instant Pot. 3. Set the Instant Pot to Sauté mode and heat the coconut milk until it reaches a boil, which should take about 10 minutes. 4. While the coconut milk is heating, mash the strawberries and mix them with the cream cheese until well blended. 5. Once the coconut milk is boiling, add the strawberry-cream cheese mixture and stir until smooth and fully combined. 6. Allow the liquid to cool for about 10 minutes before adding the bloomed gelatin. Whisk until the gelatin is completely dissolved. 7. Pour the cheesecake mixture into a mold and place it in the freezer for 3 hours to set.

Per Serving:

calories: 155 | fat: 14g | protein: 5g | carbs: 4g | net carbs: 3g | fiber: 1g

Nutty Sesame Delight Cookies

Prep time: 10 minutes | Cook time: 15 minutes | Makes 16 cookies

◆ 1 cup almond flour	room temperature
◆ ⅓ cup monk fruit sweetener, granulated form	◆ 1 egg
◆ ¾ teaspoon baking powder	◆ 1 teaspoon toasted sesame oil
◆ ½ cup grass-fed butter, at	◆ ½ cup sesame seeds

1. Start by preheating your oven to 375°F (190°C). Line a baking sheet with parchment paper and set it aside for later use. 2. In a large mixing bowl, combine almond flour, sweetener, and baking powder, stirring until the dry ingredients are well mixed. 3. Add the butter, egg, and sesame oil to the dry mixture and stir until fully combined and smooth. 4. Shape the dough into 1½-inch balls and roll them in sesame seeds. Arrange the cookies on the prepared baking sheet, spacing them about 2 inches apart, and gently flatten each ball with your fingers to about ½ inch thick. 5. Bake the cookies for 15 minutes, or until they turn golden brown. Once baked, transfer them to a wire rack to cool completely. 6. To store, keep the cookies in a sealed container in the refrigerator for up to five days, or freeze them for up to one month.

Per Serving:

calories: 173 | fat: 17g | protein: 3g | carbs: 2g | net carbs: 1g | fiber: 1g

Almond Flour Strawberry Delight

Prep time: 10 minutes | Cook time: 25 minutes | Serves 6

◆ 2 tablespoons coconut oil	◆ 1 teaspoon vanilla extract
◆ 1 cup blanched finely ground almond flour	◆ 2 cups sugar-free whipped cream
◆ 2 large eggs, whisked	◆ 6 medium fresh strawberries, hulled and sliced
◆ ½ cup granular erythritol	
◆ 1 teaspoon baking powder	

1. In a large bowl, mix together coconut oil, flour, eggs, erythritol, baking powder, and vanilla extract until well combined. Pour the batter into an ungreased round nonstick baking dish. 2. Place the baking dish in the air fryer basket and set the temperature to 300°F (149°C). Bake for 25 minutes, or until the shortcake is golden and a toothpick inserted into the center comes out clean. 3. Carefully remove the dish from the air fryer and allow it to cool for 1 hour. 4. Once cooled, top the cake with whipped cream and fresh strawberries before serving.

Per Serving:

calories: 344 | fat: 30g | protein: 8g | carbs: 10g | net carbs: 4g | fiber: 6g

Coconut Flour Vanilla Bliss Scones

Prep time: 20 minutes | Cook time: 10 minutes | Serves 6

- 4 ounces (113 g) coconut flour
- ½ teaspoon baking powder
- 1 teaspoon apple cider vinegar
- 2 teaspoons mascarpone
- ¼ cup heavy cream
- 1 teaspoon vanilla extract
- 1 tablespoon erythritol
- Cooking spray

1. In a mixing bowl, combine coconut flour, baking powder, apple cider vinegar, mascarpone, heavy cream, vanilla extract, and erythritol until well mixed. 2. Knead the mixture into a dough, then cut it into scone shapes. 3. Place the scones in the air fryer basket and lightly spray them with cooking spray. 4. Air fry the vanilla scones at 365°F (185°C) for 10 minutes, or until they are golden and cooked through.

Per Serving:

calories: 87 | fat: 8g | protein: 1g | carbs: 3g | net carbs: 1g | fiber: 2g

Quick Rhubarb Flax Cakes

Prep time: 5 minutes | Cook time: 0 minutes | Serves 2

- 1 large egg
- 3 tablespoons refined avocado oil or macadamia nut oil
- 1 tablespoon plus 1 teaspoon confectioners'-style erythritol
- ¼ teaspoon vanilla extract or powder
- ¼ cup (32 g) roughly
- ground flax seeds
- 1 teaspoon ground cinnamon
- ¼ teaspoon ground nutmeg
- ¼ teaspoon baking powder
- 1 (2½-in/6.5-cm) piece rhubarb, diced
- 1 to 2 fresh strawberries, hulled and sliced, for garnish (optional)

1. In a small bowl, combine the egg, oil, erythritol, and vanilla extract, whisking until well mixed. 2. In another small bowl, combine the flax seeds, cinnamon, nutmeg, and baking powder, stirring until blended. Then, add this dry mixture to the bowl with the wet ingredients. 3. Incorporate the diced rhubarb into the mixture, stirring until it is evenly coated. 4. Pour the mixture evenly into two 8-ounce (240-ml) ramekins, coffee cups, or other small microwave-safe containers. Microwave for 2 to 2½ minutes, or until a toothpick inserted into the center comes out clean. If desired, top with sliced strawberries before serving.

Per Serving:

calories: 303 | fat: 28g | protein: 6g | carbs: 7g | net carbs: 2g | fiber: 6g

Decadent Vanilla Crème Brûlée

Prep time: 7 minutes | Cook time: 9 minutes | Serves 4

- 1 cup heavy cream (or full-fat coconut milk for dairy-free)
- 2 large egg yolks
- 2 tablespoons Swerve, or more to taste
- Seeds scraped from ½ vanilla bean (about 8 inches long), or 1 teaspoon vanilla extract
- 1 cup cold water
- 4 teaspoons Swerve, for topping

1. Begin by heating the cream in a pan over medium-high heat until it is hot, which should take about 2 minutes. 2. In a blender, combine the egg yolks, Swerve, and vanilla seeds, then blend until the mixture is smooth. 3. With the blender still running, gradually pour in the hot cream. Taste the mixture and adjust the sweetness as desired. 4. Use a spatula to divide the mixture evenly into four ramekins. Cover each ramekin tightly with aluminum foil. 5. Pour water into the Instant Pot and insert a trivet. Carefully place the covered ramekins on the trivet. 6. Secure the lid on the Instant Pot, select Manual mode, and set the cooking time for 7 minutes at High Pressure. 7. Once the timer goes off, perform a quick release of the pressure and carefully remove the lid. 8. Keep the ramekins covered with foil and refrigerate for about 2 hours, or until they are completely chilled. 9. Before serving, sprinkle 1 teaspoon of Swerve on top of each crème brûlée and use the oven broiler to melt the sweetener until it forms a crust. 10. Let the topping cool in the refrigerator for 5 minutes before serving.

Per Serving:

calories: 138 | fat: 13g | protein: 2g | carbs: 2g | net carbs: 2g | fiber: 0g

Decadent Dark Chocolate Brownies

Prep time: 10 minutes | Cook time: 52 minutes | Makes 9 brownies

- ¼ cup cocoa powder
- 2 tablespoons coconut flour
- ¼ teaspoon pink Himalayan salt
- 3 large eggs
- ½ cup granular erythritol
- ½ teaspoon vanilla extract
- ¾ cup (1½ sticks) unsalted butter
- 2 ounces unsweetened baking chocolate (100% cacao)
- Powdered erythritol, for topping (optional)

1. Start by preheating your oven to 325°F (163°C) and greasing an 8-inch square brownie pan with coconut oil spray. 2. In a small bowl, combine cocoa powder, coconut flour, and salt, whisking them together with a fork. Set this mixture aside. 3. In a large mixing bowl, whisk together the eggs, erythritol, and vanilla extract until well combined. 4. In a small microwave-safe bowl, melt the butter and chocolate together in the microwave, heating for about 1 minute and stirring every 30 seconds until smooth. Add the melted chocolate mixture to the egg mixture and whisk until fully incorporated. 5. Gradually add the dry mixture to the wet ingredients in two batches, whisking thoroughly after each addition until completely combined. 6. Pour the batter into the prepared pan and bake for 50 minutes, or until a toothpick inserted in the center comes out clean. Allow the brownies to cool in the pan for 20 minutes before cutting into 9 squares. If desired, sprinkle with powdered erythritol before serving. 7. Store any leftovers in a sealed container in the refrigerator for up to a week, or freeze for up to a month.

Per Serving:

calories: 210 | fat: 20g | protein: 4g | carbs: 4g | net carbs: 1g | fiber: 3g

Rich and Creamy Erythritol Crème Brûlée

Prep time: 5 minutes | Cook time: 30 minutes | Serves 4

- 5 egg yolks
- 5 tablespoons powdered erythritol
- 1½ cups heavy cream
- 2 teaspoons vanilla extract
- 2 cups water

1. In a small bowl, use a fork to whisk the egg yolks until broken up, then stir in the erythritol until well combined. 2. In a small saucepan, heat the cream over medium-low heat for 3 to 4 minutes until warmed. Remove the saucepan from the heat. 3. To temper the egg yolks, gradually add a small spoonful of the warm cream, whisking continuously. Repeat this process two more times to ensure the egg yolks are gradually warmed. 4. Slowly incorporate the tempered egg mixture into the warm cream while whisking constantly. Add the vanilla extract and whisk again until fully mixed. 5. Distribute the cream mixture evenly into ramekins, filling each with about ½ cup of liquid. Cover each ramekin with aluminum foil. 6. Place the trivet in the Instant Pot and add water. Carefully position the ramekins on top of the trivet. 7. Secure the lid on the Instant Pot, select Manual mode, and set the cooking time to 11 minutes at High Pressure. 8. After the timer goes off, allow for a natural release for 15 minutes before manually releasing any remaining pressure. Open the lid with care. 9. Gently take one ramekin out of the pot. Remove the foil and check for doneness; the custard should be mostly firm with a slightly jiggly center 10. Refrigerate all the ramekins for 2 hours to chill and firm up. Serve cold for the best flavor.

Per Serving:

calories: 229 | fat: 22g | protein: 4g | carbs: 2g | net carbs: 2g | fiber: 0g

Appendix 1: Measurement Conversion Chart

VOLUME EQUIVALENTS(DRY)

US STANDARD	METRIC (APPROXIMATE)
1/8 teaspoon	0.5 mL
1/4 teaspoon	1 mL
1/2 teaspoon	2 mL
3/4 teaspoon	4 mL
1 teaspoon	5 mL
1 tablespoon	15 mL
1/4 cup	59 mL
1/2 cup	118 mL
3/4 cup	177 mL
1 cup	235 mL
2 cups	475 mL
3 cups	700 mL
4 cups	1 L

VOLUME EQUIVALENTS(LIQUID)

US STANDARD	US STANDARD (OUNCES)	METRIC (APPROXIMATE)
2 tablespoons	1 fl.oz.	30 mL
1/4 cup	2 fl.oz.	60 mL
1/2 cup	4 fl.oz.	120 mL
1 cup	8 fl.oz.	240 mL
1 1/2 cup	12 fl.oz.	355 mL
2 cups or 1 pint	16 fl.oz.	475 mL
4 cups or 1 quart	32 fl.oz.	1 L
1 gallon	128 fl.oz.	4 L

TEMPERATURES EQUIVALENTS

FAHRENHEIT(F)	CELSIUS(C) (APPROXIMATE)
225 °F	107 °C
250 °F	120 °C
275 °F	135 °C
300 °F	150 °C
325 °F	160 °C
350 °F	180 °C
375 °F	190 °C
400 °F	205 °C
425 °F	220 °C
450 °F	235 °C
475 °F	245 °C
500 °F	260 °C

WEIGHT EQUIVALENTS

US STANDARD	METRIC (APPROXIMATE)
1 ounce	28 g
2 ounces	57 g
5 ounces	142 g
10 ounces	284 g
15 ounces	425 g
16 ounces (1 pound)	455 g
1.5 pounds	680 g
2 pounds	907 g

Appendix 2: The Dirty Dozen and Clean Fifteen

The Environmental Working Group (EWG) is a nonprofit, nonpartisan organization dedicated to protecting human health and the environment Its mission is to empower people to live healthier lives in a healthier environment. This organization publishes an annual list of the twelve kinds of produce, in sequence, that have the highest amount of pesticide residue-the Dirty Dozen-as well as a list of the fifteen kinds ofproduce that have the least amount of pesticide residue-the Clean Fifteen.

THE DIRTY DOZEN

- The 2016 Dirty Dozen includes the following produce. These are considered among the year's most important produce to buy organic:

Strawberries	Spinach
Apples	Tomatoes
Nectarines	Bell peppers
Peaches	Cherry tomatoes
Celery	Cucumbers
Grapes	Kale/collard greens
Cherries	Hot peppers

- *The Dirty Dozen list contains two additional itemskale/collard greens and hot peppers-because they tend to contain trace levels of highly hazardous pesticides.*

THE CLEAN FIFTEEN

- The least critical to buy organically are the Clean Fifteen list. The following are on the 2016 list:

Avocados	Papayas
Corn	Kiw
Pineapples	Eggplant
Cabbage	Honeydew
Sweet peas	Grapefruit
Onions	Cantaloupe
Asparagus	Cauliflower
Mangos	

- *Some of the sweet corn sold in the United States are made from genetically engineered (GE) seedstock. Buy organic varieties of these crops to avoid GE produce.*

Appendix 3: Recipes Index

Made in United States
Orlando, FL
17 December 2024

55902515R00057